GUNFIGHTERS

GUNFIGHTERS

BY
COLONEL CHARLES ASKINS

A PUBLICATION
OF THE
NATIONAL RIFLE ASSOCIATION OF AMERICA

Printed in the United States of America

Published by the National Rifle Association of America
1600 Rhode Island Avenue, NW
Washington, D.C. 20036

ISBN 0-935998-43-8

Library of Congress Catalog Card Number 81-82777

NRA BOOKS — Bill Askins, *Director;* Ted Bryant, *Editor;*
Mike Fay, *Production Chief;* Betty Bauser, *Art Director*.

Dedicated to
JOHN ARMSTRONG
A hard-riding Texas Ranger

FOREWORD

The frontier was a boisterous place, inhabited by a hard riding, rough breed of men who made their own destinies as the big country was settled. These frontiersmen were open, generous, and hospitable in the main, but there was a streak of ruthlessness in them all, brought out by the hard life they led. Some were downright mean. The hardest element of frontier society was the gunfighter. Many were wanted in other parts of the Union, and all were eager to be swallowed up in the freedom of the frontier. These free-wheeling wanderers, gamblers, gunslingers, and lawmen, frolicked and fought their way into the pages of history.

It was evident the breed who were building the West were doing it on anything save idleness. Many had migrated from the plantation culture of the Old South but the past was behind them. This was Western aristocracy amaking, a horny handed gentry whose culture was the free and open kind, kindled at the tailgate of the chuckwagon, cemented in the dregs of tin-cup whiskey and the flaming mouth of six shooter and Winchester. The lusty beginning of this frontier culture has rendered it pretty much immune to the debilitating influence of too much cultivation and refinement which have done such immeasurable harm to the American fiber in past decades.

A frontiersman depended on himself, his sixshooter and a fast horse, a man's word was his bond and broken promises brought swift retribution. Life was good, but troubled; folks slept fitfully, a pistol under the pillow, and a rifle in the corner. This is the story of those times and afterwards.

CONTENTS

1

A MILD DISPUTE

Wyatt Earp ignored Billy Clanton's .44 Remington Army (it was nickle-plated) pointed at him from a distance of six feet and instead took deliberate aim at Frank McLowrey who stood off at a slight angle. Earp, probably the coolest hombre ever to ear back a hammer in a lethal gun battle, knew this McLowrey was a better shot than his compadre Clanton. Earp intended to rub out the better marksman first. His 250-grain .45 caliber slug (fired from one of a pair of Colt Model 1873 Peacemakers with 7½-inch barrels) struck the enemy squarely in the navel. It tumbled him like a headshot rabbit.

Frank had his saddled bronc standing at his shoulder when his partner Billy opened the play. He had a rifle on the near side and he clutched at the stirrup and sought to pull himself up to the scabbard and thus fetch loose his Winchester Model 73 carbine. But this was too much for the spooky caballo who, buggered at the staccato of shots and the billowing smoke, stampeded. McLowrey then drew his sixshooter.

When Wyatt Earp swung back to the youngest of his enemies (Bill was 19) he put a bullet just below the ribs. Morgan Earp, youngest of the fighting brothers, hit the cowboy only an instant before and his bullet entered within inches of that of his older sibling. Clanton fell from these two lethal rounds but propped himself against the side of the Harwood house and with his Remington across his knees sought targets.

If it might seem the Earps had all the best of it on this blustery day in latter October, 1881, near the south gate of the O.K. Corral in lusty Tombstone, let me hasten to assure you that this was not necessarily so. Billy Clanton, who had opened festivities by triggering off the first shot at Wyatt Earp from six feet, and was almost as promptly shot by Morgan Earp, was down but not necessarily out of action. He shot Virgil Earp, another of the going-hell-for-leather clan, and this bullet, fired somewhat wildly, tore through the Earp calf and fetched him to ground within a dozen feet of the gunman who was engrossed in firing at the other Earps.

Tom McLowrey, brother of the fatally wounded Frank, dodged behind the horse but when the caballo broke away he was un-covered. Doc Holliday, close amigo of Wyatt Earp, and very much a part of the lethal set-to, tossed his sawed-off Greener 10 gauge to shoulder and the load of 00-buck tore through McLowrey's right arm, sawed off 3 ribs and made sausage of his liver. The full charge of 11 big pellets lodged in the hapless gun-swinger. The yardage was nine short steps.

Meanwhile the real trouble-maker, the hombre probably most responsible for the bad blood between the Earps and the Clanton-McLowrey gang, Ike Clanton, had run away.

Clanton was standing beside Wyatt and caught him by the left arm and shoulder, apparently trying to wrestle the big mar-shal to the ground. Earp, six-feet-one and a 180 pounds, threw off the lighter man like a mastiff would shake loose a rat terrier. Noting that Ike Clanton had no gun out, Earp said contemptu-ously, "Either get to fightin' you sorry sonofabitch 'er get out'n the way."

Ike, usually never at a loss for words, took this as pretty good advice. He burst through the screen door at Fly's Photo Gallery, tore through the house at a dead run, burst out the back (passing Sheriff Behan and Billy Claiborne who were cowing there safely out of the angle of fire) and did not stop running until he got to Ignacio Mendez' cantina and dance hall on Allen Street. Ike, for all his precipitous retreat, had a narrow escape from the ever-lethal dentist, Doc Holliday. The good practitioner let loose a blast from his old Greener just as Clanton made the doorway of Fly's place. It missed.

The battle was not yet over. Billy Clanton was down, his back against the Harwood shack, his Remington across his knee, but he was still full of fight. Frank McLowrey, hit by Wyatt Earp during the first exchange, was on his knees and swung up his sixshooter. It was a S&W Schofield .45, an unusual gun for the time and place. He leveled the gun at Wyatt. But Holliday, a good man in a scrap, saw the movement and swung to cover McLowrey. His bullet struck the man amidships just as Morgan Earp shot the gunman behind the ear.

At the same time, Billy Clanton got Morgan Earp in his sights and an instant after McLowrey died, the Clanton bullet struck Morgan in the shoulder and ranged under the shoulder blades to come to rest on the far side of the body. It was a serious wound but not a killing one. Doc Holliday, very much in the thick of the fight, was shot through the hip. Actually the bullet struck his holster and was deflected, into the fleshy part of the upper thigh.

"It ain't nothin," the doughty dentist-gambler protested. And so it proved to be, a flesh wound and a trifling one.

The little photographer, Camillus Fly, whose gallery formed one side of the arena, came out just as Billy Clanton got off the last shot of the battle, the bullet which had struck Morgan Earp. As Clanton lay dying, a bulldog determination still impelling him, he attempted to cock the Remington one more time. Fly took the gun from his near lifeless hands.

The shootout was over. And a rootin' tootin' good affair it had been, maybe the most lethal in the annals of the old west. In the space of 30 seconds three men lay dead and as many more were wounded. Only the acknowledged leader of the Earp clan stood unscathed, Wyatt Earp himself. He had fired two shots and both had found their mark. He had killed Frank McLowrey and had his lead in Billy Clanton. Extreme range of the fight was 20 feet, a proximity which might have induced some gun-swingers to hurry. Not Earp. In commenting on the battle many years afterward he said, "I don't make fast draws. I pull my gun deliberately, aim carefully, and don't jerk on the trigger." These comments make out a poor case for the quick-draw sharks of screen and TV.

The eddying smoke of gunfire hung in the motionless air and into the cloud strode Sheriff John Behan. He walked up to Wyatt Earp, who he hated with a passionate disdain and demanded, "Gimme yer gun. Yer under arrest."

Earp looked down on the squatty minion of the law and with a vast contemptuousness in his voice replied "You ain't taking my gun t'day. Nor yet tomorrow neither." Without a further glance at the sheriff he went over and began to minister to Morgan Earp who was bleeding quite seriously.

Tombstone was accustomed to killings. Not a week went by when gunplay was not commonplace. But this was a ringtailed, geewhiz of a shooting spree, a murderous interplay which impressed even the gun-hardened denizens of the tough town! Sides were chosen and the miners in the nearby silver mines dropped shovel and pick and raced into town to take a hand. Word was galloped out to the Clanton ranch and Ol' Man Phineas Clanton gathered up all his cowboys and with a straggling crowd of neighbors and sympathizers headed for town.

"I'm a-goin' to hang thim bastards fer killin' mah boy," he announced to one and all when his sizeable troupe pulled to a halt in Allen Street, the main stem, and directly in front of the Oriental Saloon. The Oriental, let it be noted, was a hangout of the Earps and most especially Wyatt who had the gambling concession there.

Tombstone boasted more undertakers than doctors. There were seven of the former and but three of the latter. The bidding was quite spirited for the layout of the three dead gunmen. Finally Ritter & Ream, freely admitted as the duo most competent to really put on an elegant going-away party, got the business. The firm had a glass-sided hearse, ornately gold-trimmed and costing the very considerable sum of $8,000 in St. Louis, which carried the remains of the youthful Billy Clanton. A second hearse, not quite so elaborate, was chosen to wheel out the McLowrey boys. First however the bodies, all clothed in formal evening dress, were put on display in the front window of the Frontier Hardware & Feed Store at the corner of Allen and Fourth Streets.

Ol' Man Phineas Clanton did not enter the Oriental Saloon

and his cowboys, if they entered, were careful of voice and gesture. While two of the Earps were hospitalized in the Cosmopolitan Hotel, which served as a sick bay, the old lion of the pack, Wyatt, and the equally poisonous amigo, the redoubtable Doctor John Holliday, were very much in evidence around the Oriental. Mad though Ol' Man Clanton was he did not want to buck these formidable gun-fighters.

Virgil Earp was up and about in a matter of a week's time. Doc Holliday had a limp for 4-5 days from the chunk of lead which lodged in his thigh. But this was dug out by Doc Piggett, who was an expert at extracting hot lead and patching bullet holes and one day Wyatt, Virgil and the staunch friend, this fellow Holliday, pulled up abreast of the Cochise County courthouse.

"Billy Brackenridge brung over a warrant fer all of us." Wyatt explained. It is signed by Judge Spicer an' I reckon we'uns had better go turn our' selves in."

Billy Brackenridge, let it be noted, was Sheriff Behan's chief deputy. The good sheriff might have served the papers himself but he wanted little part of the Earp clan. He sent Billy who was a youthful chap, well liked and considered harmless. He searched the explosive Earp out behind the monte table in the Oriental and after hemming and hawing for a couple of minutes handed over the warrants.

"Tell the judge we'll be over," Wyatt acknowledged.

By this time a coroner's jury had debated the killings and had reached no conclusion. Judge Wells Spicer, an attorney elected by the itinerant population of Tombstone as city magistrate, took a full month to reach a verdict. He formally announced that Wyatt Earp and party were justified in their actions. After all, Virgil was city marshal and Wyatt was his first deputy. The other Earps and Holliday had been sworn in shortly before the quartet moved down Fremont Street to the fatal encounter with the Clanton/McLowrey combine.

Despite the fact that the Earps had a semblance of the law on their side, the facts were that this was a personal vendetta. The chances were that Wyatt and his brothers didn't give a damn whether they represented city authority or not. They were bound that blustery day in late October to kill a few Clantons and McLowreys.

The truth was the Clantons and the McLowreys had elected to play hard ball with a coterie of honest-to-god professionals. The locals, all cow rustlers and suspected stage robbers, were not gun-slingers in a class nor on a par with the Earps, most especially Wyatt Earp. Down from Dodge City, the hell-roaring terminus of all the cow herds driven up from turbulent Texas by even more turbulent cowboys, Earp had killed seven men before the fracas at the south gate of the O.K. Corral. He was the night marshal in a town where the boast was, "We serve up a dead man for breakfast every morning."

If this were not enough background, Earp had moved from Wichita to Dodge, his tenure in the eastern Kansas cow town enlivened by some 11 months as policeman and city marshal. Wichita, during its heyday as the cattle capital, had seen a million and a half bawling Texas bovines come and go, driven to market by long-haired, wild-eyed, unshaven riders intent on only one thing—painting the town a deep crimson. What they wanted was a hell-raising good time with a plentitude of liquor, monte and wild, wild women. "An' if'n a goddamn marshal gits in tha way we'uns got an answer fer that too," was the way the foreman of the XIT outfit explained it.

Earp was not so much a lawman as a gambler. He had been indicted for stealing horses just outside old Fort Gibson, the Indian Territory, but he took a long ride one night and when dawn broke he was over the Kansas line. His penchant was faro and monte and while he was in Dodge he not only pistol-whipped various recalcitrant Texans and hauled them off to the local jail but also dealt a game in the Long Branch Saloon. It was rumored as well that he had a half-interest in one of the town's more lively bordellos and, as a matter of fact, had a whore there who nightly shared his couch. Malicious gossip or not, when he arrived in Tombstone in December 1879, he lost no time in taking Sheriff John Behan's inamorata away from him—a fact of life which chilled the little cordiality the two had for each other. This damsel, Fanny Naylor, besides other obvious assets, was an amateur actress and had the lead in the stage play "Pinafore" staged at the town's leading theatre, the Bird Cage.

Wyatt came to Tombstone well-heeled financially. He shortly bought out the gambling concession in the Oriental and, if this were not enough, had an interest in the monte game across the street in the Eagle Brewery. Virgil Earp, who galloped down from Prescott, Arizona, with Wyatt, was another gunfighter. He had been a policeman, deputy sheriff and city marshall in Kansas, Colorado and northern Arizona and enroute to Tombstone with his formidable brother, was sworn in as a deputy U.S. marshal for the Arizona Territory.

Virgil was 36 at the time he struck the brawling Arizona town, and his redoubtable brother was 31.

There were two other siblings. James, who was not a gunfighter, had been wounded during the Civil War and his shooting arm was disabled. Morgan, only 28, who went about with a decided chip on his shoulder was a curly wolf. As big as Wyatt, Morgan was bad-tempered, surly and always openly looking for trouble. He had been a policeman and once he got settled in Tombstone, the older brothers got him a job as the Wells Fargo stage guard between the mining town and Tucson. This was a run of 11 hours and a route much given to ambushes by highwaymen intent on knocking off shipments of silver bullion from the mines in the nearby San Pedro Hills.

Between the Dragoon and the Whetstone Mountains was a scattering of root-hog-or-die ranches. Most of them eked out a living by dipping quite freely and with frequence into Mexico where the scrawny and inbred vacas were harried across the US-Mex frontier and sold to the Indian Service for supply to the San Carlos Apaches. No questions asked. Among the chief suppliers were two neighboring ranchers, the Clantons and the McLowreys. These worthies had been amigos since the early 1870s and oftimes they combined forces to move sizeable herds out of Sonora. Too, there was a loose sort of agreement with rustlers in the Territory that the Clanton/McLowrey menage would act as honest brokers for the sale of such livestock as was delivered to one or the other of the ranches. Both stood near Charleston, a pueblo not too far distant from Tombstone, and both were headquarters for the cow thieves, the highwaymen and assorted bully boys of that end of the Arizona Territory.

When life grew too dull on the home range the boys were wont to saddle up and lope into Tombstone and there shoot up the town. This was called hurrahing the town dwellers and woe be unto the town law who tried to put a damper on the festivities. Curly Bill Brokus, a double-dyed toughie who made a better-than-average thing of stealing cattle, rode into Tombstone late one evening and by midnight had drunk a quart of barrel whisky, had bucked the monte game and had a round at the Bird Cage where the girls were supposed to be 16 and not older. That's when Bernie Strader, the town marshal, cornered him in the alley behind the main stem, Allan Street, between 4th and 5th Streets. Curly Bill had been letting off steam by shooting at the McAlisher Co. sign which hung before the lumber yard.

"Gimme yer gun," commanded the lawman, his own .45 doing small circles within bare inches of the Brokus bellybutton. Brokus extended his .45 Peacemaker quite tamely, the stock foremost the muzzle toward himself.

As Strader reached out to take the extended Colt, Curly Bill executed the road agent's spin, a neat piece of work in which the pistol is twirled on the trigger finger and as the hammer passes under the thumb it is eared back just far enough to make the gun fire. The 250-grain slug slammed into the lawman just six degrees to port of his beltbuckle. He died at daylight. Curly Bill and his long riders eased on out of town.

Within days Virgil Earp rode into town. Although he was the deputy U.S. Marshal for the Arizona Territory he considered it not beyond the bounds of his office to accept the proffer made by the city fathers of Tombstone to act as the town marshal. The pay was high, $75 monthly. He made his brother Wyatt the deputy city marshall. The tall rangy deputy also acted as the deputy to the Cochise County sheriff, until Johnny Behan gained the office as county minion.

Behan and Earp hated each other with a vengeance. Most especially after the handsome Earp, who was strikingly good looking with piercing brown eyes and a huge down-swept moustache, persuaded the Behan light of love, a St. Louis dove only newly arrived, to move in with him.

Tombstone during the first two years of its growth mushroomed from a village of a hundred souls to a metropolis of almost 6,000. According to Judge Wells Spicer, a sort of self-designated historian, "there are two dancehalls, a dozen gambling places and maybe 20 saloons." The city magistrate elected to pass over the brothels without giving them a count. Most of the big saloons had a crib or two in the back rooms where the ladies of easy virtue could turn a trick.

Without the town, as we've noted, were a few scraggly ranches where six cows to the section was about all the range would bear. The ranchers may have been few but their cowboys made up in lack of numbers by the pure hell they raised once they hit town. This was resented by the town's people who mostly lived in tents and flimsy shacks and did not appreciate the shots that were fired. The editor of the *Tombstone Epitaph* complained after a bullet passed through his house and narrowly missed him in bed. "This has got to stop," he editoralized. The city fathers looked to the new city marshal, Virgil Earp and his deputy, the towering Wyatt, to do something about it. The feud between the city lawmen and the cowboy-rancher-rustler combine was joined right there.

If the free-wheeling antics of the outriders was not enough to make bad blood, the fact that Ike Clanton stole a race horse which belonged to Wyatt Earp (which Earp later found under the saddle of Billy Clanton) did not help good feelings. Later, Virgil as deputy U.S. marshall, trailed six mules stolen from Fort Huachucha to the McLowrey Ranch and there rode up as Tom and Frank McLowrey were blotting the "U.S." brand on the hip of each jughead. The marshal had a cavalry detail at his back and he turned the stolen animals back to the rightful owners. The McLowreys swore to get even.

The sheriff, John Behan, had been appointed by the territorial governor but he had to stand an election and he felt it behooved him to stand in with the local ranchers. He sort of winked at the cattle thievery of some of his constituents. Too, he was envious of the Earps who controlled the town. Behan's domain was outside the environs of Tombstone, and he could see that either Virgil or Wyatt would undoubtedly run in opposition to him once the elections were held.

This dislike ripened to livid hate when Behan arrested Doc Holliday and charged him with a holdup of the local stage and the killing of the stage driver. The charge was dismissed for lack of concrete evidence but Holliday, who was not the forgiving sort, stated loudly and unmistakeably that Behan had tried to frame him. The Earps agreed. Morgan Earp was not on the stage that day but enemies of the clan claimed that Morgan, who ordinarily would have been riding shotgun, purposely gave Holliday inside information on the silver shipment and had then begged off making the trip. The Earps shrugged off the innuendo.

Later on the stage was stuck up again but this time Virgil Earp in his role as deputy U.S. marshal pinned the goods on Frank Stilwell, a deputy of Sheriff John Behan. With him, according to witnesses, had been Pete Spence. When the duo were brought before Magistrate Spicer, Ike Clanton came forward and put up cash bail. Frank McLowrey heard about the robbery, the arrests and the court appearance and he rode into town wearing two sixshooters.

Whether by design or purely by chance, Tombstone was not a big town and there was only one main stem. He met Morgan Earp, and as the younger of the brothers was alone and as McLowrey had the belligerent Ike Clanton at his side together with a half-dozen cowpunchers all of them pretty well liquored up and spoiling for a fight, McLowrey bristled up to Earp and said, "You sonofabitch. We'uns is a-goin' to kill all you god' damn Earps. Any time yer ready we're going' to set tha ball t'rollin'."

This was September and the bad blood between the factions continued to boil until the 25th of October—the day before the powder-burning at the back gate to the O.K. Corral—when Ike Clanton and Tom McLowrey rode into town. McLowrey, who peddled his beef to the Bauer Meat Market on Fremont Street, planned to go pick up the proceeds of a sale made the week before. Ike, as was his wont, commenced to make the rounds of the saloons. Around midnight he staggered into the Alhambra Saloon and went to the bar where a free lunch was always available.

Doc Holliday entered and seeing Clanton, who he hated with a rattler's aggression, walked up to the cowboy and said, "You sorry bastard, go fer yer gun so I kin kill yeh." Clanton denied he had a gun, which was hardly likely. And about that time Wyatt Earp, who was in the bar, called out to Virgil who was at the far end of the long mahogany counter and asked him to draw the dentist off. This he did. But as he drew away from Ike Clanton the latter challenged, "I'm a-going to kill yah. An' that's a promise."

The next morning by midday, the head barkeep at the Oriental, Wyatt Earp's place, came to the shack where the tall man was sleeping and told him that Clanton was armed with both a six-shooter and a rifle and had said, "When them damn Earps come out there's gonna be war."

Wyatt found Virgil at Bell & Standford's general dry goods store and the two of them moved down Allen Street. In an alley off Fourth Street they found Ike, rifle in hand. But Clanton had his back to the redoubtable brothers. Virgil seized the rifle with his left hand and pistol-whipped the cowboy with the Colt .45 in his right. The whack over the ear dropped Ike to his knees.

"You lookin fer me?" inquired the marshal.

"Iff'n I'd se'd yah a sec'nd sooner I'd a'killed yah." Clanton was still pugnacious, even as he gingerly felt his head to see if he still had an ear. Virgil Earp yanked him to his feet and unceremoniously dragged him off to Justice of the Peace A. O. Wallace's court where he charged him with packing firearms inside the city limits.

Wyatt, who had trailed along behind the pair covering Virgil's back, entered the court and told Clanton, "Look, you goddamn cowthief, you have threatened my life and I want it stopped. If you are anxious to shoot this out I'll meet you anywhere, anytime."

"I'll see you," Ike bristled, "jist as soon as I git free here. Ah'm a-fixin' to kill all you goddamn Earps."

As Wyatt walked out of the little 2 x 4 office which served as the court he came face to face with Tom McLowrey. Earp said, "Git out'n my way you goddamn cow rustler." McLowrey backed up a step and his hand dropped on his gun but he did not offer to draw. He replied, "Iff'n you want to make a fight of it, we'll fight yah anywhere."

Earp answered, "Al'right—here an' now." And he cuffed McLowrey with his open palm and swinging the big .45 with its 7½-inch barrel into action struck him over the left ear. The blow fetched the cowman to his knees in the dust of the street.

Earp walked away without even so much as a single backward glance.

By this time Billy Clanton and Frank McLowrey had arrived in Tombstone. They had ridden in via buckboard and put up the team at a stable owned by Sheriff Behan. Friends were quick to buttonhole them and bring them up to the minute on the set-to between the brothers and the hated Earps.

Wyatt gathered Morgan and Virgil in a back room at the Oriental. Doc Holliday was there also.

"We're a-goin' to kill all them bastards. When we'uns walk outta here we'se gonna walk up an' down Allen until we finds em. When we does, come on a-shootin." The brothers and Holliday nodded. They walked out of the swinging doors of the saloon and marched four abreast down the very middle of the street toward the O.K. Corral. John Behan was getting a shave in the Alfrey Tonsorial Parlors at Allen & Fourth when he saw a crowd gathering at the corner. He glanced through the window and saw all the Earps, the sawed-off shotgun in the hands of Virgil plainly visible.

"Looks like the Earps are a-huntin' the Clantons an' the Mc-Lowreys," spoke Ed Heidke, the barber, cheerfully. Behan wiped the lather off his chin and bustled out to confront Virgil.

"Gimme a minute an' I'll take them guns away from them cowboys," he pleaded.

He swung off, apparently sure where to find the Clantons and their allies. About that time, Jim Meecham whispered to Morgan that the Clantons and the McLowreys were in Fremont Street and had not given up their shooting irons. The Earps and their staunch ally, the poisonous Doc Holliday moved out in the direction of their antagonists. Virgil handed his sawed-off Greener to Holliday. Just why is from this time and distance unknown. Earp was armed with a .45 as were all the others. Wyatt had two, but instead of holsters he had the guns in voluminous pockets of the great coat which he wore.

The two parties came together on Fremont between Camillus Fly's photo gallery and Bill Harwood's house. The Clantons and the McLowreys backed up against the Harwood place and the Earps walked up to within bare feet of them. From Wyatt Earp to Billy Clanton was barely six feet. Frank McLowrey was a bit farther. There the most lethal shootout the West had ever known was enacted. In the space of 30 seconds three men lay dead, three were wounded. And Ike Clanton who was responsible, more probably than any of the participants, ran away.

But Ike returned and just two months after the killing at the O.K. he waylaid Virgil one night and as the doughty marshal crossed 5th Street he took a load of buckshot which shattered his left arm. Three months later, while Wyatt and Morgan were playing a game of pool in the McCluskey Pool & Billard Parlor on Allen Street, Morgan was shot in the back, again with a load of 00 buck. He fell his spine riddled. He died before daylight.

Frank Stilwell and Pete Spence were identified by witnesses. Frank, it will be remembered, was a former deputy of Sheriff John Behan, a deputy until he was arrested for a holdup of the Tombstone-Tucson stage.

Morgan Earp's body was placed on a buckboard and hauled into Tucson where it was placed aboard the Southern Pacific enroute to California for burial. The Earps' parents had settled in California by that time and Wyatt considered it only proper to return the body to the family. Riding beside the buckboard transporting the body was Wyatt, Virgil, and the curly wolf Doc Holliday.

The train arrived late. The remains were loaded at 10:30 of the night. As the Earps and Holliday were leaving the station they rounded the platform and who did they see but Frank Stilwell, a rifle leveled at the trio. The first shot from the .44-40 tore through the greatcoat which Wyatt wore. The three shots from the 45s in the hands of the Earps all struck their mark. Wyatt deliberately walked up and shot Stilwell as he lay on the ground.

The next morning the Earp-Holliday combine rode back toward Tombstone but they detoured to the seeps behind Charleston. These seeps were a sort of springs where outlaws on the lam sometimes camped rather than to ride into town. Either at the seeps or at Pete Spence's logging camp they caught up with the third killer who had been in on the Morgan killing. They finished him off. But Spence got the word and decamped for Mexico. The score pretty well evened, the Earps and Holliday rode out of Tombstone and Arizona never to return.

2
COWBOYS
AND SIXGUNS

In 1866 an enterprising promoter by the name of Joe McCoy rode into Kansas and out to the forty-mile post on the Kansas & Pacific Railroad, where he met a jayhawker, Tim Hershey. The get-together was a propitious one. McCoy, six-and-a-half feet tall and with a brush of whiskers to do credit to Moses, was a big man with big ideas. Tim Hershey, on the other hand, was just a small Kansas cow-rancher, but his location was a strategic one. His holdings sat firmly astraddle the rail line.

Over a bottle of Indianhead whisky and a bit of buffalo ribs these worthies hatched a plan. Hershey would lay out a town, a longhorn metropolis complete with stockyards, loading chutes, pens, switches, and a railroad station—all, of course, on Hershey's property. For his part McCoy would go to Texas and advertise.

Texans fresh returned from the Civil War had found themselves rich in cattle but poor in cash. The Southwest held an estimated six million cows and hundreds of thousands of horses but no local market. In the East were millions of Yankees hungry for beef and needing horseflesh for work and play. The McCoy–Hershey stratagem was to match up Yankee needs and Southwestern resources.

In the short space of twelve months things really happened. The energetic Hershey had his town abuilding, including stockyards and loading pens, and was on hand to greet McCoy's galloping *Tejanos*—native Texans—when they threw the first of

15

thirty-five thousand wild longhorns into those pens. The town was Abilene and this was just a beginning.

The cowboys who came up the trail behind those herds were a tough breed. They contributed in no time at all to the new Boot Hill cemetery in Abilene, some of them occupying lots themselves and others adding Abilene names to the grave markers, including those of a couple of town marshals. Abilene's main drag, known appropriately as Texas Street, quickly became a Hell's Highway charged with six-shooter smoke, rotgut whisky, and wild women. During the decades that followed, from 1866 to 1895, ten million longhorns trailed into this and later Kansas railheads, and their cowboy drivers, ably aided and abetted by citizens of the cow towns, wrote "Strife" in bloody letters across the flaming skies of Kansas.

The bucko who rode up the Chisholm Trail, or the Western Trail, or the old Shawnee Trail, with a pair of Confederate Dance .44s strapped to his flanks and a Spencer, Henry, or Winchester carbine swung under a stirrup leather, come to town for just one purpose—a hell of a time! And despite the Hickoks, the Earps, and the Mastersons, he intended to have it. Product of the Civil War, veteran of a dozen brushes with Comanche and Lipan Apache, after ninety days in the heat and the dust kicked up by a few thousand cow brutes, he galloped into Abilene to paint the town red!

He aimed to play poker, monte, and faro bank with the sky the limit; he took cold if he took his six-shooter off, and no damyankee marshal was going to disarm him; he slept better on the ground than in bed, drank his whisky neat from a tin dipper, rolled his own from a sack of Bull Durham, and loped into Abilene in the same pair of drawers he had on when the herd left Bandera. And neither bath, shave, haircut, nor change of clothing was his until the stock pens slammed shut and the trail boss had shelled out the accumulated wages.

He was wicked, wild, reckless, and hardcase. He saw Abilene as his own Mecca, a glorious hell hole where cowboys gathered to hurrah the town, buffalo the marshal, and carry the soiled doves up the stairs at the Drover's Cottage. Abilene was a watering place where they served up a dead man for breakfast every morning, and the wilder, wetter, and wickeder it got, the better he liked it. The cowboy who rode up the trail in the late 1860s was spoiling for trouble. In Abilene it didn't take him long to find it.

The guns he packed were those he had fetched home from the war. Johnny Reb (whom Texas supplied in quantities that only Virginia exceeded) rode home from the war if he was lucky enough to keep his mount out of the clutches of the Union forces; if not, he just walked. Some trudged more than a thousand miles. When everything else was tossed aside, his six-shooter remained with him.

It might be a Griswold & Gunnison, the most popular of the Southern-made revolvers; or it might be the Union handgun, the highly effective Colt Model of 1860. This was the arm of the Federal forces, and Confederates hunted every battlefield to find them. It was a big gun, .44 caliber, with an 8-inch barrel and a weight only fractions under 3 pounds. Or the Texan's gun might be the Remington Model 1858, another .44, and likewise much sought after. Remington made more than 140,000 of these big revolvers during the war. Many of them traveled to the Southwest and into sin-jammed Abilene with Texas cowboys.

In 1866–67, when the half-wild longhorns were hazed out of the mesquite thickets along the Brazos and headed up the Chisholm Trail, every man put on his six-shooter in the morning like he put on his pants. But there was no manufacture of firearms in the Southwest and no money to buy them. The item of barter was the cow. A three-year-old was worth $3 on the hoof, $10 in trade. So the cowboy rode out with a sticky loop, caught the first three unbranded mavericks, slapped his mark on them with a cinch ring for a running iron, and swapped his newly acquired herd for a gun.

The pistol he swapped for was always an old gun. It might be a Colt of the 1850 era; more likely it was one fetched home from the 1861–65 fracas. The Griswold & Gunnison was a good revolver; it was a .36 caliber and a faithful copy of the Colt Navy Model 1851. It was a 6-shot with a brass frame and a 7½-inch round barrel. It was made during the war at Griswoldville, Georgia, and about thirty-six hundred were produced altogether. It was the most common Confederate revolver.

There were, however, others. The Leech & Rigdon was also .36 caliber and like the Griswold a spittin' image of the Navy Colt. There were the Rigdon-Ansley and the Spiller & Burr, and the Columbus, made at Columbus, Georgia. Altogether the several Confederate manufacturers produced about ten thousand handguns.

These shooting irons were all cap-and-ball jobs, and some of them got their owners into godawful jams due to failure to deliver the goods when the cards were down. Everts Haley in his excellent book *George W. Littlefield, Texan* describes one of these episodes, an encounter between Littlefield and a man named Watson:

Watson pulled his gun and commenced shooting at Littlefield. Though they were within a few feet of each other, Watson missed. Littlefield drew his own gun. Two chambers went off together and then the gun failed to fire. Shelton Dowell, seeing his uncle's predicament, rode up and offered his own six-shooter, saying; "Here, Cap'n, take my gun." Littlefield dropped his old gun and took Dowell's but it too missed fire. So he picked up his old gun once more. By that time Watson had emptied his own revolver without hitting Littlefield. He hid behind a big live oak tree nearby, and stuck his head around the trunk and shouted, "Goddam you, Littlefield, you ain't got me yet." But that was a little premature for Littlefield succeeded in getting his old cap-and-ball to fire and shot Watson through the heart.

George Littlefield had been a major in the Confederate cavalry. He had fetched his revolver home from Virginia with him. It was a remote Schneider & Glassick, a brass frame revolver, 6-shot, .36 caliber, with a 7½-inch octagon barrel. It was made in Memphis. Records show only a handful were manufactured, as both William Schneider and Fred Glassick put in most of the war as gunsmiths.

The revolver tossed to Littlefield by his obliging nephew Shelton Dowell was a venerable Colt Breveté, made during the early 1850s, a puny .31 caliber with a 5-shot cylinder. It was a pocket gun by the standard of the day, with a 5⅜-inch barrel and an overall dimension of only 10½ inches. That it failed to fire was not surprising, especially in view of its age and years of frontier service.

Many a cowboy of that day carried not one revolver but a pair of them. The Dodge City *Daily Globe,* a faithful chronicler of that town's powder-flecked heyday, makes countless references to the proclivity of the hardcase trail riders to swing a shooting iron from either flank. What the *Daily Globe* did not comment on was the sorry leather in which the guns were holstered. A life-long search of the museums of the Southwest, and there are scores of them, together with an everlasting search of old books, magazines, files, and ancient newspapers, reveals that the six-shooter scabbards of that day were simply awful.

The holster was a carry-over from the cavalry, the first fighting force to carry revolvers. They wore them in holsters which had a flap on top and which swung the pistol with the butt to the front. Johnny Reb returned home and carried his filched Colt, Remington, or other handgun in the same manner. The cowboy who rode the Chisholm Trail did the same. But not for long.

When the wild bunch commenced to cut each other down in the Alamo, the Lone Star, the Bull's Head, and the Longhorn saloons of rip-roaring Abilene, it was pretty quickly decided that the holster flap had better be whittled away and the gun butt swung to the rear. But even with these alterations the holsters were abominably poor. The rig did not fit the gun, and it was made of flanking leather, a kind of cowhide that is far too soft to hold its shape. As a result the scabbard was too soft, too yielding, too inclined to cling and hold to the weapon. The standard six-shooter was likewise poorly suited to the lethal new game. Barrels ran from 7 to 12 inches: fast gun-play isn't possible with guns like that. Abilene's most colorful marshal, the formidable Wild Bill Hickok, is reputed to have rammed his guns into the waistband of his trousers or into a sash, disdaining holsters.

The six-shooter in the late 1860s was a necessary item of dress for the well turned out cowboy come to town. For the business of whooping a herd of spooky longhorns across the Indian Territory, a land filled to overflowing with more than forty tribes of discontented Indians, the cowboy needed a rifle. He wanted a

repeater and preferably one that could be loaded on Monday
and shot all week!

When Lee turned over his sword, the rag, tag, and bobtail that
was once his proud army commenced the long trek homeward. There was fixed in every rebel's mind the knowledge that
the best repeating rifle on either side had been the Spencer carbine. When our rebel turned cowboy started up the trail to
Kansas in 1866, he carried a Spencer if one could be found. The
rifle was a Union arm, made in both rifle and carbine styles. The
latter was the cavalry version, and it was a good one. It held 7
cartridges, loaded through the buttstock, and was a lever action.
It was chambered for various cartridges, calibers .56–.50, .56–
56, .52, or maybe .54. Altogether more than 100,000 were
made. Only the lack of ammunition kept the Spencer from enjoying a booming popularity among the longhorn drivers.

Possibly, even more eagerly sought after was the Henry Model
1860 in .44 rimfire caliber. This was truly the great first choice
of the early drovers. Long after the Winchester Model 1866
came along, and although it was a markedly improved firearm,
the Henry was still a common rifle along the Chisholm Trail.
Verification of this is found in the records and files of the F. C.
Zimmerman Hardware, an emporium which stood at Front Street
in old Dodge and which boasted the only gunsmith in town.
Surprisingly complete data from the ledgers of a whole bevy of
gun tinkers employed by Fred Zimmerman show the Henry was
around in numbers as late as 1878. Manufacture of the Henry
ended upon the advent of the Winchester 66, but this somewhat
momentous event had little effect on the popularity of its forerunner.

Kansas markets for Texas cattle put money for new guns in
Tejano pockets from the commencement of the drives in 1866
until the last of them almost three decades later. The Winchester
Model 66 and its center-fire counterpart, the Model 73 (.44–40)
became the big guns.

The Model 66 was a great deal like the Henry. It had a brass
receiver and was offered as both a rifle and a carbine. In its
longer version the tubular magazine held 17 cartridges; the
carbine took 12 rounds. The principal shortcoming of the Henry

had been a weak extractor, prone to breakage. Too, the magazine had no wooden forend to protect it and was all too easily dented. This caused feed problems. The extractor on the Model 66 was beefed up, and a forestock offered protection to the tubular magazine.

The Model 66 with its shining brass receiver was called "Yellow Boy" by the Cheyennes. The Model 1873, when it came along, bore a close resemblance to its predecessor. Where the receiver had been of brass now it was of iron. There was a sliding cover over the breechblock to give some protection from dirt and moisture; and while the 66 had been a rimfire the 73 was a .44 centerfire. It was made both as a rifle and a carbine, in barrel lengths from 20 to 30 inches. Some indication of the tremendous popularity of this famous rifle can be gained from the fact that its manufacture commenced in 1873 and did not end until 1921: during that time some three-quarters of a million guns were made.

Buffalo Bill Cody, writing to Winchester in 1875, had this to say about the Model 73: "I have been using and have thoroughly tested your latest improved rifle. Allow me to say that I have tried nearly every kind of gun made in the United States and for general hunting and Indian fighting I pronounce your improved Winchester, the Boss."

Uncounted thousands of the Model 73 went up the trail to Dodge. Among these may have been one or more of the 136 very specially selected rifles which bore, stamped proudly on the barrel, the words "One of One Thousand." These specially-turned 73s were made from 1875 to 1878, and then discontinued. Little of the history of these 136 selected rifles is known. A diligent search a few years ago produced only 36 of them.

Jim Gillett, a famous Texas Ranger from 1875 to 1881, veteran of a score of gunfights and countless engagements with the Comanches, pretty well summed up his regard for the Model 73 when he wrote in his book *Texas Rangers,*

As soon as we were settled in our new camp on the San Saba, some of the boys obtained permission to go to Austin (state capital) to buy a case of 10 Winchester rifles. Up to this time the company had been armed with the old .50 caliber Sharps single-shot. These guns

would heat up too fast and would then become inaccurate in sending
a bullet to the mark. [Note: The .50 cal Sharps was a holdover from
the Civil War, issued to the State of Texas from government arsenals.
The state provided the Sharps at a cost of $17.50 to each Ranger.]
The new center-fire 1873 Winchester had just appeared on the
market and sold for fifty dollars for the rifle and forty for the carbine.
A Ranger who wanted a Winchester had to pay for it out of his own
pocket and supply his own ammunition. The state furnished cartridges
only for the old Sharps. Ten men in Company D, myself included,
were willing to pay the price for the superior weapon. I got a carbine,
number 13401, and for the next 6 years of my Ranger career, I never
used any other rifle. I have killed almost every kind of game that is
found in Texas, from the biggest old bull buffalo to a fox squirrel,
with the little .44 Winchester. Today I still preserve it as a prized
memento of the past.

It is cogent to realize that a Ranger of Gillett's day drew only
$40 monthly and was only paid quarterly. His satisfaction with
the 73 carbine more than compensated him for the expenditure
of a twelfth part of his annual stipend.

3 APACHES, COMANCHES AND INDIAN FIGHTERS

Texas had her Indians, none of them more wicked than the Lipan Apaches and the Comanches. There were others, the Kickapoos, the Wichitas, the Wacos, and the Tomkawas, not to forget the Caddos, but for sheer orneriness and downright cussedness the Lipans and the Comanches were winners. The Apaches were in the southwest hard against the Rio Grande, while the Comanches ranged farther northward and eastward. The lesser tribes were in the far northern reaches of the Lone Star State, and while they were on occasion a dangerous nuisance, their depredations were small indeed compared to the major troublemakers.

The Apaches of Texas, like the Comanches, were horse Indians. Other tribes of Apaches were largely foot travelers, but the Lipans soon learned that the horse was a vital factor in hunting and fighting and that there was no better nor more lucrative sport than to raid isolated ranches, running off the livestock, killing the settlers, and putting the torch to house and corrals. The Comanches, an offshoot of the Shoshones of the north, were equally appreciative of the qualities of Texas horseflesh.

Both tribes, although never allies, fought the Texans strongly as the encroaching white man pushed his longhorns into the red man's domain. Aided by the rugged desert-like nature of the country they resisted the advance of the settlers with a relentless savagery which neither gave nor asked quarter. Their reputation of being the most cruel, heartless, and inhuman savages of the entire continent was well deserved.

23

The Lipans, even after they were defeated, wanted nothing to do with the white man. During the long years of constant hostilities those few white squaw men who lived in the Apache camp learned relatively little about their hosts. The Apaches maintained a suspicious hostile reserve toward these interlopers. When finally subdued, they retained this same aloof attitude, despising their white conquerer and wanting no part of his culture.

The Apaches had long contact with white men and thoroughly distrusted them. The Spaniards and Mexicans had attempted to conquer the various tribes with small success. Between the Mexicans and the Indians there had been a state of continuous war. When the Texans commenced to push into those hunting grounds which the red man considered inviolable, he came to regard the newcomers in the same light as his old enemies, the Mexicans, and accorded them the same medicine: a raiding party at break of day, which left people dead and dying, shanty embers smouldering, and the horse herd scattered. The Mexican government sought to wipe out the Apaches by the *Proyecto de Guerra,* a law which put a bounty of $100 on the head of every Apache male. Women were $50, and children were $25. This encouraged scores of border renegades not only to collect an occasional Lipan scalp but also to gather in a good many harmless Mexican hair ornaments—a man's scalp is hard to identify after it is lifted off his head. The government found it was paying out a good deal of money but the Apache nemesis was not reduced.

From the time Texas gained her independence in 1836, there was an almost constant round of Indian skirmishing which extended for forty years. The Lipans and Comanches were raiders, given to marching long distances on their fast, light ponies and then striking in the dead of night. Isolated ranches, tiny settlements, wagon trains, travelers, and others who had all the earmarks of a poor defense were the victims. The raiders were essentially bowmen, but they coveted the white man's rifles, and these they carried away with them when a raid was staged. Over the years the brave managed to possess a Sharps, or Spencer, or Henry, and then he was trebly dangerous. Constituting some of the best light cavalry in the world, the Texan red raider was a hit-and-run warrior. He reconnoitered his objective, planned his approach with cunning, hit with all his forces, killed, scalped, and burned. He then rode off triumphantly, with loot which was usually horses. Cattle held small allure compared to the *caballo*. For in horse numbers the brave measured his wealth. To possess a hundred mounts stamped the Comanche as a big man of the tribe, not only in the possession of such obvious wealth but in stature as a raider. To take a hundred horses from the white man was no mean feat.

Texas, nearly as big as the entire country of France, had a scattered population when the red Indian was on the prowl. If he hit an isolated ranch the nearest neighbor might be twenty miles distant. It took time to gather a force to pursue the raiders. From the first beginnings as a country and later as a state, the president of the Republic of Texas and his legislature saw that a ranger force was needed to hold the savages in check. In December, 1838, President Lamar approved a law "for the protection of the frontier against the Comanches and other Indians," which provided for eight companies of mounted volunteers for six months. These men may be called the first Texas Rangers. The following January 24, a second law was approved appropriating a million dollars for the protection of the frontier against the marauders.

Tom Phelps liked to fish and so did his wife Mary. One sultry afternoon in August, 1873, they caught up their fishing poles and told the kids to stick around with grandma, who was Mrs. White, the mother of Mary Phelps. In a gladsome mood the pair trudged off down Cypress Creek. The creek ran spang through the Phelps ranch which was about fifty miles west of Austin, near Round Mountain in Blanco County. The catfish were biting on the dough balls which had been thoughtfully put together by Mary, and chatting and laughing the pair were making a holiday of the afternoon's angling.

Suddenly Mrs. Phelps froze in horror. There across the narrow stream stood a grinning Comanche. He was naked except for a breechclout and hideously painted across his mouth and cheekbones. The old .50 Sharps clutched in one hand came up slowly.

Screaming a warning to her husband, Mary Phelps dropped her cane pole and turned to flee. It was her last act. The heavy ball caught her waist high, and she was driven forward by the force of the blow. Phelps, who had been forty yards below his wife, fishing from a rock outcropping, heard the scream and the shot, and fearful of the implications, scrambled from the rock to reach his wife. He had no gun. As he ran back up stream, a brave who had been stealthily stalking him as he perched on the outjutting shelf of limestone lifted an old .56 caliber Spencer and shot him in the head. Both were scalped, Phelps lost his shoes, and the raiders thoughtfully carried away the stringer of catfish.

Dan Roberts got his neighbors together, and they agreed it was too late to follow the band that had bashed in the Phelps. The boys agreed that they would stand ready, and the next time word got around that there were Indians in their country they would take the trail. Action was not long in shaping up.

Scouts came in to Roberts within three days and told him that a big party of raiders was moving through the cedar brakes, traveling southward. Dan, who afterward became a Texas Ranger captain and was probably the best Indian scrapper that force ever claimed, rode out with Tom and Joe Bird, John Biggs, Stanton Jolly, and George Roberts, Dan's brother. After they had ridden for about ten miles they joined up with Captain Jim Ingram, Bill Ingram, Frank Waldrip, and Cam Davidson. The outfit then numbered ten and had no faint idea how many Comanches they would bump up against. Guns were pretty poor. Some of the boys had only cap-and-ball six-shooters, with an old Spencer .52 caliber in the hands of leader Roberts as the best shooting iron in the bunch.

Cutting northwestward, in about fifteen miles the riders came upon the Indian sign. There were tracks of a big band, all horse mounted; afterward the Texans found out that every horse carried a rider. The chase began. The Indians killed and partly butchered two beeves, and this meat they packed away with them. This encouraged the riders, for they knew the Comanches planned to stop somewhere and roast the beef. The Texans galloped their horses hard, pushing to overtake the marauders. After about twenty miles of the hardest riding they came out into the open. It was a flat prairie with a small round hill at the far flank. On it they saw their first brave.

On sighting the horsemen the Indian tumbled down off the mound and disappeared from view. "Ride into 'em, boys," yelled Dan Roberts as he plucked the old Spencer from beneath his knee. The other riders forged ahead of Roberts who was riding a badly fagged little mare.

The Indians, with the good strategy of seasoned veterans, had elected to make a stand not atop the hill, which was a natural defensive element, but in a ravine which angled off to the left of the incline. Their location compelled the attackers to move across open country to come to grips with them. The Texans, all inexperienced at fighting the cunning Comanche, drove into the guns of the hidden enemy. When within a hundred yards, the Indians opened fire. The Texans knew they were in an exposed and awkward position but got down off their horses and commenced to advance on foot. It was poor strategy.

Dan Roberts with the best rifle in his little platoon moved off to one flank. When an Indian stood up to shoot at the attackers in front, he exposed himself to the old Spencer. The distance was only eighty yards, and the rifleman was a good shot. He commenced to tally on the red men and saw two drop with as many shots. But his party out in front was not doing so well. His brother George took a heavy ball through the face and was out of the fight in the first minutes of firing. The Texans, brave enough, lacked an experienced leader to tell them what to do. Dan, fighting his own battle, was little accustomed to leadership, and this hurt the effort.

The Comanches were tough, seasoned, and enjoying the scrap. They were bellied down in the picayune arroyo and offered small targets. But for the flanking fire from Dan Roberts they would have suffered no casualties at all. Dan, working the old Spencer like a coffee mill, plugged two more savages. That made four. About that time a big .50 caliber Spencer ball took him through the thigh. He fell backward and lay still.

Bill Ingram, paying no attention to the whistling lead of the entrenched savages, ran to Roberts, and scooping him up as you would a child, hustled him back to cover. "Better leave me, Bill," said Dan Roberts, "I think I'm done for." The wound was spurting blood, and young Roberts believed the main artery had been severed. Bill Ingram shook his head and applied a tourniquet made of his neckerchief. The little force of ten scouts had been reduced to eight; both the Robertses were out of the fight. The Texans beat a hasty retreat taking their wounded boys and horses with them.

They fell back to the Johnson ranch, and here the wounded brothers were patched up as best the crude frontiersmen of the day could administer to them. Later they were moved home. One of the scouts rode over to Captain Rafe Perry's ranch which was only a half-mile away. Rafe, an old Indian fighter, gathered up all his cowboys and went back to the scene of the scrap. He found the raiding Comanches gone, their dead taken with them. Perry followed the trail and found where the four braves downed by Dan Roberts and his old Spencer had been buried. The band was never overtaken, and maybe the following Texans were just as glad not to catch up with these seasoned hands at the shoot and scoot game.

While the Roberts boys lay at home convalescing, the Honorable H. C. King, Texas state senator, came to see them. He was so impressed by the fact that they had organized and led the little band of Texans against the Comanches, who numbered twenty-seven, that he went before the legislature and introduced a bill to award every member of the party a new Model 1873 Winchester rifle. Dan Roberts felt that he had been amply rewarded for his part in the scrap and for the wound he had suffered. In no time at all he had joined up with the Texas Rangers, and the Model 73 went with him all up and down Texas; veterans, the two of them, of forty Indian skirmishes before they decided to call it quits. We shall hear more about Dan Roberts and his .44 Winchester as we go on.

The Comanches in this particular scrap had not conformed to good Indian tactics in electing to make a stand against the badly outnumbered Texans. The red strategy was to form a line on horseback when an attack was imminent, and when the white men charged, the line gave way in what appeared to be a pell-mell retreat. This was done with great speed, the Indians pouring the leather to their mounts and legging it at a dead run. The assault force seeing the cowardly scattering of the enemy took after them with high enthusiasm. The attacking line soon broke up into a series of pursuits, whereupon the Indians circled back and struck their now disorganized opponents from the flank and the rear. It was a basic strategy which worked time and time again. That the band which Roberts and his cowboy followers struck made a stand was uncommon.

Indians captured by the fighting Texans were usually hanged. The red man had a heaven, the Happy Hunting Ground. To get there his soul had to escape his body but the only way it could ascend to the heavens was through his mouth. If he were strangled as when hanged, his soul perished with his body. This possibility had a great deal to do with the savage fighting to the very last rather than giving up to his white attackers. Likewise the warrior who had his scalp lifted could not be a candidate for the Nirvana of his fathers. One of the striking examples of Indian bravery often occurred on the battlefield when a warrior would chance almost certain death to rescue a fallen chief and thus prevent the enemy, in this case some other tribe of red men, from reaching the body and lifting the hair piece. A brave who had been scalped was abandoned as carrion. He might be hauled away with a lasso about his heels to be dumped in the nearest buffalo wallow or left for the coyotes. There was no funeral ceremony for him. For why should there be? He could not possibly enter the Happy Hunting Grounds without his hirsute adornment intact.

The taking of scalps, common to all our western Indians, was great sport among the Texas tribes. The scalp when hacked off an enemy not only forever barred the owner from his own particular Valhalla but it enhanced the taker in the eyes of his fellows. While it was usually concluded that only one scalp was taken from a victim this was not always the case. From a full head of hair as many as three scalps might be whittled off. If time permitted the Lipan would skin out the entire head to include both ears. White men with full beards were a particular object of interest and the beard would be removed skin and all.

Colonel Richard Dodge, writing about the Indians in 1867,

tells about a "scalp" in a camp of Comanches which consisted of the head, face, chest, and belly of what appeared to be a former Mexican. The so-called scalp included in the one piece of epidermis the crotch as well. It was a common thing for the Indian to skin out the hair in the armpits of his white victims. What especial significance was attached to body hair by the savages is not entirely understood, but the fact that the full-blooded Indian grew no body hair made it somewhat of a fascination to him.

Indians on the warpath did not take captives. That is, no male prisoners. If a man fell into their hands, he was put to death at once. He might be killed in some fiendish way if time permitted, but he was not held and returned to camp unless it was decided to let the squaws torture him. They were experts at this game, and when a prisoner was turned over to them they might prolong his death agonies for two or three days. Killing him little by little. Stripping the skin from his body in small bits, or cutting off nose, lips, eyelids, ears, and the genitals. Sometimes splinters of pine filled with pitch would be jabbed into the poor wretch and then set on fire. The Indian was utterly cruel, neither knew nor felt any compassion, and the screams of the tortured were music to his ears.

Women prisoners were a different thing. When taken, the brave making the capture was the nominal owner, but he had to share his prize with all the braves in the marauding band. Each ravished the prisoner until he was satiated, and this went on whenever the band stopped or went into camp. Once back in the main encampment the hapless creature was at the mercy of all the bucks in the enclave. She might be loaned out to the friends of the brave who had captured her, or she could be sold or traded. Usually she was taken into the teepee with the savage who claimed her, and here she was beaten by the squaws and kept at ceaseless toil. When the Indians wanted peace with the whites, they would offer to exchange these outraged captives for a promise to let the tribe go without punishment.

Texan tribes did not burn their captives. But for pure fiendish methods of killing while yet prolonging the death to the utmost they were probably without equal, and especially the Apaches who were utterly devilish.

Jim Gillett, who has been mentioned before, was in Captain Dan Roberts' Ranger company in 1875. Roberts was by that time enlisted in the Frontier Battalion of the Ranger force, and Gillett, a raw recruit, was a member of Company D. Word reached the Ranger encampment that some fifteen Comanches had raided the John Gamble ranch and run off forty-two head of riding stock. The Ranger force sent after the redskins numbered fifteen men and was led by Roberts. The Comanches had some sixteen hours and sixty miles head start of the Rangers.

It was significant that Captain Roberts selected for his party the ten men who had only weeks before ordered the new Winchester Model 73 rifles in Austin. These rifles were .44-40; some were carbines, others had the longer barrels, but the canny Ranger leader knew that in a fight with the Indians the repeaters might very well be the decisive element. Jim Gillett had, like his comrades, invested a full month's pay for his Model 73. He shoved it in the scabbard and climbed aboard his Coley hoss.

Besides the commander, Roberts, the riders included Sergeant Jim Hawkins and Privates Paul Durham, Nick Donnally, Tom Gillespie, Mike Lynch, Andy Wilson, Jim Gillett, Henry Maltimore, Jim Trout, Bill Kimbrough, Si Crump, Ed Seiker, Jim Day, and John Cupps. Two pack-mules were laden with extra rations and a hundred rounds of spare cartridges for each man in the group. The first day the scouts covered sixty miles. They had reached Kickapoo Springs where they went into camp. There was no sign of the raiders, but Roberts who by this time was a seasoned Indian fighter was playing some hunches.

The next morning long before the dark shadows had given way to the moving sun, the party was up and riding. Roberts led his men on a southwest course from Kickapoo Springs. The pace was maintained, a hard five or six miles an hour. At noon the trail of the Comanches was crossed and the pace was quickened. When the trackers pulled up to rest and graze their horses, they selected an unfortunate site. The hobbled animals got into a nest of rattlesnakes, and two were bitten, one of them Old Rock, the iron-bottomed gray of Roberts. Neither mount could go on, and neither could they be abandoned. Jim Day's horse, Chico, had also been bitten, so Captain Roberts detailed Day to remain

with the stricken animals. Because it would have been foolhardy
to leave one man alone in that Indian country he also detailed
John Cupps to stay with him. The fighters had thus been reduced
to thirteen effectives. Day and Cupps remained with the horses
and although they never did catch up with the trackers they did
nurse the two sickened saddlers until both were on the mend and
finally moved them back to the permanent camp on the San Saba.

The Rangers had no spare horses, and their leader was now
dismounted. He quickly resolved that dilemma by shifting the
pack from one of the mules, overloading the second, but pro-
viding himself with a mount. The pack mule did not swing
along with the speed of Old Rock, but Roberts continually goaded
him, and the pursuit did not slacken.

The next day, having ridden sixty miles despite the loss of the
two horses, the trail was resumed. The Rangers rode up on a
maverick mare that had been stalked, shot, and butchered by the
band. This was good news. The rangers had by this time followed
the Comanches for a hundred and fifty miles, and during that
long time the Indians had never stopped to build a fire. The meat
stripped from the carcass of the mare would induce them to hold
up and cook and eat it.

The trail took the pursuers and the pursued by this time to
the head of the South Concho River and the Pecos on the west.
Here the raiding party had built three fires and cooked the ribs.
Captain Roberts reckoned the meal had been eaten right after
daylight. That night was a dismal one for the Rangers. No fires
were allowed and the horses were close-herded. Roberts believed
he would overtake the horse thieves on the morrow.

In the saddle by first light the group had hardly ridden five
miles when they sighted the Indians. Roberts made ready to
fight. He had his boys discard all the gear on their saddles,
including coats and slickers. Except for their intrepid leader
Dan Roberts and Sergeant Hawkins, none of the Rangers had
ever fought Indians before. The inexperienced men tightened
cinches and wondered about the outcome.

Captain Roberts ordered the little squadron not to draw the
Winchesters nor even a six-shooter until he gave the command.
His plan was the acme of simplicity. He rode his troopers in

column of two directly up in the rear of the redskins. The Indians, feeling secure after all the miles they had put behind them, were remarkably careless. The Rangers drew up within four hundred yards of the rear guard before they were discovered.

When the raiders saw the attack force so close to them they did not stampede. In a twinkling they had all dismounted and just as rapidly caught up fresh mounts. Not a shot had been fired. They then pulled off to a little rise and formed a battle line. Each brave held his horse, stood behind him, and leveled his rifle over the saddle.

Captain Roberts brought his fighters around into a skirmish line with plenty of interval between Rangers and advanced at a slow trot until he was within a hundred yards of the silently waiting Comanches. He then gave the command to dismount. "Fire low," he ordered in a calm voice. "Kill as many horses as you can. Every Indian we dismount we can hunt down and kill later." In an instant with Model 73s going like merry hell the Rangers had killed three horses and knocked over an Indian. The Comanches were firing hot and hard but their shooting was atrocious, a common fault of the Indian. (Said General Crook, "If the Indian had ever realized what the rear sight was for we would never have conquered the West.")

When the first round of fire from the steady-going rangers had commenced to spill both horses and riders, the old chief, Magooshe, gave a signal, and every brave jumped to the back of his standing pony and got the hell out of there. "Go after them," Roberts yelled. The Rangers swung aboard, and the race was on! Jim Gillett took after a horse which was carrying double. He gave Coley, a game racer he had fetched into the rangers with him, his head and after a couple of hundred yards was rapidly closing the space between him and the fleeing Comanches. He glanced back over his shoulder and saw that Ed Seiker was trailing him. He felt better when he saw that. The Indian riding double would turn occasionally and holding his rifle in one hand would get off a shot at Gillett and Seiker. They did not return the fire. After some time the brave dropped the rifle in the grass. He hoped this prize would induce his pursuers to stop and gather up the gun. They passed it by. In another hundred yards he

deliberately dropped what looked like a fine rawhide rope. It
did not tempt the Rangers. Having dropped his rifle the Indian
now took down his bow and commenced to lob arrows at his
enemies.

When Gillett had pulled up to within twenty yards of the
badly winded Indian pony, he suddenly pulled old Coley to a
rocking halt, vaulted off his mount, and took a quick snap shot
at the other horse. The big .44 caliber ball caught the paint right
at the junction of head and neck, not only severing the spinal
column but passing through the brain as well. The poor animal
turned head over heels like a jackrabbit. The Indian on behind
hit the ground on his feet and ran off to the protection of a little
clump of trees. Gillett swung back aboard his horse and was again
in hot pursuit. As he passed the horse he had killed he glanced
down at the first Indian and was astounded to see he was a white
boy of about sixteen years, with carrot-red hair. Despite his surprise he did not pull up but went on to finish things with the
Indian runner.

He saw within a few yards the savage looking out from behind
a small tree, his bow at the ready. A snap shot from horseback
struck six inches high. The Indian then broke and ran, and Ed
Seiker, who had by this time ridden up, put a bullet between his
shoulders. Gillett and Seiker approached the brave and found he
had been wounded in an ankle, his bow was almost shot in two,
and he had only three arrows remaining.

The two then turned back to find the white boy who apparently
had been unhurt in the shooting and subsequent spill from
the dead horse. He had disappeared. When the Rangers all
gathered again, Captain Roberts detailed several of them to help
search for the white boy. He could not be found. Years later
he turned up at Fort Sill in Oklahoma. His name was J. H.
Lehmann, and he had hidden in the grass while the Rangers were
searching for him. He said he was afraid he'd be killed by them.
When the Rangers quit the area he had walked away and made
it to Menardville.

The fight had not produced many casualties. The Rangers
had killed only the Indian shot down by Gillett and Ed Seiker,
had wounded several others, and had rounded up fifty-eight

horses and mules and all the stock stolen from the Gamble and other ranches. A search for the rifle dropped by the brave when he was making a run for it was to no avail. Cartridges on his body showed it was a Henry. Gillett, now quite fond of his Winchester 73 and knowing it was the forerunner of his own carbine, wanted it badly.

Jennie, the pack mule, turned loose when the fight started could not be found. This was another disappointment because she had not only all the spare cartridges but also all the rations. A long sweep failed to find her. The Rangers concluded she had trailed off after the fleeing savages. Six months later Ed Seiker piloted a troop of the U.S. Cavalry through the area and came upon Jennie's remains. She had been shot in the head and died right there. Her pack saddle with the pack intact was still cinched in place. Seiker found that the food was all eaten by varmints but the cartridges were intact showing the carcass had never been found by the Indians.

The Rangers rode into Wash DeLong's ranch on the headwaters of the South Concho the second day after the fight. They were long and lank from almost forty-eight hours without food, and the hospitable DeLong, happy to have Rangers in his midst, butchered and barbecued a steer and fed his hard-riding guests.

4

CHASING VICTORIO

Indians of the Southwest had several great leaders. Among these were Victorio and Geronimo. Of lesser stature was Nana who was a lieutenant under the wily Victorio and learned Indian fighting at his shoulder. Both the old chieftain and Nana were corralled by U.S. troops and together with their followers were removed to the Mescalero reservation in southern New Mexico. Here the old Apache chafed under the restraints of reservation life. He spent his time talking of war to his young braves. Nana, who had all the told killer's instincts, was active in keeping alive the bitter hatred which all felt toward the white man.

One dark night 125 of the Indians, including squaws and children, made a forced march which took them across the Rio Grande below El Paso. The Apaches, led by Victorio and Nana, did not pause until the choked canyons of the Candelaria Mountains had swallowed them.

Victorio knew precisely where he was going, and he pushed his little band hard until they reached a series of great natural tanks in the very tops of the sierra. Here there was water and feed. Here was also a natural fortress, a spot where he could watch the goings and comings along the main road between Juarez (El Paso del Norte) and Chihuahua City. In his sight as well were the Mexicans' pueblos of San Jose and Carrizal.

In no time at all Victorio sent a little band of his raiders, numbering only six or seven selected renegades, down on the sleepy little pubelo of San Jose. The Mescaleros ran off a small remuda of saddle stock kept close-herded at the village.

37

No one was killed because there was no resistance. The pony herd when it was stampeded awakened a good many villagers. The next morning after they had cut the sign of the raiders and realized it was a small party, they sent a hurried messenger to nearby Carrizal for reinforcements. There were assembled, under the leadership of Don Jose Rodriguez, some fifteen stalwarts. All were mounted and all were armed. The rifles were a motley array. Most were gotten from the Mexican government and were Remington rolling-block breechloaders, firing the .40-44 cartridge. There were two .44 Henrys in the group and two shotguns, both muzzle-loaders. At least one rider had a muzzle-loading rifle. Don Jose, the *jefe,* wore two six-shooters. These were both brand new, purchased in El Paso, and were the new Colt Model 1873. Both were destined to wind up in the hands of Victorio.

The horse herd left a wide, easily followed trail. The Mexicans rode in a gallop and soon swung into the foothills. The sign shortly struck a well-worn Indian trail and wound upward, passing over a crest which had on the one side some abrupt cliffs and on the other a boulder-strewn hillside. Victorio watched the approaching horsemen and wise old strategist that he was—he had by that time fought more than two hundred skirmishes— put forty or fifty of his warriors in the cliff's face. On the other side of the trail he placed a dozen rifles, hiding his braves among the boulders. The Mexicans crowded into the saddle between the peaks, and as they were about to drop over the crest, the Apaches laced it to them. Don Jose was a good commander, and as the Indian fire, all directed from the open hillside, whistled among horses and riders, he had his little platoon dismount and move off to the flank toward the cliffs. This was what Victorio had anticipated.

As the Mexicans sought cover at the base of the precipitous bluffs, the warriors above them poured down a murderous fire. The Apaches by this time—it was 1879—all had rifles, and for the most part these were breechloaders, with a sprinkling of repeaters. The bewildered and frightened Mexicans were caught. Caught and killed to a man.

Jim Gillett, who by this time was stationed at Ysleta, a small town on the Rio Grande below El Paso, went over the battlefield a few days after the ambush and found one spot where an Apache had squatted behind a rock outcropping on the hillside and fired twenty-seven shots into the huddled posse. The cartridges were .45-70, fired no doubt from a captured Sharps.

When the company of Mexicans did not return to San Jose and Carrizal, the villagers were worried and alarmed. A second group of riders was assembled, fourteen of them, and set out to find their missing fellows. They had no choice except to follow the trail of the first detachment. Victorio had known they would do this, and he had elected to bushwhack the second riders exactly as he did the first. He let them ride full into the pass between the two peaks in the Candelarias, and when they were caught between his two lines, he fired the first shot from the new Colt six-shooters he had unstrapped from the body of Don Jose Rodriguez.

Two Mexicans tried to escape. One was shot down before he had ridden a hundred yards. The other was caught about six hundred yards back along the trail. Seeing he was surrounded, he dismounted, tied his horse to a yucca, and fought to the last. He had fired thirty or forty shots before he and the horse were killed. The yucca was shot to doll ribbons. Jim Gillett had retrieved these empties. He said they were all .44 rimfire cases, an indication that the rifle was the Winchester forerunner, the Henry, patterned in 1860 and first manufactured in 1862.

The loss of twenty-nine men from the two tiny Mexican hamlets practically decimated both of their male populations. It also spread consternation throughout all of that end of Chihuahua. The authorities in Juarez, the largest town, gathered a strike force of almost a hundred rifles. This company was recruited at Zaragoza, a *pueblo* below Juarez, and moved on to Don Inocente Ochoa's rancho. The Mexicans were under the command of Jose Ramos. The Rangers, who had a permanent camp just across the Rio Grande, under the command of Lieutenant Baylor, were invited to join the punitive expedition. Baylor gathered up ten of his stalwarts and rode across the Rio to take the trail.

At nightfall the company rode off toward the Candelarias, putting out scouts and with flank guards. They were uncertain whether or not the cunning old Apache would not attempt to

ambush even a party of this size. At midnight they halted, and
the scouts reported back that no sign of the Indians had been
found. At daybreak the company rode onto the scene of the two
massacres, and thence onward and upward to the camp of the
Mescaleros, a camp now abandoned by Victorio. Cutting sign
about the foot of the sierra they found that the Indians had
moved out westward and southward. After a council of war with
the Mexicans it was decided to turn back. The force returned to
Zaragoza, and the Rangers forded the Rio Grande to their
camp.

No more was heard of Victorio and his killers until the follow-
ing spring when the grass was good and the waterholes all filled
with the rains of the early season. He renewed his raiding and
killings then. He and his marauders were first reported sighted at
Lake Guzman in northern Chihuahua. Thence he was trailed to
Borracho Pass near the Rio Grande, and in a couple of days the
Mexicans sent word to General Grierson at Fort Davis that the
Apaches were making for the Eagle Mountains in Texas. The
army sent word to the Rangers of these movements and asked
Lieutenant Baylor to put his buckos into the field in an effort to
come to grips with the killers.

The U.S. Cavalry galloped off toward Eagle Springs, and
Baylor rode off toward the Eagle Mountains with thirteen men.
At Fort Quitman the Rangers tried to get in touch with the
cavalry via telegraph. Victorio, fully aware of the role played by
the singing wires, had thoughtfully cut several hundred yards
of the line, dragged it away, and uprooted poles along with the
copper. Lieutenant Baylor and his Rangers rode into two troops
of cavalry at Rattlesnake Springs. The Rangers had found a
place where Victorio and his cohorts had chopped out the
telegraph line. The sign here indicated a sizeable force.

The Indians were moving so fast that they kept well in front of
both the cavalry and the Rangers. They looped back around the
combined force, and just outside Fort Quitman they waylaid the
stage. It was driven by Ed Walde, who afterward became a
Ranger and a good one, and had as its only passenger a retired
general officer, Ben Byrnes. The stage was pulled by two small
Spanish mules, not the usual four or six but only the single team.

As the stage rounded a bend in the road, in a tight little box canyon only scant miles from Fort Quitman, Walde was suddenly confronted by Victorio and his entire force. There were at least a hundred savages in the trail.

The driver did not panic. He whipped the little mules around and made a run for the stage station. The Apaches raced after him and shooting and riding pursued the careening coach for miles. General Byrnes was killed, but somehow, and pretty miraculously, neither Walde nor the mules were hit. After this attack the Indians sallied over to Jesus Cota's ranch and ran off a sizeable herd of his best beefstock, first shooting and scalping his cowboy. When they tried to force the cattle across the Rio Grande, a good many of the played-out cows mired in the quicksand. These the heartless renegades butchered without bothering to kill them. The U.S. Cavalry had to give up the chase on the banks of the international stream. Victorio was heading again for a sanctuary known only to him.

Don Ramon Arrandas got together a force of Mexican volunteers, and as his recruits gathered, he sent an urgent invitation to Lieutenant Baylor at Ysleta to join with him in running down the Indians. Baylor accepted the invitation and with thirteen Rangers again entered Mexico and joined up with the forces of Arrandas. The combined company numbered about one hundred. It was a poorly armed group. Many of the volunteers had only pistols; there were no less than twenty shotguns and a sizeable number of muzzle-loaders. Arandas, the leader, was well armed. He was a wealthy cattleman, living below Juarez, and had a new Model 73 Winchester and a pair of Smith & Wesson revolvers.

The company put out scouts and flanking guards and moved off toward the Rancheria Mountains. They struck the Indians' trail, but it had been partly obliterated by a recent rain. The next morning, at Lucero, it was reliably reported that Victorio had swung around and was within a few miles of Carrizal, the little pueblo where the year before he had so successfully accomplished the ambush of the town's male population. The full Ranger force together with seventy of the Mexican volunteers made an all-night march to head off the murderous old redskin, but at dawn they found the Indians had pulled back. A heavy rain then washed out the sign, and this forced the entire party to march back to San Jose. Here they waited the arrival of General Joaquin Terrazas.

When General Terrazas put in an appearance, he had with him two hundred well-mounted cavalrymen and a hundred infantry soldiers. These were regular army troops, and they made a good impression on Jim Gillett. The cavalry was armed with Remington .40 caliber falling-block rifles and Remington Model 1858 revolvers .36 caliber. The infantry had the falling block .40 caliber rifle but no sidearms. The mixed battalion was well mounted and uniforms were of good quality, and all the equipment of man and beast was in excellent condition. The infantry, recruited from the interior of Mexico, trotted along behind the cavalry and had no trouble in keeping up. As a matter of fact when the going got rough the foot soldiers could easily outdistance the horsemen.

Gillett looked over the Mexican force and was impressed by their good military appearance. He had many misgivings about such a large group ever catching up with the wily Victorio. If the old chieftain observed the battalion from afar, he would simply break his braves down into small detachments and send them to the four winds. Flee and rejoin at some distant and inaccessible spot in the vastness of the Sierra Madre Range.

General Terrazas rode four white horses. He was more than six feet in height, of commanding appearance, and trailed by innumerable aides who led three of the white mounts while the imposing commander bestrode the fourth. The battalion quit San Jose to the vivas of the little settlement, all eager to put an end to the Apache menace. The rangers marched near the head of the column and made Rebosadero Springs where they camped. Then they marched forty miles to Borracho Springs where, twenty miles west of the pass, the trail was picked up. It was followed into the Los Piños Mountains, and after about seventy-five miles of steady pursuit, Victorio turned southward heading into deepest Chihuahua.

General Terrazas then called a meeting and told Lieutenant Baylor and his other allies of the border hamlets near Juarez that since it appeared they were going to be drawn farther and farther from their homes, all were free to quit his command and return if they liked. The Rangers took this as a pretty broad hint that the Mexicans wanted them to drop out of the chase. There was no international agreement either between the United States and Mexico or yet Texas and Mexico for the Rangers to operate on the south side of the Rio Grande. To go several hundred miles into the sister republic, even though in a common pursuit, was without precedent. Baylor and his thirteen men turned back.

The very next day General Terrazas' scouts rode in and informed him that Victorio and his entire band were at Tres Castillos, about twenty-five miles southwest of the Los Piños Mountains. The Mexican force moved out at the double. The old Indian, with his usual perspicacity, had located his camp in the high mountains where he could look back over his trail. He saw Terrazas and his cavalry for hours before they came within range.

Victorio made no move to run for it. He had sent away Nana and fifty braves on a raiding foray. He had remaining in camp about a hundred warriors and of course all the women and children, as well as several hundred horses. There were almost five hundred horses and mules. Why this redoubtable leader, veteran of hundreds of skirmishes with both the Mexicans and the Americans, elected to sit tight until he was completely surrounded by the Mexican cavalry no one from this time and distance can reasonably understand. It was wholly out of pattern. Most certainly he did not believe his hundred fighting men could successfully stand off a force of three hundred. His deep understanding of his foe, a knowledge built of a lifetime of implacable fighting, must have told him that here was no pick-up force. The actions and the attitudes of the well-disciplined troops spread out below him must have plainly written that this was a fight which was bound to go ill with him and his followers.

Directly after nightfall, General Terrazas, having listened to his scouts, disposed of his troopers so that he had three sides of the Indian encampment surrounded. He waited until first light before he commenced the assault. Victorio had not been idle.

He knew that he was in for a tough battle and that he could not flee. Indeed he seemed to relish the thought of a fight to the finish. Just what was going on in his wily old brain will never be known. He deployed his braves in a close-in defense, a perimeter bristling with Winchester, Henry, and Spencer repeaters against the single-shot rifles of the attackers, and mounted a white horse to check his outposts.

Terrazas had moved his scouts in quite close. With Victorio nicely silhouetted against the morning sky, one of these fellows laid his rifle across a piñon limb and, although the shot was a long one, fired. His comrade, rifle cradled on a huge boulder nearby, fired at precisely the same moment. Both bullets found their mark. Victorio was struck in the thigh and through the ribs. He died almost instantly.

The old leader had been within sight of his entire following when he tumbled from his horse. Nana was away; the band had no other leader. Terrazas closed on the Mescaleros. Eighty-seven braves were killed, and all the women and children were captured.

When Nana heard of the loss of his band, he took his fifty warriors and crossed the Sierra Madre to Sonora where he joined forces with another notable old scoundrel, Geronimo. Together the pair raided up and down Mexico, with frequent forays into Arizona, and unquestionably killed more humans than any other guerrilla group in the history of Indian warfare.

General Terrazas was lionized after his notable victory over the Apaches. A grateful government gave him such huge grants of land in Chihuahua that he finally possessed one of the largest ranches in North America, if not the largest. The general was so elated over the outcome of the battle that he sent a messenger after the Rangers. He caught them at Fort Quitman but his news caused nothing save dour faces among the *Tejanos*. They had missed being in on the kill by only thirty-six hours. After all the many days and fruitless miles on the trail there was little rejoicing.

5

QUANAH PARKER

A few miles north of the Canadian River in the Texas Panhandle was the ruins of an old Bent trading post. It was called Adobe Walls, not the original name, because it was abandoned in 1844, and the store, warehouses, private dwellings, mission, blacksmith shop, and other structures, all built of adobe and rock, had gone to ruin. The adobe brick walls, many of them five feet thick, still stood.

During the Civil War the Kiowas and Comanches became increasingly troublesome and took to raiding with a great deal of regularity along the Santa Fe Trail. An attack in 1864 on a wagon train near Pawnee Rock, Kansas, in which five settlers were killed and five small boys carried off by the Indians, incensed General Carlton who had the western Kansas district. He ordered Kit Carson, who was campaigning against the Navajos, to break off and punish the Kiowas and the Comanches.

Carson had about four hundred troops in his command. These were volunteers from New Mexico together with a sizeable group of Ute and Jicarilla Apaches. He struck a Kiowa village and drove the Indians to the vicinity of Adobe Walls. Here the Kiowas got reinforcements, and it took all Carson and his ragtag force could do to stand them off. He had two twelve-pounders, and these he mounted within the thick walls of the old fort and put up a defense for two days and nights. Finally during the third night he ordered a retreat. Adobe Walls was to see more fighting before it crumbled into the dust of the Texas Panhandle.

The old fort had been used by the U.S. Cavalry as a sort of

45

way station on patrols into the lands along the Canadian River. It was not regularly garrisoned, but the corrals were kept in shape so that cavalry stock could be turned out when a scouting party moved through that area. By 1874 without any maintenance the buildings were further fallen to ruin. The buffalo hunters were thick through the Panhandle country by this time, busy decimating the southern herd. Adobe Walls became a rendezvous for them. There were stores where they could buy rations, powder, primers, and lead, also salt and tobacco. There was a blacksmith shop and a saloon and a small number of settlers who catered to the needs of the drifting buffalo hunters.

Quanah Parker was the big chief of the Comanches. He preached a war of extermination against the white man. He traveled around to the councils of the Kiowa, Arapaho, and Cheyenne and urged them to join with the Comanches in their holy war. Besides Quanah Parker the Comanches had a powerful medicine man, Isa-tai, who told them during the ceremonial sun dance that he could make them immune from the white man's bullets. The Indians believed him. As a first target Quanah Parker led his people against Adobe Walls. It held twenty-eight men and one woman. There were seven hundred Comanches, Kiowas, Cheyennes and Arapahoes in the attack party.

Among the regulars at Adobe Walls in June, 1874, were Jim Langton and Fred Leonard who ran a lively business in buying and shipping buffalo hides. Jim Hanrahan had a trading store, and Tom Keefe had started up his smithy in the old chapel. Fred Leonard had used two corners of the old adobe walls and finished out a corral with cottonwood posts, and in this enclosure he ran a wagon yard. Besides, he had a mess house for hunters and freighters.

Captain Arrington with a detachment of his Ranger company rode through Adobe Walls and warned the traders that the Indians were concentrating for no good on Deep Creek, a branch of the Colorado River, to the south. His warning was little heeded. It was talked over and the conclusion was that the Indians might be going on the war path but they would confine their devilment to isolated camps of buffalo runners. Adobe Walls, considered the residents, was too tough a nut to crack.

Quanah Parker moved his seven hundred warriors out of the Deep Creek bivouac under cover of darkness and by two hours before first light had them in attack position before the old tumbled-down post. Inside the settlers were sound asleep. There were no guards posted, no dogs about the cabins to bark the alarm. About that time Providence got into the picture. The regulars around Adobe Walls all slept in Hanrahan's store. At about 3:00 A.M. the ridgepole which supported the roof commenced to crack and pop ominously. It held a weight of branches and dirt, and the strain was too great. Everyone was awake on the moment, and two of the sleepers climbed upon the roof and began to shovel off some of the dirt before the ridgepole broke completely in two. This stirring about aroused Tom Keefe who walked outside his chapel smithy, relieved himself, and gazed off toward a buffalo herd about a half mile out on the flats. He watched the bison and his curiosity was aroused. The entire band, and it was a big herd of hundreds of animals, was drifting at a fast walk directly toward the settlement.

This was not like the buff, who by this time were feeling the steady pressure of the ever-booming rifles of the hunting army, and Keefe, an old buffalo runner himself, thought it mighty strange. He continued to watch the oncoming herd. At about this time, Elias Watson and his partner Joe Ogg, hunters both of them, decided since they were awake to go rustle their horses and thus get an early start. They left the corrals of Fred Leonard and struck off at an angle from the oncoming bison. They had scarcely gone a hundred paces when they noted the movement of the band. At about the same moment they silhouetted some of the buff against the skyline and saw they were mounted Indians. It had been Quanah Parker's strategy to bunch his braves closely and approach the Adobe Walls as though they were a herd of bison.

Watson and Ogg turned and ran. Tom Keefe at the same time had decided what was going on, and he bolted for Langton's, shouting at the top of his lungs. He crashed through the buffalo hide door with bullets and arrows chipping adobe dust around his head. Watson and Ogg made it to Hanrahan's. The Indians had hoped to ride directly into the old fort before they were dis-

covered. Only the threat from the ridgepole in the store had
alerted the whites. Quanah Parker, a brave Indian, was in the
forefront of his attackers. He rode at Leonard's door and was
shoving his way inside when one of the buffalo hunters shot him
through the chest. This put him out of the fight, and it took a
lot of spirit out of his followers who had been assured by their
medicine chief, Isa-tai, that they were impervious to the white
man's lead. Parker did not die and afterward became a friend of
the white man.

There were ten men in Hanrahan's, five men and one woman
in Langton's, and twelve in Leonard's. A pair of brothers, Ike
and Shorty Shadler, were asleep in their wagon. For some reason
the first noise of the attack did not awaken them. When they
did come alive, they found they were literally engulfed in raging
Comanches. Both were promptly shot and scalped, and the
Indians dragged their bodies into the wagon yard and draped
them over the corral fence for the defenders to see.

When Quanah Parker was shot, his nephew Stone Calf took
over command of the seven hundred rampaging warriors. During
the morning hours he divided his force into two attack parties,
and these separate groups commenced a long series of attacks
trying to force the doors of the buildings. By a fortunate circumstance the defenders were in positions where they could cover
each others' flanks, and this greatly aided the common defense.

Besides the regular residents of Adobe Walls there was a considerable contingent of buffalo hunters in the place. Among them
was none more famous than Bat Masterson who afterward became the city marshal of old Dodge, Kansas. Along with him
was Billy Dixon, who was a buffalo runner of renown. These
gentry hunted with .40 to .50 caliber rifles of Sharps, Ballard,
Remington, and other makes. These were heavy rifles weighing
fourteen to sixteen pounds, were fired off a cross-stick rest from
the prone position, and were equipped with excellent sights and
very light triggers. It was common practice for buff hunters to
take along a lighter repeating rifle, not for shooting buffalo which
required the .50 caliber but for taking small game and for
standing off the Indians and white outlaws who were wont to
raid the isolated hunter's camp. Both Billy Dixon and Bat

Masterson had Winchester 73s during the battle at Adobe Walls. Whether there were other 73s in the camp, history doesn't indicate, but it is fair speculation to assume there were. After all there were seven hundred Indians against twenty-eight white men, and certainly to stand off those odds the frontiersmen had to shoot like hell! Hotter and faster, certainly, than could have been done with the ponderous and slow-to-load buffalo rifles.

Stone Calf, young and untried, anxious to gain stature in the eyes of his fellow Comanches, led a head-on charge against Hanrahan's store. He took fifty braves with him. The Indians rode right up to the door and tried to push it in. Stone Calf was shot twenty times, and dead Comanches were counted all the way from the corner of the store back to the wagon yard. Lee Tyler, who had been firing from one of the windows of Hanrahan's, was killed during the melee.

Adobe Walls Creek ran through a little stand of cottonwoods about two hundred yards down the hill from the settlement. The Indians got into these trees and kept up a constant drumbeat of gunfire against the exposed doors and windows. While this contingent was hammering away, another band took advantage of the tall buffalo grass which grew almost against the old building. The Indians wriggled up behind Leonard's store and took cover behind a great tall stack of buffalo skins. They were attempting to work up close enough to set the roof on fire.

Billy Dixon, who spoke Comanche like a Comanche, heard the Indians shouting to the others in the trees and realized their game. He unlimbered the .50 caliber rifle, putting the .44 Winchester aside for the moment, and commenced to drive the big 500-grain slugs completely through the piles of buffalo skins. He killed an Indian pony and drove the redskins away.

The Comanches and their allies then circled the settlement, hanging on the offside of their racing ponies, and firing under the horses' necks. This was a bad tactical error. The defenders were all accustomed to shooting running antelope, and once they set a big buffalo gun to swinging it maintained a steady lead. Horse after horse was tumbled by the deadly aim of the forted-up white men. The Indians pulled off to hold a powwow.

This war council brought on the most famous shot of the

Adobe Walls siege. The chiefs gathered on horseback on a distant ridge. Billy Dixon gathered up his buffalo gun, guessed off the range at a thousand yards, ran the vernier sight up to the mark, laid the ponderous octagon barrel over the window of Leonard's, and let drive at a big Indian astride a baldfaced paint horse. The Comanche fell out of the saddle as if he had been struck by lightning. Afterward Dixon stepped off the yardage, along with others who had stood off the Indians, and it was found to be 937 long steps.

During the night the defenders abandoned Hanrahan's place and took up posts in Leonard's and Langston's stores. They dug a well during the night and barricaded the doors. Thaddeus Reed was dispatched to Dodge City to get help. He managed to slip through the Indian lines and made good his escape. It would take him three to four days to make the ride, and the hunters did not have much hope that he could bring reinforcements in time to help them.

The third day of the fighting, the Indians gave up their frontal attack and stood off and peppered the 'dobe walls from the protection of the trees along the creek. Bill Olds climbed up to the roof of Leonard's store and was shot in the head. He fell through the trapdoor at his wife's feet. That night buffalo hunters, having heard the firing, commenced to infiltrate Adobe Walls. Before morning there were a hundred of them within the walls of the several stores where the defenders were holding forth. The arrival of these unexpected reinforcements cheered the weary party very much; a barrel of whisky was tapped, and everybody had a round of red-eye. After two more days during which the Indians had not sallied forth, had fired no shots, and had not been in evidence, Frank Huffman and Bob Roberts, a couple of the buff hunters who had joined the defenders on the third night, went out to reconnoiter. They climbed out on a little rise about a hundred yards from the old chapel and looked around. Indians hidden in the cottonwoods along Adobe Walls Creek promptly killed them both.

After ten days the Indians moved out. Cautious reconnaissance by the whites established that the area was clear of the Comanches and their cohorts. Adobe Walls was abandoned and the entire party marched off, some going to Dodge and others treking into Fort Griffin. Thaddeus Reed got to Dodge in three and a half days of hard riding, and when he informed the military there that twenty-eight men were fighting seven hundred Indians, his story was not believed. Eighty-five Indians were killed according to a later story of Quanah Parker. After the white men had all departed, the Indians came back and burned Adobe Walls leaving nothing standing save the walls of 'dobe and masonry.

6

SETTLING ACCOUNTS

The night before the battle which wrote finis to the checkered career of old Victorio, a number of his braves saw the handwriting on the wall. They knew full well that the wily old chieftain had finally played his hand out. They had observed the combined battalion of horse-mounted troopers and infantrymen on the plain below their hideout, and as old campaigners themselves they had small illusion about their chances. They deserted. There were twelve braves and four squaws with four children. They escaped the massacre that befell the Mescaleros at the hands of General Terrazas and his command.

This little band stirred up unshirted hell for the next twelve months. In consideration of the few numbers—but an even dozen—these Apaches were real devils. They killed isolated settlers, raided stage stations, ran off horses, mules, and cattle, did not hesitate to tackle the U.S. Cavalry, and kept both the Texas Rangers and the military almost constantly in the saddle.

The first move of these escaping renegades was to strike out for the Rio Grande and Texas. Their destination was the Eagle Mountains. In due time they were reported at Paso Viejo, which is near the present town of Valentine. Word was gotten to the cavalry about the movements of the Mescaleros, and a scout was commenced under the command of a fresh-out-of-West-Point youngster, Lieutenant Mills. His troops were all Negroes out of the famous Tenth Cavalry. With Mills were four scouts from the Ysleta Indians.

The troop made camp at Paso Viejo despite the advice of Simon

Holguin, the ranking Indian scout, who pointed out that the
Apaches in crossing from Mexico very frequently pulled into
Paso Viejo because of the plenitude of both grass and water. He
advised the lieutenant to pull two or three miles back from the
pass and thus avoid an Indian attack at daylight. Mills, inexperienced with Indian skirmishing, told the old scout in no
uncertain terms that he was not afraid of the Apaches. They
would camp right there.

The next morning the troop rolled out, ate breakfast, packed
their mules, saddled their horses, and stood by ready for the
command to mount. In the night the twelve Apaches had snaked
their way into the very middle of the cavalry camp. The Indians
fired at almost point-blank range. Most of their rifles were
Henry, Winchester, and Spencer, and the first volley was followed
by a second and a third. At the first fusillade Simon Holguin was
struck in the head and killed. Six soldiers fell moments later.
The remainder of the troop fled. The remaining scouts, all
nephews of old Simon, stood their ground and fought off the
Apaches, more to save their uncle from being scalped and
mutilated than for any other reason.

The next place the killer band struck was less than twenty
miles west of Van Horn, a small cow town, some thirty miles
north of the ambush of the cavalry. Here they swooped down on
a wagon train. Lying on either side of the trail the Apaches
waited until the wagons were in a low saddle, and then they
opened up from either flank. At the first round of fire, Tom
Graham's wife, who was walking, tried to reach a Winchester
which was lying on the seat of the wagon. As her foot struck
the wagon tongue, she was shot and killed. Graham was struck
in the thigh, breaking the bone. Another party member, Dick
Grant, was shot in the head and died.

The marauders then wisely turned southward and crossed into
Mexico, lying low there for weeks at a hidden spring known only
to them. After resting their horses and permitting them the
scanty grazing about the waterhole the band again went on the
rampage. They moved up to Ojo Caliente Springs on the Rio
Grande, and here were spotted by Mexican goat herders. Word
was hurried along to the cavalry at Fort Quitman. A detail of

eight men in charge of a sergeant was sent on a week's scout to see what they could turn up. The troopers marched down the Rio Grande and after three days turned back. They camped the night at Ojo Caliente.

The next morning the little detachment rolled out, made coffee, ate their iron rations, gathered their horses which had been close herded all night, and prepared to saddle. At that precise moment the Apaches opened up. They had crawled up on three sides during the night and waited for daylight. The Apache had a fear of a night fight and invariably waited for the light of the day to do his killing. The fire of the Indians, armed with repeating rifles, the Henry .44 rimfire and its counterpart the new model 73 Winchester in .44 centerfire, was too much for the Springfield carbines. The latter, the Model 1873, single-shot with poor extractors, and inclined to jam, were no match for the lever guns of the savages. Every man in the cavalry detachment was killed save one. He escaped on foot. After two days without food or water he finally reached a cavalry outpost and reported the massacre.

Again the little band of terrorists faded into the vastness of border Mexico. Not, however, before they cruelly tortured three of the colored soldiers who were wounded and not killed outright. These hapless victims were turned over to the women for torture before they finally died. The eight horses and two packmules together with eight hundred rounds of .45-70 ammunition and all the rifles and the sergeant's .45 revolver were taken. The depredations then ceased for almost two months.

One sunny afternoon the stage was coming through Quitman Canyon. On it was the driver, a lad of twenty named Morgan, and the sole passenger, an El Paso gambling man, Enos Crenshaw. The Indians killed both. Baylor, in command of the Ranger company at Ysleta, recently promoted from lieutenant to captain, gathered up fifteen men and with himself at the head rode off to see what he could do about the continual threat of this little gaggle of Mescaleros. Baylor and his Rangers picked up the trail of the Indians at Ojo Caliente and followed it into Mexico. He did not hesitate to cross the Rio Grande knowing full well he had the blessings of all the Mexicans including the government.

The sign took them into the area where the year before General Terrazas had put an end to old Victorio and his followers. It then turned eastward and headed directly for the Rio Grande again.

The Apaches forded the river, stopping now and then to kill, butcher, and barbecue a horse. When Baylor and his riders reached the Rio Grande and saw that the Indians were headed for the Eagle Mountains, he checked up. Between the river and the distant sierra was a broad flat plain where the keen-eyed Mescaleros could look back over their trail and see the pursuers. The Ranger pondered this and decided they were several days behind the killers and would not be spotted if they undertook to ride out on the bare mesa. The crossing was made in daylight and that night the lawmen made camp in the lee of the Eagles.

At first light the Rangers were up and stirring. After a skimpy breakfast of coffee and parched corn, the latter eaten as they moved out, the little force commenced to ascend the mountains. Within four or five miles they came upon the Apache camp. It had been quit in a hell of a hurry. The Indians had seen the Ranger force approaching and had run, leaving behind saddles, blankets, moccasins, and other gear. They had been making ready for a celebration, for the Rangers found a horsehide sunk in the ground and in it was twenty gallons of mescal. Now mescal is a fiery concoction, made from the mescal cactus, and a favorite of these Apaches who gained their name "Mescalero" from their propensity for getting incandescent on the fermented juice of the roots of this desert plant. At the camp site the Rangers also turned up letters, express receipts, and other items taken from the stage.

It had been freezing cold the night before and the ground was frozen. The Holguin brothers, who were scouting for the Rangers, got down on hands and knees and tried to pick up the trail of the fleeing savages. It was to no avail. The Indians had seemingly vanished. Baylor turned and rode off toward Eagle Springs in the hopes of again picking up the trail where there was better tracking.

At Eagle Springs quite by chance Baylor and his party bumped into Lieutenant Nevill with nine Rangers. Nevill told his commander that he had seen the trail only that morning and it was heading for the Diablo Mountains. Baylor and his riders had eaten all their rations, and Nevill had only food enough for his nine Rangers for the next five days, but the two officers decided to ride after the Mescaleros and trust to luck about the rations.

Just as Nevill had presumed, the Indians had traveled fast across the flats before the Diablos, chancing their being seen by the pursuing Rangers. Once they got into the broken country that formed the foot hills of the Diablo Range, they had paused long enough to kill and eat a horse. They had no water, but there was snow on the ground in the Diablos, and they melted this for drinking.

The Indian sign ran around Chili Peak, a very well known landmark in the Diablos. By this time the Rangers were pushing hard. At Apache Tanks the little force cut off and watered their weary mounts and filled all the canteens. Then they pushed on. The trail pulled away from the higher country of the mountain range, and the Indians had gone out to the edge of the sierra where they could command a tremendous sweep of country. Feeling somewhat safer they made camp and slept the night. They had wisely selected a craggy canyon where in case of surprise they could drop into its rocky interior and thus elude the nemesis at their backs.

The next camp was not more than a dozen miles from the first. The Apaches had no food with them. When they traveled for twenty-four hours, they would have to slit a horse's throat, build a series of tiny fires, and broil the meat. Some of it was hastily jerked, smoked, and carried along. On this camp they killed one of their last horses and had a feed. They were by this time almost all unhorsed, having killed and consumed the team from the stage plus their own sorry and worn-out animals.

The Rangers held to the trail. The uncanny sense of the Holguin brothers to pick up the sign even when the Apaches held to bare rock kept the officers continually moving forward. Baylor felt they were only hours behind their quarry, and he and his fellows were eager to come up with the savages.

The trail had been steadily going north when quite abruptly it turned eastward, plunging the pursuers and pursued into the vastness of the Sierra Diablo. The Rangers came upon a spot where the Indians had eaten. This time they had not slit a horse's throat but had dined frugally on the smoked horseflesh from the last camp. They had again eaten snow to quench their thirst. Nothing had been done to water their played-out ponies. The Apache was a cruel man, never more heartless than in his attention to the horses, burros, and mules that he used up. It was often said in the West that a hard white man would ride a horse until he was ready to drop and then abandon him. A Mexican would come along and ride the same horse for another week and then leave the poor critter to die. The Apache would then pass and take up the same horse and ride him every day for a month until the broken-down *caballo* would literally die on his feet.

The Indian band passed over a high mesa, and when the rangers came to this crossing, they wisely made camp in a tiny canyon waiting for nightfall to follow out the trail. They were sure that if they tried to pursue the trail across the open mesa the Apaches would most surely spot them. The Rangers made a dry camp and spent a restless night.

The next morning the camp was in the saddle before dawn. On the far side of the mesa the scouts got their noses down to within inches of the ground. After some quartering about, they picked up the trail and moved out. The Indians had turned north.

Moving slowly and watching ahead very intently, Baylor was not at all surprised to have one of his scouts say in a low voice, *"Alli estan los Indios,"* pointing ahead. About a half mile away were the fires of the Apaches.

Captain Baylor dismounted his troop, left five men to guard the horses, and with the remainder of his command crept forward. By keeping the ridge between them and the Indians the Rangers managed to approach within a couple of hundred yards of the enemy. Baylor was armed with the Model 73 Winchester as was Lieutenant Nevill. Both also carried the new Colt Model 1873 six-shooter, as did the remainder of the command. Of the twenty-three men who constituted the combined force, all but three had purchased the Winchester .44-40 rifle. The three, all new Rangers, still had the old issue Sharps .45 single-shot. These were among the five Rangers detailed to hold the horses.

Baylor sent Sergeant Carruthers and seven men around to the left flank, while the rest of the force followed the captain who continued the undetected advance. The Rangers were finally within a hundred yards of the Indian bivouac. It was then barely sunrise. The Indians bestirred themselves, and several braves arose from the pallets where they had been sleeping. The Rangers, on the command from Baylor, commenced to shoot up the camp. The Apaches broke and ran.

Sergeant Carruthers with his flanking fire was in an excellent position. The first shots from his seven Rangers dropped three Indians within yards of their campfire. The others ran, but one after the other were brought down by the deadly fire of the Texans. One Apache ran blindly up the mountain, in view for a good four hundred yards. Practically every Ranger in the party had a try for him. At least a hundred shots were fired at him but he finally won the crest and disappeared from view. Carruthers and several of his detail followed this buck for a mile and a half and found he was losing a lot of blood. But he was never overtaken.

Another Mescalero was knocked down and appeared a candidate for the Happy Hunting Ground when suddenly he scrambled to his feet and went over the ridge after his fellow savage. Over the hill to the tune of Sharps and Winchester. Another Apache stood his ground, but when the Rangers approached him they found he was head shot and did not know what he was doing. He died within the hour.

The women suffered. When the Indians took to their heels, it was barely light and it was difficult to tell men from women. Two women were killed outright and a third was mortally wounded and died later. Two of the four children were killed in the fusillade and a third was shot in the foot. The fourth woman was shot three times in the hand, and she and the two children were captured. She was evacuated together with the children to Fort Davis for medical treatment.

Some three or four braves escaped. The remainder were all dead. There was a lot of loot. There were two Model 73 rifles, a Remington carbine, a .45 six-shooter which had belonged to the sergeant who had been killed at Ojo Caliente, and a .41

caliber Colt double-action revolver. There were six cavalry saddles, taken from the colored troopers killed at Ojo Caliente, and women's and children's clothing evidently belonging to Mrs. Tom Graham who had been shot and killed during the attack on the wagon train. There was a brand new Mexican saddle with fresh blood in the seat, and more than a hundred yards of new calico in a bolt. Where it had been looted the Rangers could not decide.

There was no water for the horses at the scene of the battle so Baylor headed for Apache Tanks, a ride of thirty miles, where he watered the mounts and refilled all the canteens. Then the little force turned homeward, back to Ysleta almost a hundred miles to the northward.

This was the last battle in force put up by the Indians. For another decade there were troubles with the Lipans but none on a scale of that staged by this last bitter remnant of Victorio's Mescaleros. The Rangers turned their attention to those Mexican border raiders and the white outlaws who were kicking up merry hell in the brush country along the Rio Grande.

7

McNELLY'S RANGERS

Texas had some great Rangers but none perhaps was more outstanding than a little fellow named McNelly. Captain L. H. McNelly was a Civil War veteran, a cavalryman who had specialized in hit-and-run raids, a daredevil who was only in his teens when the war commenced and barely into his majority when he was mustered out. Slight of build and of medium height, he had few outward appearances to point up the veritable tiger that lurked beneath. McNelly was an honest-to-God, hard-core toughie, every bit as ruthless, quick to fight, and ready to kill as any of the hard cases he corralled during his turbulent days as the leader of the Special Force of Rangers sent into southwest Texas in 1875 to curb lawlessness.

McNelly was not new to law enforcement. During the carpetbagger days of Governor Davis he had served with the notorious state police. This force had been organized by Davis to replace the Rangers. For nine years after the end of the war Texas had no Ranger force. It had instead the state police, an organization that brought a good deal of discredit on law enforcement in the Lone Star State. McNelly as one of four captains of the police was unquestionably the best of the lot.

He was commissioned by the elected governor to organize a company of Rangers and go into DeWitt County to restore law and order. McNelly, who lived in Washington County, selected his minions from around home. These were young Texans whom he knew personally. Some of them had fought on the Confederate side with him, and he knew he could depend on them.

The time was July, 1874, and Texas was a poor state still recovering from the carpetbaggers. She had not yet struck oil nor developed the cow business to its later opulent state, but still she had the funds to provide each of the newly sworn Rangers with a brand new Colt .45 six-shooter. As for rifles the best that could be done was to hand each recruit the old Sharps rifle. A good many of McNelly's men were well aware of the short-comings of this old single-shot and had their own .44 Henry and the newer Winchester .44-40 center-fire which had just appeared in Texas. This company was to immortalize itself along the Rio Grande during the year ahead. As a part of the reward for its exemplary dash and bravery it was given Model 73 rifles by Captain Richard King, the owner of the great King Ranch. More about that later.

The Special Force was marched into DeWitt County and there had aplenty to do. There were various factions in the neighbor-hood, each warring with the others. Joe Tumlinson had seventy-five well-armed men at his back, and he was one of the major-domos. Another hell-raiser was Bill Taylor who had a band of bravos. He went aboard a river boat at Indianolo and killed Sutton and Slaughter, two enemies of the opposing clan. This deed set the country on fire, and McNelly was kept busy during the autumn and into the winter trying to restore order. By spring he had put the lid on things to some extent, but when he was called away he was one of the first to confess that the lid might blow off the minute the Rangers rode out of the river bottoms.

General Steele, the adjutant general of the state, thought he could use McNelly and his buckos to better advantage down on the Rio Grande. Here was indeed a sticky situation. Along the Rio Grande from Brownsville northward was an area sparsely populated with infrequent towns and pueblos on either side of the river. It was brushy, with a growth of mesquite, chaparral, and live oak, with grassy mottes here and there, little water, and no cultivation. It was cow country, ranch land given over to raising the longhorn and the scrub ponies of Texas. It was a prime range for the Mexican rustler. He rode over in numbers and rounded up and drove back across the Rio Grande in de-fiance of the sheriff and his posse—in fact in defiance of the military, which was mostly infantry and could not hope to catch up with these swift raiders.

The theft of livestock had reached astronomical proportions. The King Ranch, the biggest land spread in all Texas, was the heavy loser. Thousands upon thousands of head of cattle and many horses were hustled across the Rio Grande annually. Most of the Mexican rustlers rode King horseflesh. King beef graced the market places of all the sizeable towns and cities from Matamoros, hard by the mouth of the Rio Grande, to Mexico City well within the interior. Even as McNelly rode into Brownsville where he would make his headquarters, a ship was standing off the Mexican coast waiting to take aboard four hundred cows for shipment to Cuba. Brand markings on these close-herded bovines were all *Tejano*. The herd was held by a Mexican band of one hundred, all riding horses with gringo brands.

The *jefe* of the rustling ring was General Juan Cortinas who operated along the river both above and below Brownsville. Cortinas was a revolutionary, a politician, and a land owner. He was a power on both sides of the Rio Grande, and harm done to any of his gang members was sure to bring back retaliation. Cortinas could muster fifteen hundred rifles whenever he elected. Into this hornet's nest rode the little Ranger, McNelly, and his forty valiants. Forty against fifteen hundred. The pueblo of Brownsville, while on the Texas side of the Rio Grande, was virtually a part of Mexico. The population was mostly *latino*. There were forty-three Americans living there when the Rangers arrived. It was April, 1875.

In June McNelly got a report that fifteen raiders had crossed the Rio Grande eight miles below Brownsville. They were aimed at rounding up several hundred head of cows and would shove the rustled stock across the river at Arroyo Colorado. McNelly sent Lieutenant Robinson and eighteen Rangers to the crossing and instructed him to put out some scouts and see if they could make contact with the raiding party. In no time at all the scouts had captured one of the rustlers. He was Rafael Salinas and he talked. He said the gang was headed by Emilio Lerma and Jose Maria Holguin and that they had been ordered by General Cortinas to stage the raid in the La Parra district and to move the stock into Mexico over the Arroyo Colorado crossing. Salinas had been left behind to guard the crossing. The next day the scouts picked up another rider. He was Incarnacion Garcia, an advance guard, who said that the rustlers were moving about three hundred head of mixed cows, calves, and other young stuff in a high trot for Arroyo Colorado. They were due to ford that night around midnight.

McNelly by this time had taken over command of his little detachment of Rangers, and they had moved in on the crossing site, arranged along either side of a gently sloping motte which ran down to the river. They waited until 2:00 A.M. when word came from a scout that the herd was passing around them about four miles to the east. McNelly gathered up his fighters, and they made a wild ride through the mesquite to throw themselves between the herd and the Rio Grande. About seven o'clock the Rangers rode up on the Mexican cow thieves. The bandits were still some miles in the lead, and they discovered the Rangers about the same time that the lawmen spotted the cattle and drovers. The rustlers put the stock into a run, but the Rangers pushed their horses to the limit and fast gained on the thieves. The Mexicans drove the badly winded stock onto a little island in the center of a great marsh, and they all dismounted and took a stand at the far side of the island.

The Rangers had to advance across six hundred yards of water and mud some fourteen to twenty inches in depth to come to grips with the outlaws. McNelly, an old cavalryman, deployed his little force as skirmishers; at a walk they commenced to negotiate the swamp. Not a Ranger fired a shot nor spoke a word. The water and muck was too deep to go faster than the slow pace set by the little leader.

As McNelly tells it:

On arriving I found them drawn up in line on the south side of the marsh which was about six hundred yards wide and filled with mud and water about twenty inches deep, and behind a bank four or five feet high. I formed my men as skirmishers and rode into the marsh, not allowing my men to unsling carbines or draw their pistols. As soon as we struck the water the raiders commenced firing on us with Spencers and Winchester carbines. We advanced at a walk, a

more rapid gait being impossible, and not firing a shot or speaking a
word and keeping our line well dressed.

On our nearing the position they held perhaps within seventy-five
or one hundred yards, they mounted, wheeled their horses around
and galloped off. When we got out on hard ground we pressed forward and soon brought ourselves within shooting distance, fifty or
sixty yards. The Mexicans then started at a full run and I found our
horses could not overtake them. I ordered three of my best mounted
Rangers to pass to their flank and press them so as to force a stand.

As I had anticipated, the Mexicans turned to drive my men off but
the Rangers held their ground and I got up with four or five men
when the raiders broke off. After that it was a succession of singlehanded fights for six miles before we got the last one. Not one escaped
out of the twelve that were driving the cattle. They were all killed.

I have never seen men fight with more desperation. Many of them
after being shot from their horses and severely wounded three or
four times, would rise on their elbows and fire at my men as they
passed. I lost one man, L. B. Smith of Lee County. We captured
twelve horses, and rifles, pistols, saddles and 265 head of beef cattle
belonging in the neighborhood of King's Ranch, Santa Gertrudis.

This was McNelly's report to General Steele. The official report to the adjutant general did no more than mention the work
of the scouts which McNelly used so successfully. One of these
was such a bloodthirsty old cuss he is worthy of mention. A
Mexican, Jesus Sandoval, he was signed on by the Ranger captain at a regular's pay. He was provided with six-shooter and
rifle and had his horse evaluated to be paid for by the state if
killed. Sandoval—called "Kasoose" by the Rangers—was held
in high regard by his fellows even though he was not a regularly
enrolled Ranger and more than that was a Mexican in a day
when all the brown-skinned brethren were regarded with deep
suspicion by the gringos.

Jesus Sandoval bore a deep grudge toward all Mexican bandidos. He had owned a little *ranchito* above Brownsville on the Rio
Grande where he lived contentedly with his wife and teen-age
daughter. A band of Cortinas' bully boys rode through the country, and they found the head of the household away from the
jacal. They went in and threw the women on the floor and raped
them. Then they came outside and set the little home on fire.

When Sandoval returned home after a couple of days all he found was ashes. The ashes of his home and his loved ones. He took the warpath.

For the next three years the brushy trails on either side of the Rio Grande were haunted by the grim killer. He would lie in wait for days, and when one of Cortinas' bravos rode through he was roped, thrown, and hanged. Jesus seldom shot one of his enemies. He strung them up. In no time at all word spread up and down the river, and the hardcase riders got so they moved in company. The bigger the crowd the better. Sandoval then gave up the mesquite ambush and moved into the pueblos where he made a specialty of the silent knife in the dark shadows of corral and cantina.

His signing on with McNelly was as natural as his thirst for revenge. One would feed the other. With the Rangers he could move into the open and kill the bandidos whom he hated with a terrible ferocity. When he captured a spy for Cortinas, or one of the other scouts brought one in, the agent was always turned over to old "Kasoose." He would take the rustler and mount him up on an old paint horse and lead him under a tree. With his hands tied behind his back, Sandoval would drop a loop over his head and tighten it around his neck. He would then throw the loose end of the rope over a limb and tighten up on it, fairly lifting the captive out of the saddle. A little of this and he would talk quite freely. When the prisoner was ready to tell his story, old Kasoose would jerk him off the horse and take him over to Captain McNelly. The captain could not speak Spanish but he had an interpreter named McGovern who would question the spy and pass the information along to the Ranger leader. After he had been tapped for all his knowledge he was turned back to Kasoose.

Then the revengeful, brooding old Mexican would again lead out his spotted horse, mount the captive up on him, and take him back to the tree. Here he would fashion a hangman's noose and drop it around the hapless prisoner's neck. The end of the rope was passed over the limb and securely tied to the trunk of the tree. Sandoval had by this time compelled the bandit to stand up in the saddle, the loop tight about his throat. Old Kasoose would then hit the pony a sharp rap across the rump, and the horse would leap out from under the Mex. The fall usually broke his neck. McNelly had been sent into southwestern Texas with explicit orders to take no prisoners among the bandidos who were raiding across the river. It isn't on record that he exactly put his blessing on the doings of his executioner, but he did not put any damper on him either. They understood each other. Rafael Salinas, the first of the rustlers captured at Arroyo Colorado, and Incarnacion Garcia, the advance guard on the return of the rustled cows, both got the full benefit of the Sandoval treatment after they had told their stories.

The bodies of the dead rustlers were loaded into ox carts and trundled into Brownsville where all were identified as Cortinas' bravos. The population of the town was strongly pro-Cortinas, and there were many threats from both sides of the Rio Grande to shoot down all the Rangers. When it is realized that General Cortinas could muster more than a thousand stalwarts at a whistle, this was no idle threat. But McNelly and his Special Force lawmen took it all in stride. If they were perturbed by the possibilities you could not see it in their demeanor or word. They continued to ride just as many patrols, and old Kasoose kept his loop swinging. Instead of working near Brownsville the rustlers moved up the Rio Grande about a hundred miles to Las Cuevas. This is near the present town of Rio Grande City.

McNelly had by this time recruited a number of spies, and he had most of the agents on the Mexican side of the border. A number of them were actually riding with the raiders. Through this network he knew almost immediately when the shift in operations was being moved up-river. He promptly moved with it.

The Special Force went into camp in the chaparral near the present town of Edinburg. McNelly, who had contracted tuberculosis while fighting as a Confederate cavalryman, was ill. He returned to his home in Washington County and went to bed. He did not remain either in bed or at home for very long. Word was passed to him that the rustlers had rounded up two hundred head of cattle in Cameron County and hazed them over the Rio Grande. These were for sale in Monterey on the Mexican side.

McNelly had left Lieutenant Robinson in command while he was at home. On the sixteenth of November, Cortinas raiders gathered another herd and started it for Las Cuevas Crossing.

A Mexican ranchero rode into the Eighth Cavalry camp at Edinburg. There was a troop of cavalry there under Captain Randlett, who was informed of the movement of cattle and drovers. Las Cuevas was fifty-five miles away. Why the Mexican informer did not search out the Rangers who were encamped in the area is not known but very probably he was fearful of old Kasoose and his sticky rope. Captain Randlett gathered a force of local citizenry consisting of Mexican and Texan cowboys and set up a leisurely pursuit. He got to the Las Cuevas just as the bandits had made the crossing. The cavalrymen killed two of the riders and wounded a third. There were fifty cows bogged in the mud on the far bank. About that time a detachment of thirty scouts arrived to reinforce Randlett from Fort Ringgold. The captain had been given orders by General Potter, who had command of the area, to pursue the bandits into Mexico. However, he frittered away the hours of daylight and did not pursue the rustlers. In explanation later on he asserted that night came and he did not want to execute the crossing in the darkness.

Before morning more cavalry arrived under the command of Majors Alexander and Clendenin; the latter was the immediate superior of Randlett. He listened to the recital of all that had been done and promptly countermanded General Potter's orders to cross the Rio Grande in pursuit of the cow thieves. About that time McNelly rode into the camp. He had one Ranger with him; his men were fifty-five miles away. He informed the army officers that he would send for his Rangers and that very night would cross the river in pursuit of the thieves. Only three miles back from the Las Cuevas Crossing was Las Cuevas Ranch owned by the notorious Juan Flores, a self-styled "general." The rustled livestock, once pushed across the Rio Grande, was held at this rancho for sale to buyers from the interior. It was his intention, the Ranger assured the cavalrymen, to ride up to the Las Cuevas corrals and gather and return the Texas cattle.

McNelly's messenger rode into the Ranger camp near Edin-

burg at 2:30 in the afternoon. Lieutenant Robinson, who was
in command, got the detachment together and instructed his
men to take forty rounds for the six-shooter and forty rounds
for the rifle and nothing else. He informed the little detachment
when it was all drawn up in columns of twos that they had to
make the fifty-five mile ride in not more than five hours. Those
were McNelly's orders. The wagons were left in charge of a
guard, and the Special Force set off guided by old Kasoose who
knew the country like a book. The ride was a terrific test of man
and horse. The detachment rode at a gallop most of the time and
pulled up at Las Cuevas in something less than five hours.
McNelly was awaiting them.

The Ranger captain told his hard-riding troopers that they
were going to cross the Rio Grande directly after midnight. He
would get, he said, a hundred soldiers to accompany them. The
cavalry had dragged along two Gatling guns which would be
tremendously effective against the estimated three hundred
bandits staged around Las Cuevas Ranch. McNelly was aware
of General Potter's orders to pursue the raiders into Mexico if
they were caught in the act of cattle stealing. He felt confident
that the force on hand and its commanders, Alexander, Clendenin, and Randlett, would obey the orders of the general officer.
In this he was mistaken. He returned to his little force directly
after twelve o'clock saying that they would have to go it alone.

Despite the reluctance of the military to share the crossing with
the Rangers, McNelly felt that when the situation grew acute
they would respond. He proposed to force the crossing and
push inward to the Las Cuevas Ranch where his little force
would be outnumbered by at least ten to one (there were thirty
Rangers). He hoped to catch the bandits by surprise, capture a
building before they could gather their forces, and hold this
redoubt until the U.S. troops relieved him.

He informed Alexander and Clendenin of his plan. They
shook their heads in amazed disapproval. McNelly was obdurate
and stuck to his guns, informing the pair that he knew what
General Potter had ordered be done. Reluctantly the pair finally
acquiesced and agreed that if the Rangers were cut off and in

danger of annihilation they would cross their troops and come to the relief of the Texans. McNelly asked no more. He turned and strode off to prepare his force for a night crossing of the Rio Grande.

INVADING MEXICO

McNelly had by this time been in southwestern Texas for almost a year. He was intimately familiar with the situation there, its numbers of bandits, the size and scope of their operations, and the vast distances involved, and he realized that it would take years for his little force of Rangers to bring the thievery and killings to a halt. He had a better plan and in this he was joined by others.

On the Rio Grande the navy had a gun boat, the U.S.S. *Rio Bravo*. It was under the charge of Commander Kells who was operating on orders directly from the Navy Department. His contacts included both General Potter, who was stationed at Brownsville, and McNelly. According to John L. Haynes, collector of customs at Brownsville, there was a plot to place the *Rio Bravo* in position where it would be fired on from the Mexican side of the river. If Kells could not induce the Mexicans to fire on him, then McNelly was to take a force of Rangers to the south side of the Rio Grande and do the shooting himself! Or if this was not feasible, McNelly was to drive a herd of cattle onto Mexican soil, preferably in the vicinity of Las Cuevas Ranch, and then the gunboat would open up on the rancho. The scheme was to incite the United States to war against Mexico. Little is known today of the full ramifications of this plot, but certainly McNelly was much in favor of it. He could see that if the United States brought its full force to bear on Mexico it would contribute immeasurably to the solution of his problems. He pushed his little force across the Rio Grande on the night of the nineteenth of November,

1875, perfectly aware that if the U.S.S. *Rio Bravo* was not fired upon, maybe the fact that a force of Texas Rangers had invaded the country of Mexico would so incense the government it would take some drastic action. These were abrupt means, but they would enable him to achieve his ends.

Since the cavalry had fired on the Mexicans, killing two and wounding one, as they forced the stolen herd across the Las Cuevas Crossing, the bandits had avoided the river banks. McNelly felt reasonably certain that he could make the ford without drawing fire from the hostiles on the far bank. The river was deep in the main channel and would swim a horse, the current was sluggish, and the shallows on the far side were a bog of bottomless mud. Many of the rustled stock had been so exhausted by the long forced drive that they had stumbled and gone down in this ooze and drowned. McNelly took two Rangers with him and crossed the river to reconnoiter. He prowled up and down the shore line and finally found a place where he thought men and horses could come ashore without danger of floundering in the mud and rushes.

At an hour after midnight the first Rangers crossed the Rio Grande in an old dugout. They led one horse with them that swam alongside. The men carried with them only their sidearms, a *morral* filled with the eighty cartridges they had fetched from the Edinburg camp, and some skimpy rations. Once they reached the far bank they had trouble getting the horse onto firm ground. He floundered and would have drowned if the Rangers had not tailed him up. The boat returned for another contingent of the intrepid troopers. The shuttle went on until 4:00 A.M. when all thirty rangers and their indomitable commander were on the far shore.

There were only a half dozen horses. It was found too difficult to bring the mounts through the slime on the far bank, and the Rangers came over without their horses. No sooner had the last boatload of Rangers made the crossing than McNelly set off at the head of his little detachment over a deeply rutted trail that broke off toward the southwest. Las Cuevas was three miles from the river, and if the command were to hit the rancho at daylight, it would have to do it pronto. The cover was higher than a man on horseback and was quite dense. Except for the trails which threaded here and there it would have been tedious and time-consuming to have broken through the chaparral.

After an hour and a half of foot slogging the Rangers broke into a clearing. They recognized it as Las Cuevas from many descriptions. There were corrals, a complex of them, and on the far side a scattering of dwellings. McNelly gathered his people about him and told them to kill all the men they ran across, sparing the women and children. Deployed as skirmishers the Rangers hit the houses at a dead run.

They killed five men. Old Kasoose on his paint horse, which had swum the Rio Grande successfully, was in the lead and gunned down two of them as he swept into the settlement. Scarcely a shot was fired by the defenders, who were taken completely by surprise. Then McNelly got an unwelcome surprise. The Mexican guide who had been gathered up at the crossing told them that the ranch was not Las Cuevas, their objective, but Las Curchas, and Cuevas was a half mile distant. McNelly instantly realized that his plan to fall upon the opposition at daylight and push into a house in the Las Cuevas compound was now aborted. The firing would have alerted the defenders, a force estimated at three hundred well-armed and mounted desperadoes. He swung his arm in the wide arc of the cavalryman. His force moved out. They took the trail toward Las Cuevas knowing full well they were outnumbered by ten to one and had an enemy that was even then making preparations for their arrival. Hot preparations.

McNelly's report to General Steele is of interest:

Before daylight on the 19th, I started for the ranch, found what I supposed was Cuevas, charged it, found five or six men there and they seemed to be on picket. We killed five of them and then proceeded on my way to Cuevas (half-mile distant) and about three miles from the river. On getting about one hundred yards from the first house I found about two hundred and fifty or three hundred men drawn up in line. About a hundred mounted and the rest on foot. They occupied the ground and the corrals between me and the first house of the ranch. I at once saw the utter impossibility of taking a house by assault, as the firing at the other ranch had given them notice of our approach. After exchanging shots for about ten minutes I fell back taking advantage of a few bushes on the side of the trail to conceal our movements from the enemy. I left Sgt. Hall with four mounted men to hold them in check as long as possible. They made no attempt to follow us and we reached the river all right.

During the fighting at Las Cuevas the Rangers killed four men. The attack had been a fizzle. McNelly had not only not gotten into a house which he had hoped to hold until he could be relieved by the cavalry on the Texas side of the Rio Grande, but neither had he retrieved the stolen cows nor punished the rustlers. He had, however, along with his lack of success, some amazing luck that his miniscule force had escaped without a single casualty. The natural thing to presume was that once he reached the river again he would cross without delay to the safety of the Texas shore. He never even considered such a move.

McNelly deployed his force along the river bank and put out pickets in the direction of Las Cuevas. He knew the Mexicans would quickly decide his command was a small one and would lose no time in following the retreat, hoping to trap the Rangers in the water as they were fording. Sure enough, a force of twenty-five well-mounted Mexicans burst into the old abandoned fields before the Ranger position. The charge was led by "General" Juan Flores, the owner of Las Cuevas, and the biggest bandido of the whole motley crew.

The Rangers held their fire until the riders were within seventy-five yards of their line: then they fired. General Flores fell off his horse with two bullets through the body. He died almost instantly. McNelly charged the attackers, and his fellows ran at his shoulder. The Mexicans were driven back to the cover of the high chaparral. When the Rangers got to Flores they found he was armed with a new Smith & Wesson six-shooter which sported ivory handles and was engraved and gold-mounted. McNelly shoved the gun into his waistband and motioned his men to fall back on the river.

During this charge forty cavalrymen crossed the river under the command of Captain Randlett. McNelly at once attempted to induce the officer to follow him for another advance on Cuevas Ranch. Randlett said that he would stick with the Rangers at the river's edge, but he could not go beyond without orders from Major Clendenin, his immediate superior.

About this time the Mexicans got unexpected reinforcements. A force of two hundred infantrymen marched in from Camargo. This indeed was serious. There were now not less than five hundred armed men opposing the thirty Rangers and the forty soldiers who had joined them.

From eleven in the morning until five that afternoon the Mexican forces carried on a series of attacks on the combined Ranger-military command which had dug in along the open fields before the river. McNelly was all for driving inward and taking Las Cuevas, but on this score Randlett remained obdurate. He was having some second thoughts about his temerity in crossing the river in the absence of his commanding officer. Instead of listening to the impetuous Ranger captain, he was giving a good deal of thought to pulling back across the Rio Grande.

About this time the Mexicans came forward under a flag of truce and requested a parley. Randlett went forward to treat with them. McNelly would not discuss terms. He demanded the return of the cattle which had been rustled and the rustlers who had driven them out of Texas. The note carried by the Mexican emissary promised that the cattle would be delivered the next day to Ringgold (Rio Grande City) and that every effort would be made to arrest the thieves, and it asked that the Rangers and soldiers retire to the Texas side of the boundary. In reply, Randlett promised to hold the fire of his troopers until nine the next morning provided the two hundred infantrymen that had just arrived from Camargo be withdrawn a distance of three miles and that the flag of truce be left flying.

About this time Major Alexander, who outranked Randlett, appeared on the Texas side of the Rio Grande and without any consideration for the situation peremptorily ordered Randlett and the cavalry to return to the United States. This left McNelly and his Rangers alone in Mexico.

When the Mexicans saw the military had withdrawn, they then treated with McNelly. He informed them that he would have his cattle and his rustlers before he budged. The Ranger was informed that the cattle were near Camargo, a town in the interior, and could not be returned that evening. The negotiators then asked for an extension of the cease fire until the morning. Mc-Nelly agreed to make no advance during the night if the bandits would bring in two horses captured from the Rangers during the fight at Las Cuevas. McNelly further told them that he would permit the flag of truce to be flown and would respect it to the extent that when he again started to fight he would give them an hour's notice. This was from a man who was faced by five hundred well-armed enemy! Thirty men at his back and these valiants down to twenty cartridges per man. With this situation confronting him he had agreed to give his opponents sixty minutes notice before he attacked.

Night settled down upon the scene. McNelly had his bully boys deployed along the line of chaparral above the river and some distance from the banks of the stream. Despite the truce the Texans really believed that the Mexicans, steadily augmented by incoming outlaws who had heard of the fight going on and wanted to be in on the finish, would try to overwhelm them during the hours of darkness. McNelly reconnoitered.

He crossed the Rio Grande in his leaky old dugout canoe and gathered rations for his hungry cohorts. He scouted up and down the river and found a spot beneath a four-foot bank where he ordered that a trench be dug for a last ditch stand. "We'll fight them along the line of brush and if they get too much for us we'll fall back to this trench and fight here until we all die," he grimly informed his followers. The night wore on and the pickets, posted toward Las Cuevas, were tense and alert. Bill Callicott, telling about it afterward said he was on guard and saw a *bandido* stealthily edging down one of the cow trails. Callicott raised his Winchester to plug him and as he put pressure on the trigger he saw, just in the nick of time, that it was a cow! He eased back on the trigger. McNelly got off a message to the adjutant general of Texas, William Steele, which read as follows: "From Mexico near Las Cuevas. I crossed the river on the nineteenth and marched on Las Cuevas, killed five men before reaching the ranch and several afterward. On arrival at the ranch I found about three hundred men. After a few shots I retreated to the river as the U.S. troops were ordered not to cross. The Mexicans followed me to the river and charged me. They were repulsed and as they seemed to be in force some forty U.S. soldiers came over. The Mexicans made several attempts to dislodge us but failed. United States troops withdrew to left bank last night. The Mexicans in my front are about five hundred. What shall I do?"

News of the stand made by the Rangers had by this time not only reached Brownsville but had gotten as far as Washington. General Potter who was in command of this whole sector of the frontier got off a hurried message to Major Alexander, as follows: "Advise Capt. McNelly to return at once to this side of the river. Inform him that you are directed not to support him in any way while he remains on Mexican territory. If McNelly is attacked by Mexican forces on Mexican soil do not render him any assistance. Keep your forces in the position you now hold and await further orders. Let me know whether McNelly acts upon your advice and returns. Signed Potter."

The State Department then got into the act. The consul at Matamoros, on the Mexican side, Thomas F. Wilson, wired his commercial attaché at Camargo this message: "I understand McNelly is surrounded and treating for terms of surrender. If so go to him immediately and advise him to surrender to Mexican federal authorities and then you go with him to this city to see that nothing happens on the way. Instructions have been sent from here to authorities in Camargo to allow you to act in this matter. Signed Wilson."

Lucius Avery, the attaché at Camargo, lost no time in hurrying across the river at Fort Ringgold and thence to the Las Cuevas Crossing where he could see the Rangers lounging about on the far bank. He crossed to parley with their leader. "Nope," McNelly informed him, "We may be surrounded but we have not surrendered and we don't intend to. Go back and tell the state department this is a matter between the Texas Rangers and a passel of outlaws and I'll handle it without any help." Avery, nonplussed, returned to the Texas bank. This was the afternoon of November 20.

At four o'clock of that afternoon, McNelly hauled down the white flag which had flown between the forces since the evening before. He sent word that he would attack within the hour.

He would fight unless the cattle and the cattle thieves were turned over to him. The Mexicans held a hurried consultation. After a discussion which ran dangerously toward the end of the hour's grace given by the little Ranger commander, they came back and agreed to round up all the cattle and arrest the thieves and deliver them both at Rio Grande City the next morning at 10:00 A.M.

With these promises and the withdrawal of the forces in front of him, McNelly commenced a leisurely crossing of the Rio Grande. Not a shot was fired; there was no hostile gesture from the bravos who had gathered to wipe out the Rangers. In all the history of the Texas Rangers there was never a more daring display of sheer bravery and intrepid action than the performance of the Special Force during these two days in Mexico. The fact that they could have been overwhelmed by the sheer numbers of the opposing forces, that all would die if the battle was joined, the lack of support by the army, the opposition of the sector commander, General Potter, and the censure of the State Department did not deter the indomitable little terrier, McNelly. To him his duty was quite clear. Texas cows had been stolen and must be returned. And the thieves punished. He had gone about his duties to these ends with a oneness of purpose that brooked no obstacles. Once the Mexicans had agreed to return both livestock and culprits he returned to Texas soil. That his actions had been heroic or out of the ordinary he did not presume to dwell upon. He would have expected as much from any Ranger caught in the same web of circumstance.

The next morning quite early, McNelly and his party rode up to Rio Grande City which lies opposite the Mexican pueblo of Camargo. He waited patiently until 10:00 A.M. but no cows appeared. He then sent word to the Mexican officials to deliver the cattle and the rustlers as promised. At first they demurred saying the cows would be ready the next day. McNelly would have none of that and demanded that the cattle be forded at once. Finally a herd of about seventy-five cows, held by twenty-five Mexican vaqueros, was pushed down the river. The vaqueros refused to force the herd into the water and make the crossing.

There was a ferry, and McNelly loaded up with ten of his

buckos and crossed to the south bank. He confronted the cowboys, all of whom were armed, according to Bill Callicott, with
six-shooters and Winchesters, and demanded through McGovern,
his interpreter, that the stock be put to swimming. The coffee-
colored leader of the vaqueros shook his head and grinned down
insolently at the diminutive ranger.

Now it is best to let Bill Callicott tell what happened: "The
captain then told McGovern to tell the sonofabitch if he didn't
deliver the cattle across the river in five minutes we would kill all
of them—–and with that every man in the Ranger force fell into
line and cocked his rifle—if you ever saw cattle put across a river
in a hurry those Mexicans did it. And in less than five minutes!
All the stock made it save one old cow, she was too tuckered out
to go into the water. We roped her and gave her to the ferryman
as pay for taking us over." Thus in a twenty-four hour period
McNelly had twice invaded the Land of Mañana and came away
with what he sought. The stolen cows. He had hardly expected
the Mexican authorities to surrender the thieves.

The next morning the Rangers sorted out the various brands
on the cows held in a corral outside Rio Grande City. It was
found that thirty-five of the seventy-five cattle belonged to the
King Ranch. McNelly sent four of his rangers, George Durham,
Ed Pitts, Bill Callicott, and W. L. Rudd, to return the critters
to Captain Richard King, the owner of the great King spread.
When the Rangers and their little herd reached the Santa Gertrudis, King himself made them welcome. He took them in and
fed them royally, meanwhile saying that of the thousands of head
of cattle that he had seen rustled to Mexico these were the first
cows he'd ever gotten back. He offered the Rangers fresh horses,
money, and rations and finally went into his armory and came
out with four brand new Model 73 Winchesters which the troopers were delighted to accept. The Model 73 cost a full month's
pay and to be offered the highly prized firearm as an outright
gift was a sure way to the fighting lawmen's hearts.

9

KING FISHER AND CRONIES

In 1876, while McNelly was bringing Texas law to the Rio Grande near its mouth, things were not going so well north of him. In a vast area between Castroville and Eagle Pass there was an outlaw named King Fisher who ruled the hundred or so badmen in his country and took what he wanted. The sheriffs avoided him, the courts feared to take action either against Fisher or any of his henchmen, and honest ranchers saw their stock rustled before their eyes in broad daylight. Those in league with the King hired gunmen to ride up to the homes of their enemies and shoot them down. Assassinations were so common that many went without any indictments being drawn—killings done for gain, to even old grudges, or just for the hell of it.

The county judge of Maverick County was threatened and so feared for his life that he dared not sleep at home. A rancher and his sons followed the trail of some stolen horses and rode up into a ranch corral where the horses were penned. A cowboy came out of a nearby lean-to and asked them to get down. When they dismounted he shot all three while their backs were turned. Rustling of stock was the principal business of the outlaws who threw their herds into pastures along the Nueces River and later drove them quite openly over on Devil's River where they sold to buyers who came down from the Kansas railheads to pick up the stolen beef. The honest citizens complained that times had not been so precarious when the Lipans and Comanches were on the warpath. Despite their plight few indeed had the temerity to lodge complaints against the desperadoes.

King Fisher, the chief of the outlaws, was a gunfighter, a swashbuckler, and an exceedingly deadly hombre. In his middle twenties, he was a veteran of forty gun battles, all of which he had won. Asked one time how many men he had killed he said, "eight, not counting Mexicans." He always dressed in the height of cowboy fashion, and it was once claimed that he had killed a tiger, property of a traveling circus, and had a pair of chaps made from the skin. A two gun wearer, his six-shooters were invariably nickle-plated, engraved, and sported ivory handles. Of good family, Fisher had a wife and three children and lived at the end of the only road which ran into his domain. At the boundary was a sign which read, "This is King Fisher's Road. Take the other one." Most travelers did.

McNelly heard about the situation up in King Fisher's country and asked General Steele for permission to move northward and clean it up. The affirmative nod from the adjutant general was quick in coming. McNelly had not been too busy at Brownsville through the winter months of 1875–76. He and his men were spoiling for action. They moved out, and a short distance up the Rio Grande, near the town of Edinburg, they struck the trail of ten Mexican rustlers who were shagging a herd of stock toward the river. McNelly and his company put their horses into a hard gallop and reached the crossing place. There were still remnants of the herd on this bank and also some five or six of the rustlers. A fire fight immediately boiled up, and in the shooting four of the thieves were killed. Two others escaped to the far shore, one of them wounded.

McNelly then got in touch with the Eighth Cavalry which had a squadron at Edinburg. McNelly asked Captain H. J. Farnsworth, who headed the squadron, to go with him into Mexico and retrieve the stolen livestock. The cavalry leader refused, telling the Ranger it was contrary to standing orders. Mexican guides that McNelly had with him told him that the herd was being held only three miles from the Rio Grande on a ranch called the Sabinisto. The doughty little leader crossed the river with three of his men and searched in those spots where the guides had told him the stock was being close herded. He could not find the cows. He suspected the cattle had been driven into the Mexican pueblo of Reynosa. There was a force of Mexican soldiery in Reynosa, so he thought it the better part of discretion not to invade the town seeking his lost herd.

He rode back across and rejoined his force. The group rode into Edinburg and there McNelly sent word over to the *alcalde* of Reynosa, the town mayor, to come over and treat with him. The *alcalde* did, and the Texan told him that he wanted the cattle returned to this side together with the rustlers. Nothing came of the negotiations, and McNelly's only satisfaction was the knowledge that he had put some of the outlaws out of the cow rustling business permanently.

From Edinburg to Fort Clark, McNelly broke his company down into small squad-like groups, and in a formation of skirmishers they moved northward. In this way they covered a good deal more ground and were more capable of apprehending the outlaws who were skulking in the brush. The company made its headquarters at Fort Ewell and made its extended patrols from this central point.

Once settled the first thing Captain McNelly did was to stage a raid on King Fisher's ranch. This had never been done before, and it was a well-known fact that any lawman who had the temerity to ride into the home grounds of the formidable King was in for real trouble.

Taking ten men with him, McNelly closed in on the headquarters. He moved by night, using all his savvy as an old Confederate raider to bypass the guards which Fisher had flung out about his rendezvous. The second night of the movement McNelly and his troopers ran smack into a group of rustlers at a lake some eight miles from the King Fisher Rancho. In the fight that followed, three were killed and a fourth captured. Before the night was over, the prisoner tried to escape and was sent to join his departed brothers. The Rangers were in position around the King Fisher spread by daylight.

Captain McNelly rode boldly up to the front door and shouted for Fisher to come out. One of his gunfighters came boiling around the corner from the direction of the bunkhouse. He was instantly covered by McNelly's gun. "Drop it or I'll kill you," said the steely-eyed little Ranger. The gunman looked at the odds and decided it was good advice. He dropped his six-shooter and stood sullenly. King Fisher came out of the house and tamely submitted to arrest. He had been arrested before, and he knew that he controlled the courts and intimidated the judges in that corner of Texas.

McNelly fanned out and gathered up nine of the outlaws who were living in the bunkhouse. He moved them guarded by his ten Rangers to Eagle Pass. There they were lodged in jail much to King Fisher's disgust. The next day during a preliminary hearing the local justice turned all of them loose. King Fisher rode around to see the Rangers after he had been released and laughed in their faces.

The remainder of McNelly's boys had gathered eight hundred head of stolen stock and moved it into a collecting point. The local cattle inspector refused to examine the brands, and the sheriff would not issue subpoenas for the arrest of the rustlers. McNelly was compelled to turn all the stock out on the open range.

This was all very disheartening to the Rangers and their fearless leader. He had driven to the very heart of the King Fisher empire, had arrested the King himself and with him his stalwarts, had escorted them to jail, along with hundreds of head of stolen beef, and for thanks had seen all of them released. His report to General Steele was caustic and bitter.

McNelly had contracted tuberculosis either during his years with the Confederate cavalry or later while in the Ranger service. There was no cure for the dread disease in those days and because he drove himself relentlessly, never asking his men to attempt any task that he would not do himself, he steadily grew worse. He had been compelled during 1876 to return home for periods of rest and for treatment by his doctors. His condition deteriorated and as is typical of tuberculosis, after a stage of the disease had been passed, he grew worse more rapidly.

During October he and five of his men escorted five members of the Sutton feud party to jail at Galveston. It was the gallant little captain's last official act as a Ranger. He rode directly from this detail to his home and was never active thereafter. He died eleven months later at the age of thirty-three.

After jailing the Sutton feuders, McNelly was relieved of his command, the Ranger company was reorganized, and Lee Hall was put in command. When word got around among the decent people of Texas that Adjutant General Steele had dismissed the intrepid McNelly there was a tremendous wave of protest. Steele, by way of defense, lamely stated that McNelly's medical bills had claimed one-third of all the costs of the Ranger company. The abandonment of this courageous officer by the State of Texas to die alone without the support of his organization and his state is a black blot on the history of Texas. L. H. McNelly was one of the greatest Rangers in the history of that famous outfit. He was a hard man, a tough man, and a valorous one. He was given an assignment to bring order to the Rio Grande. He knew and his superiors were aware when they detailed him to the border that he would have to fight. He did in a no-quarter show. He showed little mercy to the outlaws who crossed him, he expected the same in return. If men had to be killed in the discharge of his duty he killed them. If hard rides and dauntless pursuits were the orders he rode cheerfully and willingly. He asked a lot of his men and they gave unstintingly. He never asked more than he gave himself. He literally killed himself in his devotion to his state and its problems.

Farther up the Rio Grande is the Big Bend. This tremendous loop formed by the meandering stream has always been a wild and desolate stretch of Texas. Barren and dry, for the most part it is a desert land. First used for cow ranching, it is little changed to this very day. In the late seventies and early eighties it was a stamping ground for those outlaws who had been harried on westward and for those who had taken it on the lam from the Lincoln County War of New Mexico. These badmen flocked into Fort Davis, and among them were some hardcase customers who robbed the stage with regularity, shot up the only saloon in the nearby town, and finally held up the leading mercantile store, the trading post of Sender & Siebenborn. This latter robbery was too much. The local citizenry put in an appeal to Captain Roberts, who had his company of Rangers over in San Saba

County. The captain responded by detailing Sergeant Seiker
and ten Rangers to Fort Davis.

On the Rio Grande below Fort Davis is one of the oldest and
certainly one of the hottest spots in Texas. This is a little town
called Presidio. It was then and is today a hotbed of *contrabandista*. In the seventies it was the crossing place for cattle
rustled across the bald expanse of the Big Bend; later it was a
prime location for the crossing of contraband arms and ammu-
nitions for the recurrent Mexican revolutions which were commonplace throughout the end of the last century, extending
for three decades into this. During the days of the Volstead Act
it was a trouble spot for the border guardians against the steady
pressure of wet goods. It is to this very day a favorite crossing
for aliens who seek to enter the United States without being
properly immigrated.

Seiker and his stalwarts mounted a long-range patrol in the
direction of Presidio on July 1, 1880. It was a long, hot ride
from Fort Davis, and because the patrol was to be a ten-day
affair, they took along a pack mule to cargo the rations, both
food and extra ammunition, for the swing. When within about
twenty miles of the pueblo, the Ranger force struck a pack outfit
consisting of four men, all armed and mounted, with a string
of pack horses. The Rangers attempted to ride up to the other
party but when they got within about two hundred yards the
strangers broncoed and rode for the high mountains, shooting
back as they tore off.

This looked like the kind of a sortie they had come seeking,
so the Rangers fanned out and the chase commenced. The outlaws, when they got into the rocks, fell off their horses, took cover,
and began to shoot in dead earnest. Their fire was lethal. During
the first moments of the fight Ranger George Bingham was shot
through the heart and Ranger Duffy Carson had his hat shot
off, a stirrup leather cut, and his mount wounded. He wounded
one of the gang, and this hombre, despite his wound, kept right
on with his lethal marksmanship. In telling about it later, Ed
Seiker said, "When this one stuck his head up from behind a
big rock to take aim, I let him have it right between the eyes with

my .44 Winchester." Seiker then told his boys to charge the "forted up" outlaws. This they did, and the rustlers—which they proved to be—surrendered. In commenting on this, the Ranger sergeant said, "I didn't know Bingham was dead at the time or I'd have killed all of them. We had them disarmed before anybody told me we had lost George. It was a good thing I wasn't told 'til afterward." Seiker and his boys rode back to Fort Davis and lodged the prisoners in the stockade. He was relieved by Lieutenant C. L. Nevill and thirteen men. Nevill intended to base on the fort permanently after that, so Ranger Sergeant Seiker and his buckos shoved off to rejoin Company D.

On October 20 Corporal R. G. Kimball, also of Captain Robert's Company D, rode into Fort Davis with a badly wounded horse rustler. He had made quite a ride. With him he had Bill Dunham, another member of the Roberts command. They had left camp on September 20 and had taken up the sign of a band of horses rustled from Fort Terrett. Kimball, who was in command, had five Rangers with him. They had ridden in a trot and a gallop for ninety miles until the herd was crossed at the Horsehead sandbar on the Pecos River. Here because of the killing pace, four of the Rangers had foundered horses on their hands. They did not know whether all their mounts were going to die or were too stove up to move, or whether with a week's rest along the grassy banks of the Pecos, they would recover. At any rate they were finished in the race to overtake the rustlers and the stolen livestock. Kimball was made of the kind of stuff that shapes great Rangers. He did not hesitate; he pushed on, following the trail at the same gallop-trot. With him he had the only man whose horse was still capable of going—Bill Dunham. The fact that there were four outlaws in front of them—odds of two to one—did not deter the Texans. They kept up the killing pace.

After a half day's ride in which they had made more than forty miles, they rode into a ranch and swapped horses for new mounts. The old rancher had just run up a bunch of broncs for the commencement of the fall roundup. The Rangers, thus fresh mounted, kept up the same ground-eating gait. According to Bill Dunham, "That dam hoss I swapped fer bucked every mile of the way from Trelway's place to the Carter Ranch." Here

they had made another sixty miles, and again they picked up
fresh mounts.

They were now within sixty miles of the New Mexico line. It
was pretty apparent to both Rangers that the rustlers were
driving hard to get out of Texas. The Rangers made a seventy-
five-mile night ride galloping all the way and got to Pope's
Crossing. There they learned that the rustlers were behind them.
They had traveled so fast they had swung ahead of their quarry.
They turned back and had hardly gone more than six or eight
miles before they bumped squarely into the herd and its drivers.

Two of the rustlers took it on the lam. They put spurs to
their horses and headed for New Mexico. The other pair fell
off their mounts, unsheathed their rifles, and made a fight of it.
Both Kimball and Dunham and a cowboy named Bill Smith
who had elected to go along when the rangers rode through the
Carter ranch were all armed with the Model 73 .44. They killed
the horses and then shot one of the outlaws through the lungs
and the other through both thighs. The fight was over almost
as soon as it had begun.

The Rangers had ridden almost five hundred miles, had been
in the saddle for fourteen days, and had swapped horses a total
of seven times. They moved the lung-shot rustler to a nearby
ranch where he lingered for forty-eight hours and then died.
The other was bandaged and loaded aboard a spare horse and
the long trek commenced back to the San Saba country. It was
closer to drop back via Fort Davis and this they did, arriving
on October 20. The horse thief was locked up in the jail hospital.
He finally recovered completely and after trial was sentenced to
Huntsville Prison.

Farther up the turbulent old Rio Grande there was yet another
Ranger company. These were Baylor's Rangers, encamped at
Ysleta, which is just outside El Paso. Lieutenant Baylor and
his boys had been into Mexico after Victorio and his Mescalero
Apaches and returned to home base for the Christmas holidays.
It was December, 1879.

Into their camp one day rode two mining engineeers, a couple
of fellows named Andrews and Wiseall. They had a light spring
wagon pulled by a fine light team and tied behind the wagon

was a sturdy Morgan-bred saddler. Beneath the wagon trotted a black-and-yellow shepherd dog. The pair were well armed, and it was obvious from a glance at their outfit that they were equally well heeled financially. The Rangers invited the travelers to stay in camp and celebrate the holidays with them. But Andrews and Wiseall declined with thanks. They were headed for San Antonio, almost six hundred miles distant, and were anxious to reach their destination before cold weather became too intense. The duo discussed which route they should travel, and Lieutenant Baylor strongly suggested that they should travel down the Rio Grande to Fort Davis and then strike eastward for San Antonio. This was a bit longer but it was much safer. The hazards of being caught up by roving bands of Apaches, loose from the Mescalero reservation not too many miles to the north in New Mexico, was still quite real.

Despite the advice of the Rangers, the engineers elected to strike out to the east of Ysleta, traversing the old Butterfield stage route. This ran through Hueco Tanks, about thirty miles to the east, then to Alamo Springs, through the Cornudas Range and onto Crow Flats. At Crow Flats, some eighty miles away, was an abandoned stage station. This route took the travelers on a course parallel to the southern New Mexico boundary and kept them in a country which was traversed by the Apaches as they came and went from the reservation to their hideouts in Mexico. Andrews, spokesman for the pair, said that he had business on the Pecos in southeastern New Mexico, and it would be necessary for them to swing by en route to San Antonio. After a week's pleasant stay with the Rangers the two-man party pushed off. The shepherd dog in the interim had made friends with all the lawmen, and they told him adios along with his masters when he stationed himself, as he had come, beneath the spring wagon and trotted off into the sunrise. Little did the Rangers know what was in store for the party.

By trotting the team the partners had covered the eighty miles to the old abandoned station by midday of the third day. They pulled into the yard, unhitched and unharnessed the horses, and pulled the saddle off the third horse. After putting hobbles on the animals, they turned them out in a flat near the station. They went inside and hashed up a meal.

Suddenly they heard the unmistakable shrill yips of the Apaches and looked out to see a party of twelve or fourteen rounding up and hazing their horses off into the greasewood brush. They grabbed up their Winchesters and threw lead after the raiders, but the range was long and the galloping redskins made fleeting targets. Realizing the seriousness of their predicament they barricaded the old station, which was sturdily made of adobe, and prepared for a siege. They waited tensely until darkness fell. Nothing happened. They expected the Indians would wait until dawn of the next day and hit them then. It was the Apache way. The Indians were fearful of the darkness and waited out the night to strike just as dawn came. Andrews and Wiseall reckoned that was what would happen to them. They decided to clear out while the darkness hid their departure.

They rigged a couple of dummies, placing one at each of the two windows. They commanded their dog to remain on guard. He whined and nosed their hands and told them he wanted to accompany them but both scolded him and ordered the obedient shepherd to hold fast. When the darkness swallowed them, their faithful companion was mounted guard on the wall about the stage station.

The men had to make a choice whether to turn back toward the ranger camp or go forward to the first settlements along the Pecos in New Mexico. The latter was a bit shorter so they elected to go forward. They tramped all night, fearful virtually every minute that the Apaches would be coming behind in pursuit. By morning they had covered twenty-five miles and were deep in the Guadalupe Mountains.

They did not stop with the coming of the sun but continued to march. Directly they climbed into a saddle of the sierras and ran smack into an Indian ambush. Why the redskins did not kill both of them at the first exchange was something of a mystery. The white men stayed together and took refuge on the top of a steep little hill where they had a good command of all the approaches. They did not have too much ammunition, but both were armed with Model 73 rifles. By carefully husbanding their dwindling supply of .44 cartridges they held off the Apaches. Just as night was drawing down upon the hapless pair, a brave showed himself within thirty yards. Andrews promptly killed him. Then the pair jumped to their feet and ran off down the mountain, miraculously managing to remain together even though it was dark and the sides of the mountain covered with thorn and big boulders.

Deciding that the route to the Pecos was too hazardous, they turned back toward the stage station. And as they had done the night before they managed to reach it just as the sun was rising. Their faithful Shep was overjoyed to see them. They had left him with a side of bacon and some shelled corn. There was an alkali-tainted spring within a hundred yards of the station, and the dog could water there. The pair retrieved the bacon and cooked a meal, the first in more than twenty-four hours. Their shoes had completely worn out as a result of the traverse of the mountains, and they had to wrap their feet in gunny sacks which they had carried on the spring wagon.

The next morning they set out on their back trail to walk the eighty miles back to the Ranger camp at Ysleta. Again they commanded their despairing canine friend to stay in camp and mind the wagon and their property. They tossed him the remnants of the bacon and invited him to eat the shelled corn. Hardly a diet for even a frontier dog. The shepherd sat on the wall about the station and watched his masters walk off into the mirage which continually shrouds Crow Flats. Six days later the pair staggered into the Ranger bivouac at Ysleta more dead than alive. Their feet were a mass of blisters, cuts, and bruises. They had virtually starved the last three days of their trek and had been without water for the last twenty-four hours.

One of the first things they were asked was the whereabouts of Shep who had won over practically every Ranger in the command by his amiability and friendliness. The engineers told their tale and Sergeant Jim Gillett had no trouble in getting ten volunteers to ride with him to Crow Flats to see if Shep survived and to return the spring wagon and other belongings of the travelers.

Also, if luck held, to punish the renegades who had gone south with the horse flesh.

Gillett and his fellows rode into Crow Flats in two and a half days. All of them were anxious to push on as fast as they could to see what was the fate of the gallant canine.

Imagine the relief of the hard-riding, hard-fighting, hard-shooting Rangers when they rode up to the stage stop and out came Shep! He barked and cavorted, and even though every rib could be counted, there was no evidence of the bacon rind, and most of the shelled corn was gone, he was alive and well. Every Ranger got down and gave him a hearty greeting and Shep responded. He knew he was among friends. The Rangers had fetched along a team of horses and the day following they harnessed the team, hitched it to the spring wagon, and with Shep— a big feed in his belly—sitting proudly atop the load of his masters' possessions, the return to Ysleta was begun. The faithful dog had remained for fifteen days at the station where he had been commanded to stay on guard.

10

RINGTAILED TOOTER

Texas had its share of gunfighters, there can be no doubt of that. Some were immortalized in story and legend, and others have been given scant notice by the chroniclers. One of the most remarkable of the Lone Star gun swipes was a fellow with the rather commonplace name of Ben Thompson. Ben has hardly been given his due when the stories are spun about the efficacy of his smoking six-shooter. He was a ringtailed tooter, and if you want to tally the men he helped to shuffle off this mortal coil, or the hairbreadth escapes he had from death, or the rampages he went on, always ending with the demise of some citizen, then Thompson must rank along with the top gun hawks.

Thompson lived longer than most. His years reached the considerable number of forty-one. Most gunslingers hardly attained such a ripe old age. King Fisher was only thirty-two when he met his end, and Sam Bass, the train robber, was only twenty-six. Ben had been going to the wars for twenty years by the time his luck ran out. A long time when you consider his career of blood and mayhem. When he finally wound up in the morgue he had gotten himself into one of these situations where he was asking for it. He had done that before, generally under the stimulus of a quart of red whisky. Before, he had managed to shoot his way clear. When Thompson was liquored up his reactions were still just as fast as when cold sober and his concentration was maybe even better. Most fighters get a trifle befuddled after they have been soaking up the one hundred proof

93

stuff for a day and a night. Not Ben Thompson. He got faster on
the trigger, more deadly on the aim, and infinitely meaner.

When he was gunned down he was in company with King
Fisher. We have already noted this West Texas firebrand. He was
the head of a hundred outlaws in that vast expanse from Castroville to the Rio Grande. He was a gunfighter, a killer, veteran of
forty battles, and victor of them all. He had been arrested by
McNelly and his Rangers and had laughed at them. The jail
wasn't built that would hold him. He held sway over his land
and his courts. He was thrown in jail by the Rangers one day
and as promptly released the next. Then an interesting thing
happened to King Fisher. He went straight.

He sluffed off his ragtag following of rustlers, robbers, and
killers and commenced to ranch as an upright, if reformed, citizen.
He gave over his night riding and his killings, stayed home at
night, and was the model *Tejano*. In the course of some five or
six years he was regarded as a staunch member of the community. So upright and stalwart, as a matter of fact, that he was
appointed a deputy sheriff at Uvalde. The public memory is
short, as is obvious in the case of this remarkable Texan.

Ben Thompson was no admirer of the new King Fisher. There
had been friction between them, and Ben had threatened to gun
down the new Fisher. For his part King Fisher was not forgetting
the bad blood, and while his lethal pair of six-shooters had been
holstered for some time, he was quite cheerfully willing to fetch
them into action if it looked like Ben was going to make his play.

This makes all the more peculiar the fact that this pair died
together. Not at the muzzles of each other's guns but standing
shoulder to shoulder against a common opposition. It is one of
the eternal mysteries.

Ben Thompson was an Englishman, whether by direct birth
or by descent is hard to say. Some contend that he was born
in the midlands of the Tight Little Isle, and others say he first
saw the light at Lockhart, Texas, which is more probably true.
At any rate Ben was old enough to fight in the War Between the
States, and after this bloodletting he enlisted in the army at
least twice. He was a miserable soldier and first killed his sergeant

at Fort Clark. When the lieutenant, a man named Jason Haigler, sought to arrest him he was fatally wounded in the neck. Ben then mounted the first horse he found on the picket line and without saddle or bridle, riding only with the halter, made it to Del Rio and safely across the Rio Grande. He remained in Mexico until his enlistment ran out.

With his enlistment finished he calmly returned to Fort Clark. It was some sixteen months later, and without being questioned about the double killing, he re-enlisted. He was never brought to trial, indeed was never threatened with court martial or punishment. He was a nuisance to the military as he had been before. He had been stealing rations when apprehended by the sergeant. He went back to thievery, to bootlegging to the soldiers, and to running a monte game on the post. He finally deserted and went downriver to Laredo. He crossed to the Mexican side into the pueblo known as Nuevo Laredo, and there tried to flimflam a pair of Mex gamblers who saw through his duplicity. They reached for their guns, but Ben had been anticipating them, and he beat both to the draw. He killed them and barely managed to reach the Texas side of the river ahead of the bravos who had seen the shooting and were anxious to tack his hide up on a handy adobe wall.

Ben rode into Austin, the capital of Texas, and there he hung his hat. He was a gambler by bent, and Austin offered plenty of action. He was a saloon keeper, and together with dispensing the redeye and dealing a monte hand he found an atmosphere conducive to his free and easy style. From those early years until his demise in 1884 he claimed the capital as his headquarters, although of course there were interludes when he was temporarily out of town. There was that time when he tried his level best to kill Adams Brown. He had shot Brown three times. The victim did not die but had a warrant sworn out for Thompson. A jury of his peers heard the evidence and decided Ben was decidedly in the wrong. They sentenced him to two years in the penitentiary. In those days there were no such things as paroles and pardon—Ben did the full time.

There was another occasion when he got into a hassle with another toughie named Red Coombs. This hombre was an ex-

buffalo runner, a gunfighter, and a real hardcase. He was gunning
for Thompson, and Ben was on the lookout for him. They met
in the Ace of Diamonds Saloon. Coombs saw Thompson coming,
hauled out his six-shooter, and took good aim just as Ben came
off the street. The carefully triggered shot was a miss. Ben was
somewhat blinded by the darkness of the bar and the bright flash
of the recoiling .45, but he knew all the signs and cheerfully
hauled forth his old hawg-leg and let one go at the center of the
smoke cloud. It drilled Coombs spang through the brisket. He
was dead when he slumped to the floor. A coroner's jury never
left their seats to exonerate him for that execution.

Ben had an amigo in Austin named Phil Coe. The latter
owned the ornate Rawhide Saloon on Congress Avenue. Ben ran
the gambling for Phil and the two were bosom compadres.
Finally Coe drifted up the longhorn trail to Abilene, and there
he established a new saloon, the Bull's Head. When Ben came to
town he bought a share of the place, and he and Phil were
partners. Wild Bill Hickok was the town marshal, and he hated
all Texans. They in turn wanted to kill him. Coe and Wild Bill
were making a play for one of the better looking harlots, Jessie
Hazel, and this led to an even more personal vendetta between
them. Especially after the saloon keeper moved the lady into his
quarters over the Bull's Head.

One night Phil Coe and a bunch of his Texas cow-driving
compatriots were out on the town. They had made the rounds
of the bawdy houses and had soaked up enough whisky to float
a dead Comanche. Out on the single thoroughfare, Texas Street
it was appropriately dubbed, Coe unholstered his six-shooter and
ripped out a series of blasts toward the Kansas skies. Wild Bill
was instantly on the scene. There was a town ordinance against
shooting off any guns in Abilene. Hickok shouted at Coe to drop
his gun. The Texan turned on the marshal, the gun held hip-high,
and pointed at Wild Bill. It was a fatal move. Hickok shot
twice. Both bullets struck the saloon man and he died before
morning.

Ben Thompson was laid up with a broken leg when his friend
and partner was gunned down by Wild Bill. He could not take
up the fight for he was flat on his back, the result of a spill off

his horse. He swore he would kill Wild Bill when he got on his feet again. When he was quite recovered he rode the other way. Back to Texas. Just why, after the war talk he made, he did not ride into Abilene and search out the executioner of his amigo Coe, Ben could never quite explain. It is likely he had some doubts as to just what the outcome might have been.

He rode back to Austin and found that the saloon and gambling hall that he and Coe had managed so successfully had fallen on evil times. He sold out and again returned to Kansas, this time to Ellsworth, a cattle shipping center. Here he and his brother Billy opened another saloon and gambling joint. In no time at all they were feuding with the local law, all of whom were imported by the citizenry and were sworn enemies of the Texans. One day a fight started. Billy, who habitually stayed about half liquored-up, shot and killed the sheriff. This inflamed the town, and only the intervention of those Texas cowboys who arrived with a series of trail herds served to get the younger Thompson mounted and headed out of town toward Texas. Ben stuck around and stood off the crowd that gathered. He had taken no part in the actual shooting and was exonerated by a jury which heard the evidence.

He traveled after that. He went out to Leadville, Colorado, where he plied his profession of card dealing. After a time he drifted back to Austin as he always did. As Ben grew older he took more and more to the solace that redeye brought him. It was seldom that he was not in his cups, if not drunk, then drinking. When he was sober—which was rare—he was pleasant enough, but when he got sufficiently incandescent he was exceedingly dangerous, not only to strangers but to drinking partners, old friends, and anyone who was handy. He was abusive, insulting, and vindictive and was continually trying to maneuver the other fellow into a quarrel so that he would have an excuse to go for his gun. People got so they avoided him. This hurt his feelings and made him all the more bellicose.

One night he went into the Senate Saloon which was owned by Mark Wilson. Ben had been tanking up all afternoon, and by the time he pushed through the swinging doors of the Senate he was rip-roaring drunk. He and Mark Wilson had bad blood between them, and both knew it was only a matter of a little time until their differences would have to be worked out in the curling smoke of a forty-five.

Wilson, in anticipation of the forthcoming fracas, had been made a special policeman and had armed himself. Ben walked up to him, cuffed the saloon man over the ear, and cut his head with a heavy ring he wore. Wilson, without offering to strike back, turned on his heel and went into a back room. He reappeared in the space of ten seconds, armed with a sawed-off 10-gauge. He threw up to shoot at Thompson but Ben, with the uncanny speed and precision that had never deserted him, was first. He neatly clipped the top of Wilson's heart with his first ball.

The barkeep, who had sworn he would stand by his boss, Wilson, thought he would be next. He whipped out a six-shooter stowed behind the bar. Ben swung over to swap lead with him, and the bartender discreetly dropped behind the counter. Thompson calculated where he was hiding and thumbed two quick slugs through the flimsy partition. Both struck the man in the back. He lingered for three weeks and finally died.

Ben was charged with double murder, duly tried, and just as promptly acquitted. He then ran for city marshal. And was elected! It is pretty hard from this time and distance to know just how the thought processes of the good citizens of the state capital must have been geared to deliberately turn the reins of law enforcement over to one of the most notorious gunmen the Lone Star had ever fostered. But that is precisely what they did. It is even stated that Ben made a good town marshal. At least there wasn't any play at trying to buffalo the chief of police!

Down at San Antonio, seventy-five miles south of the capital, was a friend of Thompson's, a saloon man named Jack Harris. He had a bar and gambling place called the Vaudeville Variety Theatre. In addition to liquor and cards he ran a specialty stage show. The Vaudeville was a hot spot in the city and attracted a huge patronage. The other partners in the place were Joe Foster and Billy Sims.

Jack Harris was one-armed. He had lost his arm during the Civil War, when he fought with General Albert Sidney Johnson, acting as scout and guide. Before the war Harris had been in the campaign of 1857 against the Mormons in Utah. Despite the loss of his arm, the left, he was rated as a crack pistol shot. Asked one time how he would handle a shotgun he took out a pair of friends; they marveled that he could hit quail on the wing with the one-handed grip. "If I can hit a bird on the wing I reckon I can hit a man standing," he often remarked. Jack Harris was a tough frontiersman, ready to fight, ready to shoot, and not a gent for anyone to try to impose upon.

He and Ben Thompson had known each other during their war days. They were friends. Amigos up until the time when Ben came down from Austin and got into an extended poker game at a table managed by Joe Foster. At first Ben lost heavily. Then he commenced to win, and he got back a part of what he had lost. He then decided to withdraw from the game with his winnings. Foster asked him to make up what he had previously lost. Ben got mad, cursed Foster, and told him the game was crooked. He gathered up all the money in sight, pulled his gun, and backed out of the Vaudeville. That was the end of the friendship between him and Jack Harris.

Harris proclaimed that Thompson was a tinhorn and a crook and was not welcome back in his place. He backed Joe Foster and said that not only was Foster an honest dealer but that anyone else who tried Thompson's approach would have him to deal with.

Ben went back to Austin and his job as city marshal. He was not long in hearing the talk that Jack Harris had made against him. Those who carried the word also added that Harris said he would kill Ben if he ever returned to San Antonio. This sort of a challenge was too much for the pugnacious Thompson. He got aboard the train and returned to the Alamo City, thoughtfully stowing a couple of quarts of squirrelhead whisky in his luggage to keep him in proper humor for the forthcoming showdown. When he got to San Antonio he was well lubricated and in an exceedingly belligerent mood. He sent word to Harris that he had arrived and what was Jack going to do about it?

Cooler heads got hold of Ben and kept him in his hotel room. He finally got so stiff he fell asleep, and they stowed him in bed. The next morning for breakfast he had a waterglass full of whisky, and before he went down on the street, another. Whom should he bump into but Jack Harris. Ben did not go for his gun but strode up to Harris and wanted to know if Jack had been looking for him. "I wasn't looking for you, Ben," said the imperturbable saloon keeper, "but I was waiting for you. If you had came into my place last night I'd have killed you." He then turned on his heel and walked away. Ben would have probably shot Harris in the back then, a thing he had no compunction about doing, but his hand was caught by a deputy sheriff who had been dogging his footsteps since he quit his hotel.

Ben had three more hookers of redeye, and then he marched boldly into the Vaudeville and up to the bar. He told the barkeep he understood that there was a squad waiting for him, all shot-gun armed, and headed by Jack Harris. The barkeep just grunted. Ben told the bartender to carry word to Harris that he would shoot it out with him and all his hired guns. The bar man just grunted again and unimpressed informed Thompson if he had any messages to deliver to Jack Harris to go find him and deliver them personally.

Later in the day and still marching under a double load of the demon rum, Ben again entered the Vaudeville together with a friend. He looked around and spotted Jack Harris at the foot of the stairs, partially hidden behind a venetian blind which covered the door at the foot of the staircase. In his hands was a sawed-off 10-gauge. Ben called out, "What are you going to do with that shotgun, Jack?" and with these words he went for his six-shooter. Before Harris could swing the smoothbore to his shoulder, Thompson had shot him twice. Once on his feet and a second time as he tumbled backward from the effects of the 240-grain slug. Harris died within the hour; both shots had penetrated his chest.

Thompson was tried and acquitted of this killing. That he had been the aggressor, that he had deliberately baited Jack Harris, that he had repeatedly gone into his place of business seeking a fight, that he had made threats heard by dozens were all con-sidered but discarded by the jury. It was early Texas. Both men were bitter enemies, each had made threats against the other, both were armed at the time of the fatal shoot out. Ben was turned loose and caught the train for Austin. When he got back home again he was fired as the city marshal.

A year went by. Almost another passed. Ben continued to gamble and to raise hell. He had lost most of his friends because his drinking never let up, and his comrades of other days wanted little part of him because he was so mean and ornery when in his cups. He made a specialty of hoorahing saloons, and the police had a deathly fear of running him in.

One day King Fisher came to town. Fisher was by this time a deputy sheriff at Uvalde, a rancher with a big spread and a sizeable herd of legitimately owned livestock. He had put his old outlaw days behind him, and although he still had a formidable reputation as a gun-swoop, he had not added any notches in some years. He bumped into Ben Thompson. Ben was drinking and was in an evil humor. However, when he met King Fisher he professed to be glad to see him. Fisher had some doubts about that. The two had never been friendly and had, as a matter of fact, some differences that were sufficiently big to make them decidedly suspicious of each other. It is likely that Ben Thompson had plans to get Fisher drunk and to kill him. To gun down a fighter of the reputation of the notorious King would be a big feather in his cap.

King Fisher, who was sharp about the mental perambulations of a killer of the stature of Ben Thompson, must have sensed what the latter had in mind. That he went along with Ben, tossing off drink for drink with the foxy ex-marshal but all the time watching for the forthcoming gun play, is simple indication that in all probability Fisher was welcoming the try when it came.

After hitting a half dozen saloons the pair conceived the idea of boarding the train and going down to San Antonio. Just why Ben wanted to go to the Alamo City is not known, but he was so far along in his cups by that time that undoubtedly he wanted to return to the scene of his last killing and swagger there before the eyes of King Fisher and the startled citizenry who had not forgotten the shooting in the Vaudeville.

The pair of well-lit gun hawks quit the train at eight of the evening and headed for a bar. There they had two rounds of drinks, and then they entered a local theatre where they watched a performance of *East Lynne,* the tear-jerker of a bygone era. Coming out, Ben caught King Fisher by the arm and guided him toward the Vaudeville Theatre where twenty months before he had gunned down Jack Harris. The Vaudeville was now owned and operated by Joe Foster and Billy Sims. Neither were any friends of the notorious Ben, indeed both held a cordial hatred for the man. At the same time King Fisher was another case altogether. When clearing up his misdeeds, Fisher had been lodged in the San Antonio jail for nine months, and Joe Foster had passed him tobacco, candy, writing materials, and other things. King felt only a sense of gratitude toward the saloon owner for his kindness.

If it was the intention of Ben Thompson to go into the Vaudeville and to there finish off Joe Foster and Billy Sims as he had done their former partner, he could not have discussed his lethal intent with his running mate Fisher. Certainly King would not have agreed to any such play where his benefactor Foster was concerned. It is still likely that this was what Thompson had in mind when he deliberately set foot inside the saloon where he knew full well only enemies awaited him. It is just as probable that he also nurtured the plan to kill King Fisher if the shooting started and the opportunity afforded.

The pair walked in and took tickets for the balcony where they could sit and drink and watch the girls on the stage below. Ben saw Billy Sims, and he asked him over to the table to have a drink with them. With Billy was a big San Antonio policeman, a Mexican named Coy. He also sat down with the pair. In no time at all the talk got around to the killing of Jack Harris. King Fisher, who had been in on his share of killings, said it was a poor subject and why didn't they drop it. He suggested they drop down to the bar below. All arose and started down the stairs. About that time, before a foot had actually been set on the steps, Joe Foster showed up. Ben asked Foster to come and have a drink with them. The little gambler refused. When Thompson put out his hand to shake, Foster again refused. This enraged the volatile Thompson who scooped out his gun and drove the muzzle into Foster's mouth. Coy instantly caught the six-shooter around the cylinder so that it could not be fired.

Coy, a big bruiser, bore down on Thompson and they both fell to the floor. King Fisher was either thrown down or dropped to keep out of the line of fire. Both Foster and Sims were firing. Coy contended afterward that he did not shoot a single time. In seconds Joe Foster had a bullet through the leg, a shot that killed him in a few weeks. Both Ben Thompson and King Fisher were dead. Coy, the policeman, turned over a six-shooter to the coroner which he said had belonged to Thompson. It had been loaded with six rounds; all were fired except one live cartridge.

The coroner's jury found that Ben Thompson had been hit three times. When the body was returned to Austin for burial it was found the erstwhile gunman had been struck by eight bullets. Five of these had been fired from behind and above. The bullets were .44-40 caliber, and all were taken out of the skull. King Fisher had likewise been hit from behind and by the same bush-whackers who had gunned down his companion. Joe Foster and Billy Sims were exonerated, although the honors were of small compensation to Foster who developed an infection in the wound in his leg and lived only a short time.

ARMSTRONG AND HALL

With Captain L. H. McNelly when he rode into the thick of things were two stalwarts, Lee Hall and John B. Armstrong. The pair had stood by his side during the affair at Las Cuevas and had proven outstanding fighting men.

Both were promoted, first to corporal and later to sergeant. Hall outranked Armstrong by virtue of longer service, and when a vacancy for lieutenant opened up he was first in line. The increasingly serious illness of McNelly was well known to General Steele, who was paying for the medical costs from the Ranger budget. With the forced retirement of the gallant little leader in October of 1876, Steele looked about for another officer to step into his shoes. Lee Hall stood logically in line. He was given the command in the fall of 1877. McNelly died a month before the appointment. John Armstrong was elevated to lieutenant and was second in command of the Special Force.

During 1875–76 the pressing need had been for control of the Mexican raiders, and the energetic drive of McNelly had put a damper on these depredations. Now with seventy-seven in prospect the adjutant general directed his field forces to concentrate on the internal lawlessness. And there was plenty of it. Banks were being robbed, stages were held up, cattle was rustled, horses were driven off, and gunmen shot it out with each other and freely lent their ordnance for hire. Sheriffs were afraid to take action, judges were intimidated, district attorneys were fearful to draw up indictments, and decent people knew not what to do

105

or which way to turn. There was aplenty for the company of Hall-Armstrong to do!

The Ranger headquarters in Austin compiled a book which was known simply as the "Fugitive List" which contained three thousand names and descriptions of wanted men, most of them for major crimes such as grand larceny and murder. Every Ranger outfit had these books on hand, and the lawmen put in their time studying names and outlines of the wanted outlaws. Many had rewards on their heads, and it was a standing practice for the Ranger who nailed a desperado to collect the reward. Salaries were only $40 monthly, and if a wanted man could be picked up who was worth $500 the Ranger was vastly enriched.

DeWitt County had been the scene of a long-standing feud between two factions, the Taylors and the Suttons. Both sides had numerous relatives and even more adherents and went gunning for each other not showing any slightest hesitancy about how they reduced the opposition. Bushwhacking from the trail, shots through the window, and shots in the back, were common.

A good many innocent people were caught up in the crossfire and killed. One of the most regrettable was the death of Dr. Brazzell and his son. The doctor had given assistance to a member of the Taylor faction. In retaliation the Suttons dragged him from a sickbed, took him a few hundred yards from his home, and in company with his son, shot both. Lee Hall, with five Rangers, went in to arrest those gunmen of the Suttons who were known to be the killers. He found them at a wedding celebration; the Sutton headquarters were decorated not only for the wedding but also in preparations for the Christmas holidays which were only three days away. The Rangers surrounded the house which was full of dancing rollicking gunfighters, all imbibing freely and none more so than the bridegroom who was one of the wanted men.

Hall burst in the front door, six-shooter in hand, just as his officers crashed in the back and appeared at the windows, all armed with the .44 Winchester. It was a tense moment, and only the calm voice of the steely nerved Ranger leader saved the party from a lead-slinging holocaust. "We're here to take five of you to jail. For killing Doctor Brazzell. Step away from your dance partners and line up against the wall. Any man that makes a move for his gun will be killed." He motioned with the cocked and leveled revolver.

The Suttons, hardcase killers, used to buffaloing the local sheriff, and secure in the knowledge that they were here in greater strength than the Rangers they saw, hesitated. Lee Hall stepped inside the door and cuffed the nearest Sutton over the ear with the 7½-inch barrel of the .45. That did it. The others tamely lined up against the far wall, the women huddling in the far corner. Hall disarmed the lot of them.

"Look," said Young Sutton, the bridegroom, "this is my wedding night. Can't we go on with the dance? We'll be here in the morning to go to jail." Lee Hall pondered this and finally nodded his head. The wedding party continued until daylight streaked the heavens, and not only were there no disturbances but neither did any of the accused attempt to escape. Breakfast eaten, the wanted men saddled up and escorted by Hall and his intrepid Rangers set off for the court of Judge H. Clay Pleasants.

This justice, an iron-nerved jurist who had been repeatedly threatened with death, sat in his court with a Ranger on either flank to give him protection. He heard the evidence against the Suttons and promptly refused them any bail and remanded the group to the Galveston jail.

Hall, having seen the Sutton ringleaders jailed, broke his command down into skeleton squads and sent them through the country, apprehending the lawless wherever they could. He had them report not to him but directly to Austin. He could not keep account of all his force because of their widespread activities and the lack of communications. In February he sent Corporal Hardy and two Rangers to San Patricio County because of the widespread activities of cattle rustlers. The trio captured more than twelve hundred fresh cowhides but could make no arrests because county officials were in league with the thieves.

Lieutenant John Armstrong, who was just as active as his commander, Hall, was in the vicinity of Eagle Pass, which is on the Rio Grande, and sent Lee word that a Mexican bandit was just below the town on the Texas side of the river and that he had with him a band of renegades that numbered perhaps thirty.

Armstrong had been assured by the Mexican officials at Eagle Pass that if he could drive this bravo across the Rio Grande they would finish him off.

Hall diverted three of his flying squads to the business, and led by Armstrong, the Rangers descended on the bandit's headquarters. This not only flushed the outlaw to the south side of the rio but also stampeded an assortment of badmen, both saddle-colored and white, to the mañana side of the frontier. Whether the Mexican officials made good their promise to liquidate the *jefe* is from this time and distance unknown.

Hall and Armstrong, together with Sergeant Parrott of their command, crossed into Mexico to the town of Piedras Negras, which is the counterpart of Eagle Pass. There they intended to powwow with Mexican border officials about the outlaws driven into the southern Republic by their raid. In the main plaza of the village they bumped into a gringo who was on the Fugitives List. They promptly collared him and, without the formalities of extradition or even so much as a by-your-leave of the Mexicans, hustled him over to the Texas side of the border. After that Hall went to Fort Clark. A grand jury was in session, and he went before the jury and assured them that if they did their duty, finding indictments which the evidence indicated were true, he would personally see that no man was harmed. The jury thus encouraged found bills against King Fisher and numbers of his cohorts. John Armstrong, with this evidence of law and order now in being, rode down on Fisher's stronghold and as McNelly had done the year before hauled him into jail. Among other charges against King Fisher was that he, in cahoots with Ben Thompson, had killed a man named Amos Wilson in Austin.

Like many police organizations before and since, the Ranger force was struck with a wave of economy. The word got out that the Special Force would have to be broken up because of lack of operating funds. This caused a major furore. The West Texas Stock Association held an emergency meeting and assessed its membership a total of seven thousand dollars to keep the Hall-Armstrong group in the field and operational.

In Mexico, General Porfirio Diaz was establishing himself as the new president of the country. Diaz was a dictator but the word had not been popularized in those days. He referred to his new office as the presidency. He was liquidating the opposition, and along the Rio Grande this took the shape of the forces of Valdez and Escobedo. This pair of worthies were sent fleeing and their ragtag-and-bobtail forces were scattered to the four winds. A Mexican revolutionary out of work will turn to outlawry—to raiding on a small scale and thievery in whatever direction seems to offer the most profit. The fat cattle on the Texas side of the Rio Grande beckoned to many. Raids and rustling became again almost as persistent as when McNelly had been riding in the lower Rio Grande Valley.

Hall gathered up twenty men from his scattered force and together with Lieutenant Armstrong and Sergeant Arrington made a raid on Valdez' camp about thirty miles down the river from Eagle Pass. The raid was a fizzle so far as a shoot-out was concerned. The outlaws had pickets out who fetched word of the coming of the Rangers, and about fifty of the coyotes drifted across the river. Another fifty were captured and the Fugitive List was carefully scanned to see how many fitted descriptions. Returning to Eagle Pass the Rangers then raided the town itself and picked up an additional sixteen wanted men, seven of them for murder and three for horse theft. All were moved the eighty miles to Castroville jail.

During August, Hall was back in Rio Grande City near the very crossing where in 1875, two summers before, he had invaded Mexico with the courageous McNelly. Hall and his men were in Rio Grande City a second time because a band of Mexican bandits had crossed the Rio Grande, struck the jail, and released all the prisoners. These included both Mexicans and Americans, all of whom leisurely made their way into the Land of Mañana.

Hall went directly to the *alcalde* in Reynosa and demanded the return of the fugitives. He visited the commandante of the Federal forces and renewed his demands. When the commander seemed not too impressed, Hall threatened to bring his Rangers and forcibly return the escapees. The commandante, remembering the invasion by the Texans in 1875, hastily agreed to round up the prisoners and turn them over to the Ranger. Three were collected and duly escorted to the ferry where Lee Hall accepted them. The others could not be found, having no doubt taken themselves to unknown spots in the interior of the country.

So far this chapter has been mostly devoted to the commander of the Special Force, Lee Hall. Now we would like to say something about the other half of the equation, Lieutenant John B. Armstrong. This bucko was quite as much of a going-hell-for-leather as was his leader. He had gone to the Rio Grande brush country with McNelly in seventy-five and had stood at the shoulder of the tigerish Ranger through the Palo Alto and Las Cuevas scraps. He had learned from McNelly and had agreed in thought and action with his mentor when that ex-Confederate raider said no quarter would be asked or given. John Armstrong was quick on the trigger just as McNelly had been. If the opposition wanted a shoot-out he was their man. There probably has never been a braver Ranger than this man, as subsequent events in his turbulent career will disclose.

While still operating under McNelly, Armstrong, then a sergeant, took a squad of men and rode out of Carrizo Springs headed for the domain of King Fisher. The time was October of 1876. Night caught the group some miles from Espinoza Lake where they had been reliably informed there was a camp of outlaws. Wanted men, some wanted for murder, others for cow rustling, all in the Texas crime book.

About nine at night, Lieutenant Armstrong divided his force, having heard that another bunch of desperadoes were right then camped at the Pendencia. This was King Fisher's headquarters. Corporal Williams was tolled off to lead the force on this latter hangout. Armstrong with the balance of his troop kept on toward the encampment on the shores of Espinoza Lake. When the party got within sight of the lake they spotted a wisp of smoke coming as they rightly surmised from the outlaws' camp. They dismounted, tied their horses, unsheathed the Model 73 carbines with which all were armed, and proceeded to "round up" the camp. When the ring closed in on the camp, the outlaws let the lawmen get within twenty yards and then they opened up.

The fight was a hot one for a few minutes, and then the superiority of the .44-40s in the hands of the deadly Rangers foretold the end. Three of the outlaws were killed, and the fourth was hit five times but survived. From the wounded captive they learned that six others had dodged out of camp, word having been passed along that the Rangers were coming.

From this same captured outlaw Armstrong learned of a wanted Mexican at Whaley's Ranch about eight miles from Espinoza Lake. He detailed three of his Rangers to go fetch him in. When the officers got to the ranch the Mexican had been alerted and came out fighting. He had to be killed. During the night the wounded man, despite his several bullet holes, tried to escape and in the melee was shot again, this time fatally.

In the course of a twenty-four-hour period Armstrong and his stalwarts had killed four Americans and one Mexican. They recovered fifty head of stolen horses and a small number of cows. It had been a lively time typical of the action of the Special Force and its leaders.

A little more than a year later, John Armstrong was detailed to Wilson County to arrest John Mayfield who was accused of shooting and killing Bob Montgomery. Lieutenant Armstrong took with him Leroy Deggs, a member of the company. There was a considerable reward on Mayfield's head, and both Rangers were anxious to corral him and share in the prize money. The alleged killer was a rancher, and the Rangers rode out to his ranch and found him in his corrals. When they told him who they were and that he was under arrest, Mayfield went for his gun. Armstrong and Deggs both shot together and both hit their man. Mayfield was killed on the spot.

The Rangers had not expected that the rancher would make a fight of it. They had no way of moving the body, having concluded their man would saddle a horse and ride into town with them peacefully. They were confronted with the job of rounding up a horse and tying the body on the saddle to move it to the county seat. Members of Mayfield's family had meanwhile fanned out to neighboring ranches with the news of the killing. The corral was soon filled with inflamed friends, relatives, and dangerous sympathizers. They not only would not help with catching up a horse but commenced to threaten Armstrong and his fellow officer. The pair were in a dangerous predicament. They did not want any more shooting, and it was obvious if they attempted to move the body that a gun play would be in the cards. They caught up their horses, mounted under the sights of the gathering, and slowly rode away. Mayfield was secretly buried by his family and friends, and the reward was never paid. The law required that either the man or his body be presented for payment.

If this might appear that the pair of Rangers had been buffaloed by the mob, the subsequent performance of John Armstrong puts the lie to that presumption. Armstrong captured, singlehanded, Texas' worst killer, John Wesley Hardin. It is a story worth retelling.

Hardin, a product of the War Between the States, was a killer who was constantly on the lookout for the makings of a quarrel so that he could add another notch to his gun. He is stated to have killed forty men, and this may be true. Certainly he gunned down some twenty-five or thirty, not counting Mexicans or Negroes. He was a murderer who was as wont to shoot from ambush as not, who tried never to give the other man an even break, and who when he was in his cups was as dangerous as a rattler in the dog days of August. Hardin was a member of the Taylor faction in the Sutton-Taylor feud and was an acknowledged rustler of cattle and horses. If he was involved in bank robbery, train robbery, or other crimes, it was never pinned on him. He finally shot down a deputy sheriff, Charlie Webb of Comanche County, in 1874, and this set the Rangers after him.

After this killing Hardin ducked over into Louisiana and stayed there. He was captured, returned to Texas, but escaped, and until 1877 nothing was heard of him. The state had posted a $4000 reward for his capture, dead or alive, and this excited John Armstrong. With a sum of money that large, the Ranger thought, he could start to ranching. For that was his ambition. He knew full well that the little salary he made as a Ranger officer would never be sufficient to buy the beginnings of a herd of cows. But with $4000 he could make a beginning. He went to the adjutant general and asked to be assigned to the job of catching Hardin. The adjutant general acquiesced.

A detective named John Duncan was assigned to work with

the Ranger on the case. He rented a farm next to a kinsman of Hardin's, and soon the two were on friendly terms. It has been said the neighbor was actually John Wesley's own father. At any rate there was a handsome team of young horses on the place and a spring wagon in good repair. After a time Duncan offered to buy both the team and the wagon, and the offer was so high that the neighbor finally admitted he could not sell either. They were not his, he explained, but belonged to a relative who was away at the time. Duncan, without seeming to be too anxious, raised the offer he had made. Finally his neighbor said he would write to the absent relative and ask if he would sell. By adroit maneuvering the detective got to see the address on the letter. It was sent to "John Adams" at a little town in Alabama.

Lieutenant Armstrong was promptly told of this, and he at once went to the adjutant general and secured a warrant for the arrest of not only John Wesley but also included in the arrest papers the alias, that is, "John Adams." Then he departed for Alabama, Detective Duncan with him. When he reached Montgomery he learned that not only had Hardin been hiding in the state but he was bushed up with a band of cut-throats and the gang was threatening to rob the trains. Hearing this, Armstrong held a powwow with railroad officials who when they learned of his mission offered to help him in every way they could. The first thing they did was to inform him on good authority that Hardin and some of his bully boys were right then at Pensacola, Florida. Without a moment's delay Armstrong and Duncan pushed off for that city.

It should be remembered that all Armstrong had as authority was a warrant for the arrest of Hardin signed by the adjutant general of Texas. He had no authority from either the state of Alabama or Florida, and in the event he captured Hardin he had no extradition papers. If he was forced to kill the gunmen—a mighty likely possibility—he would be in the peculiar position of a law officer operating outside his domain. These legal technicalities were brushed to the background in the mind of the aggressive Texan. He was on a hot scent, and he intended to follow it to its conclusion.

Just outside Pensacola, Armstrong and Duncan alighted and

immediately went to see the chief of police. They explained that they planned to await the return of Hardin and his fellows right there. When the train stopped to take water at the whistle stop, they would board the train and capture the outlaw. The chief and his minions pledged their help. It was decided that Armstrong would enter the car in which John Wesley and his rannies were riding and would throw down on them and cover them. At the same time the Florida officers would enter at the other end of the car and would likewise cover the wanted men. Duncan wisely decided he would stay on the station platform and would reach through the open window and catch Hardin by the arm and thus disrupt his draw.

The train pulled in more or less on time. Hardin and four of his followers were in the smoking car. The windows were open for it was a hot day. Armstrong, who was suffering from a bullet wound in his leg and had to walk with a cane, hobbled up on the steps of the smoking car. As he got to the door he hauled out his old .45. It had a 7½-inch barrel, and as he limped through the doorway he was immediately spotted by Hardin. "Texas, by God!" he shouted as he saw the six-foot frame of the big Ranger loom up in the entrance. He went for his six-shooter which he had shoved into the front of his waistband beneath a coat he was wearing. As he gripped the stock and commenced to pull the revolver, the big upstanding hammer caught in the suspenders which held up his trousers. He could not clear the gun for action. He yanked and yanked, and the more he tugged the more firmly anchored the gun became. Meanwhile the Florida officers had decided that discretion was the better part of valor. They did not pour through the rear door of the coach. Indeed, they did not show up anywhere on the train. Likewise Detective Duncan failed to reach through the raised window and catch Hardin's arm as he wrestled to get his shooting iron into action. John Armstrong was facing five exceedingly tough and determined adversaries, every one of them armed and one the most dangerous gunfighter Texas had ever spawned.

The Ranger had five or six steps to take to reach the seat where Hardin and his hardcase gang were seated. Half way to the bunch, one of them flipped up his .45 and let drive at Armstrong. He missed. The big Ranger triggered off a shot at the man who promptly dived through the window, ran four or five steps, and crumpled over dead, his heart shot in two. By that time Armstrong was on top of Hardin. Disregarding the others, all of whom had drawn their six-shooters, he grappled with the smaller man to disarm him. Hardin rolled up in the seat and kicked the Ranger in the chest with both feet. It sent Armstrong spinning, but he recovered and with a tigerish rush again pounced on his man. This time he swung the big long-barreled six-shooter over his head and brought it down on Hardin's skull with enough force to cave it in. It knocked the outlaw as cold as a wedge. The officer then swung his gun on the others, all of whom dropped their guns and raised their hands.

The train conductor who had been alerted by train officials to cooperate with Armstrong told him the train was his. The first thing the Ranger did was to get the Hardin buckos off his hands. He turned them over to local police and proceeded toward Whitney, Alabama, which was Hardin's new home. When they got to Whitney, they had to change trains for the journey into Montgomery. Hardin's friends flocked around and threatened to shoot up the train, kill Armstrong, and release the prisoner. Armstrong grimly assured them they might succeed but all they would have to carry away with them would be a dead Hardin. "I'll kill him the first move you make," he said. In Whitney he sent General Steele this telegram.

"Arrested John Wesley Hardin, Pensacola, Fla. this PM. He had four men with him. Had some lively shooting. One of their number killed all the rest captured. Hardin fought desperately closed in and took him by main strength. We are now waiting for a train to get away on. This is Hardin's home and friends are trying to rally men to release him. Have some good citizens with me and will make it interesting. J. B. Armstrong."

When the train pulled in which would take the Ranger and his captive to Montgomery, Armstrong found the railroad had put on an extra coach just for him. And with the extra car a guard with a rifle. He handcuffed Hardin to a seat and took up guard at one door and put the railroader at the other with his rifle. They got out of Whitney before trouble broke and reached

Montgomery where he placed his famous prisoner in the city jail. He went off to bed at a local hotel. Not, however, before he got off a second telegram to General Steele asking for extradition papers for Hardin.

He had scarcely gotten to sleep when he was awakened by a court bailiff who asked him to get over to court as soon as he could. When he arrived he found that John Wesley had gotten a lawyer and this worthy was about to spring him on a writ of habeas corpus. Armstrong pled his own case, describing in detail what a notorious scoundrel, killer, murderer, and gunman was the prisoner. He asked for a continuation until the extradition papers could be gotten from the Texas governor. The judge listened and locked Hardin up for a second time despite the protestations of his lawyer and the threats of the outlaw.

Armstrong then got off a succession of frantic telegrams to the adjutant general in Austin. These had their effect, and the needed extradition came through. He loaded up his famous charge for a second time and commenced the ride to Austin. His last wire was a cheerful one: "It is all day now. On our way. Papers arrived okay. J. B. Armstrong"

Hardin was closely guarded by the Rangers while locked up at Austin. He was transferred to Comanche for his trial, again carefully guarded by the Rangers. There were a good many threats by his friends and relatives that he would be released. No attempts were made. The presence of the Rangers was a bit too formidable to be bucked. The jury heard the evidence and gave Hardin twenty-five years. He was twenty-six years of age. He served twenty years of the sentence and was pardoned by Governor Hogg in 1893.

John Armstrong duly collected his $4000 reward money, and just as he had promised himself he invested it in cattle. From that beginning he became a rancher and steadily added to his holdings until his cows and acres were immense. His ranch is near the famous King Ranch of South Texas and today, some four generations later, is still owned by a John Armstrong.

12
THIRTY NOTCHES

When Lieutenant John Armstrong bent his gun barrel over John Wesley Hardin's head, he put one of the country's most dangerous killers out of action for a long time. The courts weren't so crowded in those days, and they also seem to have given some priority to defendants as notorious as Hardin. In no time at all he was before the bar and just as promptly had been stowed away for twenty-five years. In those days the business of hasty paroles and lenient pardons was largely unheard of. Hardin remained in the custody of the Lone Star State for twenty long years. Finally with only five years left on his sentence, Governor Hogg pardoned him.

During the two decades that he remained a guest at Huntsville Prison, John Wesley was the model prisoner. He did not quarrel with his fellows, was respectful and obedient to the guards, and in his spare time of which he had a good deal he studied law Once sprung from the grim gray walls he took the Texas bar examination, passed it, and became a full-fledged lawyer.

At first he went back to his old stamping grounds, but twenty years was not enough to wipe out all the old enmities. When a fight or two were narrowly averted, Hardin packed his gear in a camelback trunk and did not stop traveling until he had crossed the state. He set down in El Paso. Here, in no time at all, he had hung out his shingle, "John W. Hardin Attorney at Law."

He was forty-six years of age, about five feet, nine inches tall, weighed 145 pounds, had light sandy hair which had not gotten gray despite his years in prison, and small blue eyes, cruel and

cold, set well back in his head. Hardin had worn a gun openly
before he was corralled by Armstrong. After he got out of prison
he affected a calfskin vest into which he had sewed two holsters.
These were for a cross draw, and he carried two short-barreled
.41 double-action revolvers in this hideout.

Hardin was the son of a preacher. Born in Texas in 1848, he
was only into his teens when the Civil War drained off all the
young men for the Confederate cause. The war ended and the
carpetbaggers arrived. Hardin took offense at the influx of North-
erners, many of them Negroes. The *Tejanos* considered it a personal affront when the blacks attempted to exert any control.
The Davis government, the first carpetbagger administration, had
organized the Texas State Police. It was liberally sprinkled with
freed slaves, and these officers were the particular targets of
fellows like the young Hardin.

By the time he was fifteen he had shot and killed a black state
policeman. This got the police and Union soldiers after him, and
he carefully laid in ambush and killed three soldiers. He then
threw in with a slinky-eyed cousin, Simp Dixon, and this pair
were run to earth in Richland Bottoms. Only the ambush did not
work out very well for the state forces, for both Hardin and his
cousin each killed a man in breaking out of the circle of guns.
By this time John Wesley was sixteen and he was allergic to hard
work. He became a professional gambler, an occupation which
was essentially his only means of livelihood for the remainder of
his days. Although after he got out of Huntsville he did profess
to be a lawyer, it was precious little law he practiced. He preferred the cardboards.

Having gotten safely out of Richland Bottoms, he and Simp
Dixon split up. Hardin rode into East Texas where he in no
time at all got into an argument with Amos Bradley, another
gambling man. Bradley claimed Wes was dealing off the bottom
of the deck. Hardin called him a liar, and they both went for
their guns. Bradley, who had been planning to kill the slightly
built boy across the table from him, had a pair of derringers in
his vest pockets. He got one of these and pushed it across the
felt top almost into Hardin's navel. The gun misfired. It was

fatal for Amos Bradley. John Wesley's .45 slug struck him in the throat. Hardin thought it best to ride on out of town.

In a little town in that end of Texas, Horn Hill, the Robinson Brothers' circus set up. Hardin was only a boy in years even though he did play a man's game. He went to the circus. He did not bother to buy an admission, but simply went under the tent. A big burly guard collared him and commenced to kick him out the entrance. Hardin squirmed in his collar, whirled, and killed the canvasman before the eyes of the amazed audience. This time he left town at a high gallop. And indeed did not stop for a hundred miles.

He rode into Kosse and quickly found the biggest saloon, the fastest moving poker game, and where the whores were. He was still only sixteen but he went looking for his pleasures as if he had reached his majority. Alan Comstock was a pimp with a girl who was working the line. That Hardin was smitten with the cyprian's glamor there can be no doubt. He slept in her crib and was seen with her every evening in the Three Star Saloon and gambling hall. Comstock smouldered for three days about the activities of the kid; then he went looking for him. Hardin had been expecting him, and when Comstock burst into the room where the prostitute and he were shacked up, Hardin had his six-shooter lying in his lap. He was seated on the edge of the bed, his feet on the floor, his eye on the door. As the pimp burst the door open, John Wesley eared back the big hammer and triggered off a round that pierced Comstock's right eye without touching the lid. It went on out the back of his head, leaving a considerably messier hole back there.

In Waco, Wes got into a hassle with a barber named Huffman. It was over a race horse which Huffman and another man, Ramsey, owned. Hardin first bought the horse and then found it was lame and forced the barber to take the pony back and to return his money. This infuriated Huffman, who after having a half dozen drinks went looking for the kid. He found him in the Acme Saloon, dealing cards. Hardin, as was his wont, sat facing the door. He saw Huffman come in, go to the bar, and order a drink. John Wesley eased his .45 out of the leather and laid it in his lap. Huffman was drunk and commenced to berate the boy

from the bar, a distance of about twelve feet. Finally he turned
with his back squarely to the bar and commenced a clumsy draw.
Hardin whipped up the six-shooter which had been lying handy
in his lap and shot twice. The first shot struck Huffman almost
on his navel and the second missed and cracked the mirror behind him. He slumped to the floor badly wounded. He lived for
thirty-six hours and died.

Hardin quit town, a posse at his heels. He evaded the posse
but the sheriff in Longview captured him and threw him in jail.
He got in touch with the authorities in Waco who said they would
pay the expenses if the sheriff could deputize a couple of locals
to return Hardin for trial. In the jail Hardin bought a smuggled
.45 with four cartridges in it. He tucked the gun in his waistband
beneath his overcoat—it was wintertime—and when the guards
came to escort him back to Waco they did not search him. These
guards were a pair of tough deputies, the one, Stokes, a jailhouse
bully, and the other, Smolly, a 'breed who suggested that as soon
as they got Hardin outside town they shoot him and go back and
say he made a break for it. Stokes, who had some compunction
about cold-blooded murder, demurred.

They had to swim their horses across the Sabine River, and it
was filled with floating ice. There was snow on the ground and
on the second night they had to make an open camp. Stokes went
to a nearby farm to get some corn for the horses, and this left
Wes and the 'breed Smolly in camp alone. Hardin was tied on
his horse each day but in camp was given the freedom of no
shackles on hands or feet. He maneuvered around behind the
horses, reached under his arm where he had tucked the smuggled
.45, and hauled it forth. Smolly had his back turned. Hardin
called to him: "Turn around you sonofabitch." Smolly whirled,
going for his gun. John Wesley shot him with all the old cartridges that would fire: three went, one failed to go. He then
buckled on Smolly's gun and well-filled cartridge belt, took up
his rifle, saddled the best of the horses, and rode off leisurely. He
felt quite confident that Stokes would not take up his trail until
he could gather a posse.

He then rode home to Mount Calm where he told his parson
father all his adventures, and the elder Hardin advised him in

all seriousness to go to Mexico. Wes thought this might be pretty good advice, and so he saddled up Stokes' horse and headed for San Antonio, his idea being that he would ride through the Alamo City and thence to the border around Laredo. Hardly had he gotten well on his way, when somewhere between Belton and Waco he had the poor luck to round a bend in the road and find three state policemen in the trail. Just as though they had been informed that he would be along. Before Hardin could make even the slightest move toward his belted gun, he found himself covered by the three lawmen. They knew all about him, knew that he had shot Huffman and was wanted for not only his killing but the murder of Smolly. They commenced the long ride back to Waco. Nightfall caught them in the bush.

They made camp but because they outnumbered the slight prisoner by three to one they did not shackle him and indeed permitted him to sleep between Smith and another state policeman named Davis. The third, Ellis, was to take the first guard watch. Hardin pretended to go to sleep, but he watched like a wolf as the others unbuckled their belt guns, stacked a shotgun and two rifles on their saddles, and went to sleep. Ellis remained alert until about midnight, when the watchful John Wesley who had never slept a wink saw that his head was nodding. Gathering himself he sprang from the ground between his guards and in a single bound was on top of the stacked arms. He snatched up the shotgun just as Ellis came awake. He cut him in two with the first barrel and then swung on the sleepers who were sleepily awakening. He shot and killed Davis with the second barrel and then snatched up the six-shooter from the defunct Ellis and finished off Smith. Again he quite leisurely repossessed his own six-shooter, picked over the rifles selecting the best, did an equally expert job on the saddles and the horseflesh, and finally satisfied he had the best of the equipment offered, rode off to his cousins, the Clements.

The Clements, Jim, Manning, Gyp, and Joe, had a sizeable ranch near Gonzales. They were a tough lot—all gunfighters and killers and all considered it open season on the hated state police. If a state policeman could be shot from ambush, this was looked on as a sort of trophy hunting which could be bragged about around the chuckwagon fire. When John Wesley rode in with the story of his latest exploit, he was hailed as a returned hero. The Clements were gathering cattle for a drive to Abilene, and they invited Hardin to accompany them. This, John Wesley concluded, would be a lot better than riding off to the Land of Mañana. He'd just go to Kansas for a spell and let things cool off in his native Texas.

Meanwhile he rode into Gonzales one evening for a little fun and stayed for three days. He got into a card game and this kept him. He won at poker and lost at monte and finally decided the Mexican monte dealer was a cheat. He slapped the dealer's face with his left hand and went for his gun with the right. The dealer never had a chance. The Hardin bullet struck him under his ribs and ranged upward making its exit beneath his left shoulder blade. Gonzales was a wild town and although there was a city marshal he made no move to arrest Wes Hardin. It was known he was a cousin of the formidable Clements, and the city minion wanted no part of this combine.

Across the Indian Territory the Indians attempted to levy a tax of 10¢ per head on the livestock. In the squabble Hardin shot and killed a redskin. Again after crossing out of the Territory and into Kansas, the Osages rode into the herd and commenced to cut out fifteen or twenty steers. Again there was an altercation, a brief flurry in which the trigger-quick Hardin took the leading role. He shot and killed an Osage.

Everything was then calm until they got to Newton Prairie. Here a herd behind them got to crowding too close, and Wes rode back to remonstrate. The herd boss was a Mexican, Jose Guzman, who did not like Hardin's tone nor yet his words. He rode back to the chuckwagon and picked up a Henry .44. He returned and when he got close he opened up on the Texan. He shot away Hardin's hat brim, and then the rifle jammed. He dropped it in the grass and came on at a gallop, drawing his six-shooter as he charged.

John Wesley, for some reason, was poorly armed. He had an old cap-and-ball .36 caliber, and it was in poor repair. He could not keep the chambers in alignment unless he held the cylinder with his hand. This he did as his adversary loped closer, firing at every jump. Hardin managed to hit the Mexican in the thigh when they were almost stirrup to stirrup. Later on they came together again, and this time John Wesley was better armed. He killed Jose Guzman.

The cattle were delivered to the loading pens in Abilene, and the drive was done. Wes and the Clements rode into the far end of Texas Street to have themselves just one hell of a time. After a hundred days on the trail they were ready for all the hell-raising that the rip-roaring, sin-soaked prairie metropolis had to offer. And it offered a lot!

The town was held in check by Wild Bill Hickok. The famed city marshal hated all *Tejanos,* and they returned his cordial animosity with interest! It was Wild Bill who enforced the edict that no guns would be shot off inside the town limits. He had killed men to enforce that ordinance. John Wesley Hardin was eager to see this lawman, maybe even match guns with him. Ben Thompson was there then, and he knew of Hardin's reputation. He urged him to kill Hickok. "Why don't you kill him yourself?" John Wesley wanted to know. Ben said he'd rather someone else did it. In later years, it was Hardin's story to relate how he got the drop on Wild Bill by pulling the road agent's spin on him. And that he made him hand over his guns. This yarn does not seem to have much support in fact. The truth is that none of the ranking Texas gun-peelers wanted to match shots with Hickok. Ben Thompson had been his enemy and he had hesitated. Hardin was only a boy of eighteen when he was in Abilene, and with twenty notches on his gun and a reputation that had even then marked him as a ranking killer, would have liked nothing better than to add Wild Bill to his own personal graveyard. That he never tried him is indication of the stature of the Abilene marshal.

John Wesley did manage to get into plenty of mischief while he was cruising up and down Texas Street, tossing off a whisky here and another there, and not forgetting the floozies in the Drover's Cottage, nor yet the card game in the Bull's Head. It was in the latter saloon that he had a quarrel with a man named Tatum. They got into an argument over a poker hand, and Tatum, who most surely was unaware that the slight boy in front of him was the highly lethal Wes Hardin, reached across the table and slapped the Texan. The six-shooter in Hardin's lap roared under the table. It took the startled Tatum in the thigh, severing the femoral artery. He bled to death in twenty minutes. John Wesley, knowing of the ban on gunfire in town and sure Wild Bill would come to investigate, loped out the back door, climbed aboard his horse, and rode off to the Clements cow camp at Cottonwood. Here he felt safe surrounded by his hard-case cousins.

A rancher up from Texas, Jason Roundtree, was shot and killed—it was robbery—by a Mexican named Pablo Gutierrez, who rode off with a considerable sum of money taken from the body of Roundtree. The posse after Gutierrez rode through the Clements camp and told Hardin who was sticking in camp what had happened. He saddled up and rode with them. The murderer was caught at Bluff, Kansas. Hardin shot and killed him. He felt sure this would make him popular with the Texans in Abilene, and he concluded this public acclaim would be such that Hickok would probably forget the killing of Tatum. John Wesley rode back into town quite openly. As he had surmised Wild Bill elected to ignore him.

But not for long. Wherever John Wesley went, there developed trouble. He was asleep in the Drover's one night when he was awakened by that sixth sense which never seemed to desert him. He found that his clothes were being searched by some light-fingered gent who never knew what hit him when Hardin eased his hand under the pillow and came out with his .45 cocked and ready. He lightly touched the muzzle to the thief's neck and pulled the trigger. He then leaped out of bed, once more mindful that Hickok said no guns would be set off in the limits of the town. Hardin stepped over to the window, and there as it would happen were Wild Bill and four others just pulling up in a hack pulled by a team of horses. Not waiting to retrieve his pants which had fallen under the dead man, Hardin scrambled through the window and out on the porch. He then dropped lightly to the ground and ran down the alley. Sans pants and with his shirt tail flapping behind him. His six-shooter was still in his hand, and he was determined that if the alley was blocked by Hickok or any of his minions a shooting match would instantly develop.

Outside the town he pulled up, and in no time at all along came a cowboy who was riding back to his outfit along the creek bottom. Hardin swung up behind him and rode on to the Clements camp. He did not return to Abilene after that latest killing. Despite the fact that he had been quite within his rights in protecting his property, he was not sure that the deadly efficient city marshal would understand. He rode off instead for Texas, back to Gonzales country.

Here a pair of Negro state policemen tried to capture Hardin in a trading post. One of them covered Hardin while the other waited outside. He asked Wes to hand over his six-shooter. The revolver was proffered handle foremost, but what the officer did not see was that the gunman had his trigger finger through the guard. As the Negro reached for the handgun, it spun rapidly on the Hardin finger, the butt slapped into his palm, and the gun exploded. Exploded into the face of the policeman. He dropped, and Hardin stepped out on the porch to finish off the other who had mounted on the sound of the shot. As though he knew it was his brother officer and not the fugitive who had been shot, he was already in motion. Hardin's bullets about his sides only served to speed him down the dusty road.

This shooting brought a posse which rode after Hardin for three days. He finally laid in wait for them, and it is believed he had some help from the Clements for three of the possemen were killed. This broke up the pursuit, and John Wesley rode back to the Clements headquarters without bothering to hide his presence.

Despite the multitude of warrants out for him and the fact that he was now a marked man, a gunfighter, and a killer with more than thirty notches on his gun, Hardin fell in love and married. He set up housekeeping near Gonzales and attempted to farm and ranch on a small scale. This soon paled and he was again in the saddle, this time headed for Kingsville and the lower Rio Grande country. In the brush country south of San Antonio a Mexican rode into his camp late one evening and before it was good darkness had made a play to rob Wes. He died for his pains. Hardin had been suspicious of him from his first appearance and had taken off his belted gun and hung belt and holstered weapon on a mesquite. The Mexican, seeing this, waited until the gringo had his back partially turned and then he made his draw. But hardly fast enough. Hardin had on his two-gun vest and he whipped out one of the bunty .41s in this vest and killed the robber.

How long he stayed in the Kingsville country or when he returned is not known, but it was not many months until he was back on his old stamping grounds near Gonzales. Riding into town one day he had a few drinks and then got immersed in a game of ten-pins. The game soon resulted in a quarrel with Dudley Sublett. Words led to blows and then to gun play. Both men were hit. Sublett took a .41 slug through the shoulder, but Hardin was shot through the body. The Clements whisked him out of town, and his life was despaired of. One thing that made it precarious was that he had to be hidden in the bush and continually moved, for the news that he was badly wounded encouraged the Davis state police to come hunting him.

Finally his hideout was found by a couple of state policemen who came upon him guns drawn. Hardin killed one of the officers and wounded the other but in turn got a slug through the knee. He then surrendered to a man he felt he could trust, Sheriff Dick Regan. When the sheriff rode up to take the surrender, one of his possemen, perhaps out of animosity or from nervousness, let his gun go off. It just happened to be pointed at Wesley, and the bullet hit him in the thigh.

Regan, when Hardin was fit to travel, loaded him on a pallet in the back of a spring wagon and hauled him off to Austin where he was jailed. After some months he was returned to Gonzales to stand trial. Here he managed to bribe either the sheriff or his jailer who let him escape. He was by this time recovered from his three wounds, and he celebrated his release by going on a prolonged drinking binge which wound up like so many of John Wesley's sprees—with the killing of a man. This time it was Pat Morgan with whom he had quarreled before. Seeing him in the Spotted Horse Saloon he resumed the affair to the detriment of Mr. Morgan.

This put Jack Helms, the local sheriff, on his trail. Instead of running, Hardin waited for the sheriff, and when the smoke of the encounter had all cleared away, Helms lay dead. This put Charley Webb, deputy sheriff of Brown County, into the action. Wes had gone over to Comanche to the horse races when word reached him that Charley Webb was in town and said he was either going to return Hardin to jail in irons or cart him back in a pine box. Webb was mixed up in the famous Sutton-Taylor family feud. He was a supporter of the Suttons, and John Wesley was related to the Taylors. This angle had its bearing in the avowed intentions of Webb when he came into Comanche that day.

The two came together in the Ace of Diamonds Saloon toward the shank end of the day. Webb had on two six-shooters; Hardin, so far as appearances went, seemed to be unarmed. He was wearing his two-gun vest, a novel invention which apparently fooled a good many adversaries, this day to include Charley Webb. Hardin walked up to the deputy and asked if Webb was seeking him. "No I don't have any warrant for you, Wes," the lawman said.

"Then have a drink with me," Hardin offered. As he spoke he turned to the barkeep to order drinks, when Bud Dixon, Wes' cousin, yelled, "Look out, Wes!" Hardin turned just as Webb shot him in the side. Despite the wound he drew his right-hand gun and killed the deputy with a shot through the throat. Hardin then thought it expeditious to quit Texas. After the Webb killing a mob formed and rode after Bud Dixon and his brother Tom and lynched both of them. With them was Wes' brother Joe, and he was also killed by the mob. This was probably related to the Sutton-Taylor feud more than to the fact that Hardin had gunned down the deputy sheriff.

Wes Hardin traveled over into Louisiana but did not stop until he reached Alabama. Here he hid under the name of John Adams. He was a farmer and a stock buyer. He owned several saloons and drifted in and out of New Orleans, Montgomery, and into the state of Florida. He was an inveterate gambler, and this occupied a lot of his time. If he killed anyone during these years while he was outside the state of Texas, the shootings were done under a cloak of anonymity. No record of them holds to this day. That he was mixed up with some shady characters is obvious from the concern which railroad officials evidenced when Lieutenant Armstrong approached them with the request that they help him capture the gunfighter. Apparently Hardin had planned to hold up a series of trains, and this was the principal reason he had traveled from his home place in Alabama to Pensacola when he was intercepted by the determined Ranger.

Wes wound up in El Paso after he was released from Huntsville, but he did not go directly to the border city. He had tried Gonzales but this, he found, was probably going to embroil him in another fight and get him thrown back in jail. He took sides in an election of the county sheriff, and bloodshed before the last votes were tallied was narrowly averted. None too smart, Hardin was still sharp enough to see that he had better hunt a new home. He departed, never to return. His wife, whom he had married during the wild days of his youth and who had stuck by him through all the years of his incarceration, died and this cut the few remaining bonds.

John Wesley traveled to Pecos in West Texas. He went there because Jim Miller—more familiarly called "Killer" Miller—had sent for him. Miller was a brother-in-law of Manning Clements, and since Manning was a cousin, he could scarcely deny the plea of Miller to come to his aid. Killer Miller was in a fight with the local sheriff, Bud Frazer, and in a meeting in the street one day the sheriff went for his gun first and managed to wing Miller. Later on, during a second encounter, Miller got the better of the argument and cut Frazer in two with a shotgun. At any rate when John Wesley got the message, Bud Frazer was still very much alive and was charged with assault to murder. He would be tried in El Paso, and Miller wanted Wes to help with the prosecution.

A word in passing should be spoken about Jim Miller. His story has never been properly told. And the chances are it never will. Because no one has all the details but Miller, and he died at the end of a rope in Bartlesville, Oklahoma. Miller, as I have said, more generally referred to as "Killer" Miller, was a murderer for hire. If you had an enemy whom you wanted rubbed out you got in touch with Miller. He moved about but was usually somewhere in the vicinity of Fort Worth. For $1000 Miller would ride up to the man's ranch after dark and kill him through a window; or wait in the trail until morning and plug him between the shoulders as he rode out to the horse trap. Miller did not believe in giving the other fellow a chance. His game was the ambush, the shot from cover, the shotgun in the night. How many men he killed for pay will never be known, but it was many. He finally shot one citizen too many in Oklahoma, and a hanging posse caught up with him and three of his fellows and hanged them all in a livery barn.

Hardin came to El Paso, and whether or not he was of any assistance to the prosecution in the trial of Bud Frazer deponents sayeth not. Suffice it to record that John Wesley liked El Paso which was a wide open city, choked with saloons, honkytonks, gambling dens, whores, and gunfighters. If there was a tougher metropolis in Texas than El Paso in the late eighties and early nineties, I do not know where it was to be found. The atmosphere just suited the gunman turned legal light.

Jeff Milton was the chief of police. He was an old border officer and a good one. He had fought two score gun battles, had one arm shorter than the other from having it hit by an outlaw's slug, was as courageous as a grizzly, and utterly fearless of the riffraff that drifted in and out of the bars and brothels. Besides Milton as chief of police, there was another curly wolf who was constable of Precinct One. This was old John Selman, called "old" to distinguish him from young John Selman, his son. Of the two, old John was the ringtailed tooter. He was wearing a badge, but old Selman was a thoroughgoing outlaw. He had been mixed up in a half-dozen killings at Fort Griffin, and also in cow thievery and murder. He had considered it the better part of good judgment to ride out of Fort Griffin between days. Word had gotten to him that the vigilantes were going to string him up. Before Hardin came to El Paso, old John had burst into Tilly Howard's sporting house and there found Bass Outlaw, his six-shooter still smoking, standing over Ranger Joe McKidrict. On hearing Selman run in, Outlaw swung on him. His first shot hit the constable in the leg; so did his second. Old John then opened up, and his first shot hit Bass high over the heart. He died that night. It was by no means the first killing to be chalked up to the old gunman. Two years later Deputy U.S. Marshal George Scarborough had to kill Selman. But that is another story. Right now we are interested in John Wesley Hardin and El Paso, his new stamping grounds.

El Paso corners on three states, Texas, Chihuahua, and New Mexico. In this triangle were a couple of cow thieves named Vic Queen and Martin M'Rose. They were hard riding, active, and efficient. So successful, in fact, that the New Mexico cattle association finally offered a reward of $1000 for each one of them. They were arrested, but the pair escaped. They got away by the simple expedient of making bond and then skipping to the Mexican side of the border. Their bondsmen put up another $250 for their capture and return.

M'Rose had a girl friend who generally traveled with him. When he got thrown in the pokey she was in El Paso. After the pair skipped bond, they holed up in Juarez, Mexico, which is just across the Rio Grande from the Texas city. Mrs. M'Rose, if we may call her that, did not elect to cross over the river to rendezvous with her erstwhile lover. She had other things to do. John Wesley had spotted her, and the admiration which instantly gleamed in his pale blue eyes was promptly reciprocated by the lady. Another thing that probably influenced the newly made lawyer was that it was rumored on good authority that Mrs. M'Rose was toting $3000 in cash, the property of Martin M'Rose who dared not show his face on this side of the frontier. At any rate love blossomed handsomely between the gunman and the statuesque blonde. They moved in together, and since both liked to drink and gamble, besides finding the amoral pleasures of the new arrangement quite stimulating, they got along.

Meanwhile Wes was trying to get Queen and M'Rose extradited so that the $2250 of reward money could be collected. Finally one dark night M'Rose was persuaded to cross to El Paso to see his paramour. It was a plot. He was killed on the railroad trestle which spans the Rio Grande. Whether Hardin had a hand in the assassination cannot be established, but it seems likely he did. He was angling for the reward and wanted to get M'Rose out of the way so that the lady would be altogether his.

Things rocked along until the middle of August, 1895. About that time Wes had to go down to Pecos, and he left his beauty at home. She was bored by the inaction, got a bottle, and after consuming a good part of its contents went out on the street and commenced to whang away at street signs, store fronts, and an occasional passerby. Young John Selman, a city policeman, arrested her and tossed her in the city clink. Not before, however, he cuffed her about and cut her lip. When Hardin got back to town he was boiling mad at Selman for his treatment. He'd kill him, he said. And his old man along with him. News got to both the Selmans within the hour of the utterance.

Before dark on August 19, some three days after the statement made by Hardin, he bumped into old John Selman in front of the Acme Saloon on San Antonio Street. He told old John, "That sonofabitch you call a son is going to answer to me for his handling of Mrs. M'Rose." John Selman was not in the least afraid of Hardin. He had been bucking the hard ones for thirty years, had killed his share, and was sure of his speed with a gun. He assured John Wesley if any harm came to young John that he would hunt Hardin out and kill him.

Hardin entered the bar after the argument having told Selman he was unarmed. This was not true, as he had a pair of six-shooters in his famous vest. He walked up to the bar, his back to the door, and ordered a drink for himself and Henry Brown, an acquaintance. John Selman walked in then and strode up behind Hardin, walking catlike on the balls of his feet. When he was at arm's length he whipped out his .45 and shot Hardin in the back of the head. He fired two more shots into the body as it slumped to the floor. The second shot went through the body, and the third struck the right arm.

Selman was tried and acquitted. This despite the fact that he had shot his man from behind. He testified that he was facing Hardin at the time he fired. The coroner took the stand and said that all the bullets entered from behind. It was known that Hardin had threatened to kill both the Selmans, father and son, and this together with his reputation as a gunfighter and a killer was enough for the jury. Texas never produced another gun-twist of the formidable stature of John Wesley. The number of his notches will never be known for sure, but he gunned down between thirty and forty men.

13

MARSHALL OF EL PASO

The El Paso of the early 1880s was a boom town and like all
frontier settlements attracted the dregs of the country. With four
railroads pushing toward the city it was frantically trying to
assimilate the ever growing crowds—an assemblage of traders,
businessmen, soldiers, Mexicans, cowboys, saloon keepers, gamblers, gunfighters, outlaws, and the inevitable soiled doves of the
red light district. El Paso had forty saloons and only six stores.
It had two dozen gambling joints and two churches. It boasted
only four hotels but could have filled a dozen. It was a twenty-
four-hour town where the saloons never closed and the monte
game and the roulette wheel never ceased to go. It served up a
dead man for breakfast every morning, and all the store fronts
were liberally bullet-pocked from the hell-raising cowboys who
shot up El Paso Street.

The town had a city marshal named George Campbell. His
deputy was Bill Johnson. Campbell served the law with a light
touch. He paid little attention to the hard-riding cowboys in
town on a spree, looked the other way when there was gunplay,
and when the gals down in the cribs rolled a drunken customer,
George seldom went out and made a case of it. He just suited
the so-called sporting clique in town, and he was especially approved of by the Manning brothers, Dr. G. F., Frank, and Jim.
This trio owned a saloon and a bit farther down El Paso Street
had what was called in those days a variety theatre. They were
big figures in early El Paso and headed up the sporting fraternity.

So lax did Campbell become that the city council decided something must be done. Moving decisively they simply called him in and told him he was fired. In his stead they promoted Bill Johnson to the job. At least temporarily. Johnson was no law officer; how he had gotten to be the deputy marshal is hard to understand. He was a boozer, an alcoholic who stayed liquored up all evening and most of the day. His appointment, the council agreed, would only be until they could find a good man to take over the law enforcement for the town.

The sporting element did not like the elimination of their man Campbell as the arbiter of law and order. It was not that they minded so much that George was booted out, but they feared whom Mayor Magoffin might get to replace him. This could be downright embarrassing if he happened to be hardnosed about things. They decided to pry up hell and thus show the city council that Bill Johnson could not keep the lid on and what rightfully should be done was to hire Campbell back again. With, preferably, a good hike in salary.

One night the word was passed around to all the sporting gentry, and virtually on signal they burst out the doors of the forty-odd saloons and commenced to shoot up signs, billboards, store fronts, hitching racks, and the street. Citizens not in the know got off the streets, locked their doors, and remained away from the windows. In the morning when His Honor the Mayor and members of the city council surveyed the carnage they were dismayed. But instead of rehiring George Campbell they sent for the Rangers. Captain George Baylor who commanded Company C was in camp at Ysleta, only twelve miles down the valley from El Paso. He promptly sent up Corporal Jim Finch and five Rangers to keep order. Their appearance calmed the situation, and the sporting crowd pulled in their horns. The only trouble was that the Rangers could not remain indefinitely. Acting as city marshals was not the name of their game. After a week they were withdrawn by Captain Baylor, and the town was back in the indecisive hands of Bill Johnson.

About that time Mayor Magoffin got word of a likely candidate for the job of policing his turbulent pueblo. The fellow was up in New Mexico at Socorro and from the description sounded like just the hombre. He was Dallas Stoudenmire, an ex-Confederate cavalryman and an ex-Texas Ranger who had served with Captain Ike Waller's Company B in Colorado County. He was the city marshal in Socorro and doing a good job of holding in check the bad actors of that community. The city council, after Magoffin described his man, sent for Stoudenmire.

Within a week he swung down off the stage and without preliminaries strode in to a meeting of the council. He was an impressive sight to see, and the council looked him over and decided on the spot that he was their man. Stoudenmire stood six feet one inch in height, with shoulders like a swinging boom, great muscular arms with huge balled fists hanging below the long coat he wore. He walked with an easy grace and was quick and sure in all his movements. No guns showed at his waist and when he faced the council none could be seen beneath the coat he wore. He was a handsome man with the blue eyes of his German ancestery, an aquiline nose, and the square jaw and prominent chin of a born fighter. The hair was long and lank, black in color and carefully brushed back to fall almost to his shoulders. Stoudenmire was nearing forty when he came to El Paso.

The council fired Bill Johnson on the spot and informed Stoudenmire that he should search out Johnson and get the keys to the jail. This the new marshal proceeded to do. He was new in town and finding the erstwhile lawman was a business of visiting one saloon after the other. When finally he located the inebriated ex-marshal, Johnson refused to believe he had been deposed and likewise stubbornly shook his head when Stoudenmire asked for the keys. The burly newcomer, when he saw that polite request was getting him nowhere, reached down with those great fists of his and took hold of the drunk and proceeded to turn him upside down meanwhile shaking him as a terrier shakes a rat. The keys tumbled out of Johnson's pocket. Stoudenmire pocketed them and without a backward glance strolled out into El Paso Street.

He then commenced to familiarize himself with the town and its inhabitants. He was on the streets day and night. When he slept was a question. He might be seen at nine of the morning and at midnight. He was in and out of all the bars and gambling halls, the eating places, and the hotels. In a period of a few weeks he had a nodding acquaintance with all the saloon men and all the regular gambling habitués.

Time went on, and Stoudenmire's brother-in-law, Doc Cummings, came to town. Doc opened the Globe Restaurant, the best eating place in town. Near the Globe was the Coliseum variety theatre owned and operated by the Mannings. A few doors up the street from the Coliseum was their saloon. Trouble was to develop between Doc Cummings and the Mannings, and it was not long in shaping up. Stoudenmire, as a relative, was almost as quickly involved.

The new marshal did not come to El Paso as Wild Bill Hickok had entered Abilene, that is, with a reputation as gun-twist. So far as could be learned, he had never been involved in a killing either as a Texas Ranger or as the marshal up Socorro way. But if the newcomer had no reputation to back up his forceful manner, he soon showed the sporting crowd that he meant business. Whenever trouble developed the new marshal would be on hand in a matter of minutes, and the free and easy way he bashed heads together, pistol-whipped those who wanted to make a gun fight of the occasion, and more than anything the utterly unprejudiced manner in which he threw various ranking members of the sporting fraternity into the *juzgado* persuaded the others that here was a man not to be tampered with. They bemoaned the fact that they had lost George Campbell, and not a few offered that someone ought to kill the big sonofabitch.

Up the river from El Paso is a little hamlet called Canutillo. It is out in the country, surrounded by mesquite, chaparral, and catclaw. It is farming country now but in the eighties was ranch land. The Rangers were sent word that two dead Mexicans had been found on a ranch outside Canutillo. The ranch was owned by the Manning brothers and was managed by Johnnie Hale, the foreman. It was apparent the Mexes had been shot, murdered, and so the Rangers fetched the bodies into El Paso for an inquest.

The Rangers, always outspoken, were not hesitant in saying they believed the two dead men had been knocked off by Hale and another cowboy named Len Peterson. At the inquest were friends and the parents of the deceased, also ex-marshal Camp-

bell, likewise ex-deputy marshal Johnson, together with Stoudenmire, and of course Johnnie Hale. Just why Len Peterson was
not present since he was also a suspect, we do not know. The
inquest was presided over by a county judge who had enlisted
Gus Krempkau, a former Ranger, now a deputy sheriff, as the
interpreter.

The inquest got under way, and much of the testimony was
from Mex witnesses. Krempkau listened to their Spanish and
then informed the judge and the listeners what was said. The
testimony went badly against Johnnie Hale who fumed and got
madder and madder. He could see a case was being made against
him but what angered him was that he knew Spanish too and
he believed that Krempkau was deliberately twisting the statements of the Mexican witnesses to make Hale look bad.

Noon came and the inquest was adjourned for dinner. Krempkau went out on the street as did the others. The Rangers headed
for the Globe Restaurant for something to eat. Johnnie Hale
bristled up to Gus Krempkau and told him he was a lying sonofabitch and that if his testimony continued in similar vein after
dinner he would have him to answer to when the court was finished. Working himself into a greater rage because Krempkau
would not respond to his threats, he suddenly went for his gun,
whipped it free of the leather, and shot Krempkau through the
head.

He then turned, his gun still in his hand, and just as he whirled
whom did he see but Stoudenmire who had been only a dozen
feet away. Seeing the menacing gun, the muzzle boring straight
at his belt buckle, Stoudenmire charged down on the killer. His
six-shooters, which he carried tucked into a pair of leather-lined
hip pockets, leaped into his hands. At the full gallop he let go a
shot at Hale which passed under his arm and killed a Mexican
bystander. His second shot, triggered from the other gun, struck
Hale just below the right nipple and pitched him over on his
shoulders. He died within a few minutes.

George Campbell, no longer a law officer, and not mixed up
in the fracas in any way, pulled his gun and with the muzzle
covering the big Stoudenmire, commenced to edge across the
street, as if to escape the lethal fire. Stoudenmire caught the

movement when Campbell drew his six-shooter, and he had no sooner seen Hale pitch down mortally wounded than he turned on Campbell. He knew Campbell was no friend of his although they had never had any disagreements. He also knew that Campbell stood in well with the Mannings and very likely was a friend of Hale who was a Manning ranch foreman. If these thoughts raced through the marshal's head it was an almighty fast brain wave. In a twinkling he eared back the hammer on the right-hand six-shooter, and with Campbell's gun still menacing his midsection he fired. The shot was a fatal one. George Campbell was dead when he struck the ground.

The entire fracas had transpired within a period of a dozen heartbeats. Four men lay dead, one shot accidentally, the others gunned down by lethal intent. Even for El Paso, which was accustomed to dead men, this was pretty impressive. It served to prove to all the citizenry, both good and bad, that their new lawman was not only a deadly gunslinger but also not one to be awed by the odds. The growlings of the sporting element were hushed but vindictive. They had wondered how much bottom their new marshal really had. The demonstration had proven that he was a tough hombre.

The fact that Johnnie Hale was a Manning hireling made the killing a personal affair with the brothers. They determined to get Stoudenmire but not openly if it could be avoided. They went to work on various members of the sporting set, and through them they set up Bill Johnson to kill the marshal. Bill was told that Stoudenmire had ridiculed him before the town when he picked him up and shook him. That appointment of the newcomer as the city minion was an affront to him. Wasn't he doing a satisfactory job as city marshal before the big Teuton came to town? Johnson boozily agreed that he would gun down the formidable lawman. But not man to man and face to face. The plotters were too smart for that. This would simply get their man killed, and Stoudenmire would come off the winner of another gun play. No, they had a better plan.

It was Stoudenmire's habit to walk El Paso and San Antonio streets before midnight. He would look in on the more lively saloons and gambling halls and then go on off to bed. His route took him north on El Paso until he came to the junction of San Antonio which ran into it. He would then turn east on San Antonio and thus proceed to the end of the built-up section. At the T formed by El Paso and San Antonio was a pile of bricks, lumber, and other materials. It was piled there in preparation for the construction of a new building.

Here the conspirators stationed Bill Johnson, and just to be sure he did not miss they gave him a double-barrel 10-gauge shotgun loaded with 00 buckshot. They themselves crossed the street and took up station behind some pillars supporting the overhanging porch. As was Stoudenmire's custom he came swinging out of the Acme Saloon at about a quarter of midnight and walked directly into the ambush. At not more than thirty feet, Bill Johnson stood up behind his brick fortifications and let drive at the huge bulk of the marshal. He let one barrel go, and noting that Stoudenmire did not fall he let drive with the other. Both shots missed.

Stoudenmire, as was his wont, charged down upon the bellowing smoothbore, plucking his two six-shooters out of the leathern hip pockets. Galloping forward he fired both guns. Every shot was a hit. Bill Johnson crumpled with five bullets through head and upper chest. The sports who had observed the gun play from across the street now opened up with their artillery. With scarcely a pause to see that his first opponent was down, Stoudenmire changed direction and with both six-shooters still going like a pair of Gatlings, he charged the hidden marksmen. Seeing their bullets were having no effect on the maddened bull racing down upon them, they all took to their heels and ran. If any were struck by the Stoudenmire fire he kept to his quarters until healed and well. In the melee Stoudenmire took a slight wound in one foot.

After this shooting the big marshal moved about with a grudging respect showed him by all the sporting gentry. Here was a dangerous man, a curly wolf, a bull who knew nothing except to charge into a fight at full gallop, his guns going, his intent to kill. Not only was he cheerfully willing to join the fight but his marksmanship was somewhat astounding. Day or night he got his man. In pondering the attempt to bushwhack him,

Stoudenmire held a dozen confidential powwows with people who were on the fringe of the sporting crowd, and they told him the Mannings were at the bottom of the plot. He watched the brothers like a hawk after that. Watched them and harbored a resentment that was to culminate in a decisive encounter.

El Paso was growing, and the city council, quite pleased with its concerted effort in hiring a real bully boy for marshal, decided that with the increased size of the border metropolis a deputy marshal to assist Stoudenmire would be altogether fitting and proper. Sergeant Jim Gillett of the Rangers was hired. He had just resigned from the force after some six years of gallant service. The two hit it off from the very first. Each had a lot of respect for the other, and a close friendship soon sprung up. With a second in command to keep the lid on, Stoudenmire left town to go back to East Texas and get married. He had hardly gotten out of the city limits when Gillett became quite seriously ill and had to be put to bed. It left the town without a lawman.

Doc Cummings, as before mentioned, the brother-in-law of Stoudenmire and the owner of the town's best eatery, the Globe, took it upon himself to serve as the marshal until either Jim Gillett could get back on his feet or Stoudenmire returned. He buckled on a pair of six-shooters and then headed for the Old Boss Saloon, owned and managed by the likable Bill Coffin. The Old Boss stood on Overland Street and was only a stone's throw from the saloon operated by the Mannings.

Doc threw down a half dozen shots of redeye, and then he announced he was going to walk over to the Mannings' establishment and even scores for their attempt to ambush Stoudenmire. He had a couple more belts to sharpen his aim, and then he suited action to his words and crossed the street and walked into the Mannings' saloon. Just what happened then is none too clear for there were no unbiased witnesses. In fact there were only Dr. G. F. and Jim Manning in the place besides a bartender. Gossip had it that the actual killing of Cummings was accomplished by the barkeep. Jim Manning accepted the blame. Doc had asked for it. He had announced for all to hear that he was going to clean out the place, collecting all the Manning scalps if he could, and he had gone into the saloon, armed and with his intentions preceding him. That he was shot and killed was solely his own fault. But Stoudenmire when he returned and heard about it did not think that way. He growled deep in his barrel chest that the Mannings would pay for that killing!

He strode the streets, day and night, walloping the benighted over the head with his long barreled .45, dragging the hard customers off to his tiny jail, and all the time he kept a wary eye cast for the Mannings. And they likewise watched him. Tension grew, and the town knew that a showdown was near. Fearful when the shooting warmed up that some innocent El Pasoan would be hit, the city fathers finally persuaded the three brothers and the fire-eating marshal to sit down and sign a truce declaration. In it they agreed to let bygones be bygones and to hold the peace. It was a flimsy sort of agreement and whether either the Mannings or Stoudenmire really intended to observe its terms is highly problematical. They hated each other with an intensity which only gunfire and blood would ever erase.

Stoudenmire, who had always been a two-fisted drinker, increased his input. He was drunk every night and frequently commenced his tippling by early afternoon. When he was liquored up he got mean, overbearing, and abusive, and his ill temper was extended not only to enemies but to many of his close friends. It was an intolerable situation and grew continually more acute. Finally a delegation called upon the city council and asked that Stoudenmire either be compelled to resign as city marshal or be fired outright.

The council was not aware of the goings on of its chief minion. They called him in and asked for his resignation. He stood up and threatened all of them but in the end he turned in his badge. At almost the same time he was appointed a deputy U.S. marshal for the western district of Texas. This was a sop to his vanity and tended to soften the blow of his dismissal. The council made Jim Gillett marshal in the stead of Stoudenmire. So close was the friendship between the pair that the big German did not take badly the appointment of his deputy.

It was not long after his appointment as deputy U.S. marshal that Stoudenmire had to go to Deming, New Mexico. He rode up on the Southern Pacific, transacted the government business, and then rode the train back to El Paso. He alighted after midnight, and not having had a drink during the journey from Deming he turned down El Paso Street and went into the Mannings' Saloon. He had several whiskies and remained until daylight when he staggered out in the street. Gillett found him there, a good deal the worse for wear, and steered him off to bed.

When Dr. G. F. and Jim Manning came to their place of business that morning the bartender told them that Stoudenmire had been in the place boozing for several hours. That he had said he was looking for the Mannings and that he would be back. Jim Manning flared up at this and said Stoudenmire had broken the pact between them. He looked to his belt hardware and went out in the street and directly to the Acme Saloon, a principal hangout of Stoudenmire, stating to all in hearing that he was going to shoot it out with the marshal. That worthy was not around. He was in his room sleeping off the drunken stupor he had induced in the Manning bar.

About three in the afternoon Stoudenmire awakened, his booziness largely dissipated. He had a huge thirst on him, and he hied himself away to the Acme to assuage the great dryness in his throat. There he was told that Jim Manning had been looking for him and that there was "blood on the moon." Stoudenmire immediately announced that he would go over to the Manning place and find Jim and explain to him that he had not broken the truce between them, that all he entered the saloon for the night before was to have a drink or two. Walter Jones, one of the owners of the Acme, an ex-deputy marshal and a friend of Stoudenmire, announced that he would go with the burly marshal. They crossed to the Manning establishment.

When they got inside they found Jim Manning at the bar and Dr. G. F. playing pool. Frank Manning was nowhere in evidence. Stoudenmire went up to Jim Manning and told him that someone had evidently been telling lies about him. He asked that Jim go find Frank Manning, and he would explain his position to all of them. Jim went out in the gambling annex to find his brother.

With Jim gone, Stoudenmire turned to Dr. G. F. Manning who

put down his pool cue and approached the bigger man. Said Manning, "Stoudenmire, you have not kept your agreement with us."

"The hell I haven't," roared Stoudenmire. "Whoever says I have not is a lying sonofabitch."

With that both men went for their guns. Dr. Manning was faster. Stoudenmire, half-drunk and befuddled, fumbled his gun out of its hip pocket. The first shot from Manning struck the marshal over his right breast; it hit a pocketbook and a sheaf of letters and only caused a flesh wound. The little doctor eared back his .45 and let Stoudenmire have a second one. This bullet struck the left shoulder. Meanwhile Stoudenmire got his right-hand gun into action, and he shot his opponent in the right arm, shattering it. This caused the little doctor to drop his revolver. Disarmed, the little terrier closed on the larger man and locked his arms around those of Stoudenmire and held on with such tenacity that the marshal could not raise his gun to get in a second shot. Just how the smaller man could have held the powerful Stoudenmire—and he with an arm shattered above the elbow—is difficult to understand. But he hung on, and the two wrestled about the saloon and out onto the street, Stoudenmire trying all the while to shake loose the lighter and smaller antagonist and the latter hanging to him with a bulldog-like tenacity.

Jim Manning who had gone to find his brother Frank heard the shots, and he rushed back to the bar and thence to the street, there to be confronted by the sight of his brother and Stoudenmire locked in a grizzly-like embrace. Dr. G. F. was a slightly built, runty little man, and Stoudenmire towered above him. When Jim Manning reached the sidewalk he had a good view of the marshal's head and much below it the head of his diminutive brother. He took hasty aim and shot at Stoudenmire's head. It was a miss; the bullet hit a post across the street. The second shot, better aimed, struck Stoudenmire above the left ear. It killed him instantly.

Jim Manning was arrested, tried, and acquitted of the killing. It was the same old story of threats to get each other, a shoot-out, and the inevitable result. Dallas Stoudenmire, the fiery, the curly wolf, the hard-core, two-fisted, two-gun marshal, had gone to the well once too often. The law of averages got him. Clearly in the wrong and seeking a fight he had stacked the odds too high against him.

14

BUFFALO HUNTERS

William T. Hornaday, the eminent naturalist, believed that at the time Columbus discovered the New World the buffalo ranging over North America probably amounted to sixty million. By the time of the Civil War, Hornaday further surmised that the herds could stand an annual kill of a half million animals and not seriously reduce the overall population. Instead, by the end of the decade the bison were wiped out.

There were those, mostly military people, who had long advocated the decimation of the buffalo as a means of controlling the Plains Indians. For so long as the Indian had buffalo in plenty, he could live. The game provided food, the skins covered the teepee, robes were used for bedding, for clothing, for saddles and lariats, for bags and sacks and travois coverings. The blood was drunk, and glue, trinkets, ornaments, and eating utensils were fashioned from hoofs and horns. Even the droppings had their use. Buffalo chips, dried and hardened, were excellent materials for cooking fires.

Buffalo hides were a medium of exchange, traded by the Indians to the white man for necessities, foo-fer-ah, and whisky, for guns, powder, and shot. The American Fur Company, during the decade from 1835 to 1845, bartered for 90,000 buffalo hides from the Indians of Montana and the Dakotas. These were selected hides, taken during the winter when the skins were prime. It was estimated that to provide that quantity of selected skins the Indians had killed not less than 120,000 bison. Over a ten-year period that would amount to 1,200,000 animals.

By 1855 there was indication that inroads were being made in the herds. Randolph Marcy and W. B. Parker were commissioned by the State of Texas to go into the western portions of the state and select suitable sites for reservations for the Comanches. Parker, in writing about the survey, says that the buffalo were being killed off in great numbers. By this time the herd was divided into what were referred to as the northern and southern portions. The southern herd extended from the Platte River in Nebraska to the Rio Grande and from Old Dodge on the east to the Rockies on the west. It numbered several million animals, as did the northern herd. The idea that the population was divided by the movements of immigrants or the coming of the railroads was generally accepted. It is more likely that it was pasturage and climatic differences which separated the bison.

It was also contended by naturalists and others that there was an annual migration of the herds. The facts are, there was some movement but it did not cover any great distances. The herds would move northward in the spring to some extent and journey back south when the chill winds of the autumn brought the first hint of snow, but these jaunts were not over hundreds of miles as sometimes contended. The southern herd by 1870 was generally concentrated south of the Red River. Here there was an abundance of buffalo grass which was the favorite forage of the great game. Here, too, was gramma grass, mesquite brush for roughage, and blue stem, all having the quality of high nourishment whether green or dry.

It was here, below the Red River and generally southwest of Dodge and west and northwest of Fort Griffin in Texas, where the southern herd was concentrated. So too were gathered almost two thousand buffalo hunters. Commencing in deadly earnest in 1870, by 1879 some 5,000,000 buffalo were slaughtered. It was the finish of an animal which had once numbered 60,000,000. By 1887 but 1091 buffalo remained in all of North America.

Wright Mooar, a buffalo hunter of the seventies, did his shooting on the southern herd, and his account of the operation is typical of the procedures of the buffalo runners. Mooar was asked by W. C. Lobenstein, a trader of Leavenworth, Kansas, to furnish five hundred hides for an experiment in converting the tough buffalo to commercial leather. If the test was a success, there would be further orders for larger quantities. Wright Mooar and other hunters provided the skins.

Mooar found that he had fifty-seven hides more than Lobenstein would accept. He shipped these east on his own, sending the hides to his brother John and his brother-in-law John Combs in New York City. The pair turned the hides over to a leather-making concern in Pennsylvania for $3.50 the hide. This firm was successful in tanning the hides and converting the tough leather to a variety of commercial uses. They ordered two thousand more skins.

The five hundred hides shipped by Lobenstein of Leavenworth had gone to a company in England who likewise processed the skins and found that the resulting leather was first quality. There were orders for more hides. Thousands of them. Word spread quickly, and in a period of six months there were literally hundreds of hunters quitting Dodge, Fort Griffin, Fort Worth, San Antonio, and many other way stations. All bound for the great staked plains of what is now the Texas Panhandle.

John Mooar and Charley Wright, who had heard of the quick sale of the hides, came west and joined up with Wright Mooar. The latter would do the shooting, and John and Charley would drive the wagons, tend camp, cook, and load ammunition. The partnership signed on three skinners, bought a wagon and supplies, and set up camp on Kiowa Creek in Western Kansas.

Wright Mooar had by this time killed a lot of buffalo. His rifle was an old Springfield, the Model 1869 or 70, of .50-70 caliber, with a length of 52 inches, a barrel of 32.6 inches, and a weight of 9¼ pounds. The rifle did not kill buffalo too well. Penetration was poor, and shots had to be taken at close range or else the arching trajectory of the big .50 caliber slug would wound and not kill cleanly. According to Carl Coke Rister in his book, *Fort Griffin on the Texas Frontier,* Wright wrote to the Sharps Arms Company and ordered a special buffalo gun. "After the company had tried out two or three experimental rifles and had found them unsatisfactory it developed the much needed rifle which weighed from twelve to sixteen pounds. It was of .50-110 caliber and accommodated a long brass shell containing 110 grains of powder, which hurled its leaden missiles to incredible distances. Mooar's gun cost $150, but later when manufactured in quantity it sold for $50. The Springfield, Spencer, Henry and other rifles were also used for buffalo hunting."

The camp on Kiowa Creek did not produce any hides. Wright saddled up his horse, and with another hunter named John Webb, they drifted south, cut out of Kansas and into the old "No Man's Land" of the Oklahoma Panhandle. From thence they crossed Beaver Creek and finally forded the North Canadian River. Here they found after five days of riding that they were in a constant sea of buffalo. The military was keeping that country free of the white man as a gesture to the Comanches and other tribes who demanded the buffalo not be disturbed. Mooar and his partners loaded up their wagons and thumbing their noses at the admonitions of the cavalry rode off with four wagons loaded with camping gear and supplies. They wound up within four miles of Adobe Walls.

Wright left his partners at Adobe Walls, and they established a base camp there. He and five other hunters rode off toward the east and commenced to shoot at Gagesby Creek, an offshoot of the Washita. Here the Comanches hit their camp, but the red men did not like the taste of the buffalo guns nor yet the marksmanship of the runners. They stood off out of range and contented themselves with demonstrating. There were no casualties on either side. After shooting for three weeks on the Gagesby, the party turned southward and finally came to a halt on the North Fork of Red River. Here they shot more than six hundred buffalo. These hides and quantities of the meat were hauled back to Adobe Walls.

The remainder of the summer they hunted along the Cimarron, on the Beaver, and finally wound up on the latter stream for their winter camp. The next spring Wright Mooar, having peddled all his hides in Dodge, struck off across the Indian Territory and did not pull up until he had gotten to the vicinity of what is now Denison, Texas. He was then on one flank of the southern herd and in a country that was virtually free of his fellow huntsmen. Here he hunted for a time and then moved on westward. He had twelve wagons in his train. Six of these carried his own supplies, and the remainder were given over to freight for Fort Griffin, government supplies for the garrison. When Mooar had delivered over the consigned freight he was called before Colonel George Buell who told him he had heard he intended to shove off beyond Griffin for buffalo running. He warned Wright that twenty miles was the maximum distance he could travel. As he had done before, he ignored the order.

Wright had his brother John with him, and four other men to act as skinners. They set up a camp in West Texas and went to the shooting. At the end of the season, Mooar loaded up his wagons, each pulled by three yoke of oxen, and commenced the long trek to market with the accumulation of "flint" hides. The dried buff skin was referred to as a "flint" because it was hard, stiff, and unwieldy. When he finally pulled into Denison, from whence he had embarked months before, he found he could not sell his skins. He got in touch with Lobenstein in Leavenworth who promptly bought all of them and ordered more.

The success of the Mooar party was soon noised about, and buffalo runners all across western Kansas flocked to the staked plain for a go at the southern herd. Charley Rath, a big trader, started a wagon train south. It crossed the double fork of the Brazos and was soon followed by another train of fifty wagons in the charge of John Russell. Each train carried all the supplies needed by the hunters—rations, salt, guns, ammunition, powder, primers, lead, tools, and lumber. Also plentiful quantities of whisky. There were about eighty hunters in the two parties. These included such well-known buff men as Willis Crawford, Joe Freed, Hank Campbell, Bill Kress, and Harry Burns.

All the hanger-on element was also included for it was the intention of Charley Rath to set up a town where he could cater to the hunters. There were the painted damsels who, just as tough as the rockhard buff runners themselves, did not mind the vicissitudes of bumping along all day behind a plodding yoke of bullocks. And the gamblers and the bartenders, all ready to take the hunters' quick earned cash.

The town was called Rath City, and it set up south of the double fork of the Brazos, about fifteen miles southwest of what is now Hamlin, Texas. The town, if it could be called that, had six or seven buildings. The biggest was Rath's trading post. He had taken in a partner, a man named Reynolds, and frequently the town was called Camp Reynolds. Besides the store there were two saloons, one owned by George Aikens and the other by a man named Fleming; his was the more pretentious as he had a dance hall in connection. The town even boasted a Chinaman, Charley Sing, who had the inevitable laundry. Smoky Thompson dug a water catchment and sold water which he hauled from a creek near town. The town had a smell to it. The stacks of buffalo hides attracted flies, and as many of them were hauled in partly green the stench was terrific. No one seemed to mind. Least of all the whores who flocked into the two saloons and cajoled the passing hunters to set up the drinks or try the faro tables. Shootings were commonplace and Rath City, almost as soon as it was born, had its own boothill cemetery. There was no law. Fort Griffin was fifty miles away, and a stage ran once weekly.

Wright Mooar sometimes operated out of Rath City and sometimes out of Fort Griffin. They were by this time not only taking the skins but also butchering and selling choice cuts of meat. The Mooar boys would dig a pit, and into this pit they would put a buffalo hide which was staked to the ground at the corners. The pit was then filled with a brine made of water and salt. Then the choice cuts from the four quarters of the buffalo along with the meat from the hump were dumped into this pit and it was covered with a second skin. Four days later sugar and saltpeter were added in equal amounts to the brine. After soaking for fourteen days the meat was removed and smoked.

The smokehouse was made like a wickiup. It consisted of a framework of poles over which were stretched buffalo skins until it was quite tight. This smokehouse was a big one, more than a hundred feet in length and almost twenty-five feet in width. Within were a number of fire pits where fires of jackoak were continually kept smouldering. The smoking of the brine-soaked meat required ten days. It was then removed and hauled to Fort Griffin or Rath City, whichever was the closer, and sold. The meat curing was a sort of sideline and never reached any great proportions. As an example, in 1877 Wright Mooar sold 3700 hides but only 2500 pounds of his smoked buffalo meat. Buff tongue was considered a delicacy, much prized not only by the hunters themselves but also by the town trade. The records show that Mooar sold the C. G. Convers Company 164 buffalo tongues for 20¢ each and several hundred pounds of smoked hindquarter for 6¢ the pound.

In April, 1876, Wright and his outfit were camped in Haskell County, and here Charley Rath's business manager, W. H. West, found them. West was reconnoitering a direct route from Dodge to Fort Griffin but was under instructions to hunt out Wright Mooar and buy up a batch of hides for delivery to the Cheyenne Agency up in the Indian Territory. Mooar not only sold Rath's agent 450 selected skins but he agreed to deliver them to the Indians. Getting ready to return to his camp, Chief Whirlwind warned Wright about seventy Comanches who had stampeded off their reservation and headed back for Texas. He told him, "keep gun in one hand all the time. Coat in wagon, two cartridge belts around waist in sight." Wright Mooar thought this was pretty good advice and traveled on the alert back to Fort Griffin in June. His followers pulled up stakes in the Haskell country and came in to town.

Wright Mooar then made a trip back east to visit his parents. He had been raised in Vermont and had gone west when but nineteen years of age. The year was 1876, and on that trip to the eastern seaboard he went to New Haven, Connecticut, and there visited the Winchester Repeating Arms Company. He had heard about the new Model 1876 rifle and he wanted one. The upshot of his long visit was that when he journeyed back to Texas in October he had with him the then brand new Model 1876. This rifle was chambered for the .45-75-350 cartridge. It was twice as powerful as the Model 73 in .44-40, with its 1400 foot pounds of muzzle energy. Wright Mooar selected the musket type which had a 32-inch barrel and a magazine which would hold thirteen cartridges. With this rifle he felt he had a gun which not only would permit him faster kills on a buffalo stand but would also be potent medicine against Indian attack. His was unquestionably the first 1876 Model in the hands of buffalo hunters working the southern herd.

John Mooar, who had remained behind to shepherd the outfit, was ready to move into the winter camp when Wright put in an appearance. He had hired nine men as skinners, teamsters, and roustabout help. Altogether they had thirteen wagons, fifty-two head of oxen, and two four-mule teams. They struck out westward holding a course between the Brazos and Colorado Rivers. They passed north of the present town of Sweetwater and finally came to a stop on Deep Creek in present-day Scurry County, Texas.

It was from this site that Wright Mooar with his new Winchester 76 rifle killed the now famous white buffalo. This bull was an albino and was the only buff so marked in the entire southern herd. Albinos are not uncommon in every game species but this is the only one recorded as being shot by white runners. The Mooars shot 4500 buffalo during the next four months. They sold a ton of cured meat in Fort Griffin.

Wright Mooar handled a herd of bison a great deal after the fashion of other hide hunters. Early in the morning he would saddle his horse, take a hundred cartridges for the new Winchester 76 rifle and ride out of camp. First, however, he told his skinners which direction he was taking and precisely where he expected to find game. About two hours after his departure the skinners with a wagon would trail off in the direction he had taken. After a mile or so on his trail they would stop and listen for the booming report of the big .45-75 rifle. They approached the sound very carefully for if Wright had gotten a stand it was not to be disturbed until he was finished with the killing.

Mooar scouted the country from hill tops and slight rises, and from this camp on Deep Creek he was never long in spotting a band of feeding bison. He approached the band from down wind and tied his horse far back. If need be he wormed and wriggled forward for several hundred yards on his belly. He wanted to get within about two hundred yards of the unsuspecting animals. He could have "injuned" up to one hundred yards, but long experience had taught him that the report of the gun this close tended to upset the buffalo and make them inclined to stampede. At two hundred yards or a little farther they paid little attention to the sound.

He then looked over the grazing ruminants and carefully selected the leader. This might be a bull but was just as likely to be a cow. He shot this lead animal with a good deal of care. The buffalo had to be dropped stone dead. If it was wounded it would plunge, run, bellow, and might gore a nearby animal in its agony. This disturbed the herd and it was inclined to stampede. The smell of fresh blood always excited the bison and this, too, was to be avoided. With the first buffalo down and stone dead the others paid no more than casual attention. They would go on with their feeding and Mooar with his shooting. He fired rapidly. The new Winchester and its thirteen-cartridge magazine permitted him to fire quickly. His aim for a single day was fifty buffalo. With a little luck he could take this number from a single herd and not have to move and search out another band. When he had shot fifty he would signal for his skinners to come forward. Sometimes he would shoot so fast he would have to stop, and with the lever on the Winchester thrown open, he would urinate through the bore and follow this with a rod and a patch to wipe out the black powder residue while it was still moist. This served to clean the rifle and cool it too.

Wright Mooar never used cross-sticks to support the rifle muzzle. Not even when he had the old Sharps which weighed sixteen pounds. The new Winchester went only nine pounds and was much lighter and easier to handle. He shot off his knees or if the cover was sparse he would fire from the prone position. John, left in camp, was busy reloading cartridges for the next day's shooting. The empties were carefully retrieved and hauled back to camp at the end of the day. Pure lead was cast for the bullets. This was one of these no-choice sort of things, for the hide hunters had no way of tempering their bullets. The pure lead slugs would kill well enough if the hunter did not try to drive them through the massive shoulders. The ideal shot was behind the shoulder, through the ribs, ranging forward. Another favorite spot was behind the ear which was quite deadly if pulled off perfectly. On close stands the buffalo hunter was such a marksman that he could place his bullets into the ear at yardages out to one hundred steps.

With his fifty carcasses on the ground the hunter's chores were all cleaned up for the day. But not so the skinners'. These fellows moved up and worked with rapidity and dexterity born of long practice. They wanted to get the skin peeled before the animals stiffened up. A skilled man could whip the hide off a buffalo in about eight minutes. Sometimes there would be four skinners working together, and when a hunter had this many working for him he might exceed his daily quota of fifty. The skinner had two knives, one a ripping blade and the other a true skinner. He rolled the critter over on its back and propped the hind legs apart with a short stick which he carried for that purpose. He then slit open the hide along the belly, working from the chin to the vent hole. He then ran his cut out to the inside of the four legs. He then commenced to peel out a hind leg and with the one hindquarter finished would do the other. He then worked forward, peeling the hide from the flanks, belly, and back as he progressed. When he got the hindquarters all opened out, he might attach a team to the hide and let the mules pull it forward off the carcass. The head was not skinned out. The hide was cut off at the neck. Choice cuts of meat were taken from young cows, spike bulls, and similar young stuff. Old bulls and cows were never butchered. These cuts included the tongue, the hump, the backstraps, and hindquarters. The buffalo runners especially liked the fat around the kidneys and intestines and often opened up a young cow to claim these tidbits.

In camp the hide was laid out flat on the ground, flesh side up, and pegged. After a day or two it was turned and the hair side was exposed to the weather. This turning went on until it was completely dried. It was then folded once down the middle and baled. Bales were tied together with green strips cut from freshly taken hides. The bales were then loaded on the oxen-drawn wagons and hauled off to Fort Griffin or Rath City for sale.

Another hide hunter, Joe McCombs, partnered up with Dan Jacobs and Ed Poe; with four skinners this trio established a camp at Mocking Bird Springs, which is northeast of present day Haskell. They moved after a month or so over on the Clear Fork and remained out until May of the next year. They killed 2000 buffalo and sold the skins to Charley Rath for $2.00 for a robe hide and $1.50 for the others. The next fall they were out again taking with them in the five-wagon train which they employed some eight hundred pounds of lead and five kegs of powder. McCombs had a Sharps rifle but what the others were shooting is not known.

They went into a permanent camp on Champion Creek, south of present-day Colorado City, Texas. Here they hunted until April of the next year and again took about 2000 hides. By the fall of 1876, northern hunters were flocking into the country and almost every buffalo runner could hear the sound of other guns as he worked over the bands. During the winter of 1876–77, the party camped on Morgan Creek, west by twenty miles from the site of last year's hunting. They shot 2300 buffalo and sold the skins in Fort Griffin for $1.50 for the prime skins and $1.00 for the remainder.

In September, 1877, McCombs split off from the others, and on his own left Fort Griffin with a convoy of wagons, several skinners, and this time one thousand pounds of lead and five kegs of powder. He went into camp at Mossy Rock Springs near Signal Mountain and near the town of Big Spring, as it was afterward founded. Here he shot 4900 buffalo. Poe and Jacobs, who had gone it on their own, accounted for 6300 hides. They were not too far away from the McCombs camp. In the area were two other hunting camps, and the four parties stacked their hides together and sold all of them to W. H. Webb of Dallas who paid only $1.00 per hide. This was the last great killing year. The runners might not have realized it—but it is likely that they did—that the southern herd was largely decimated. McCombs took the field the following year, 1878, but it was his last hunt. He went into camp at Mustang Pond near modern Midland, Texas. Here he shot only 800 bison during the winter. In later years discussing his hunting McCombs reckoned he had shot 12,000 buffalo.

The Fort Worth newspaper *The Fort Worth Democrat* in a January, 1877, issue said that there were sixteen hundred hide hunters in the Fort Griffin area and that in May of the year before there came into Fort Griffin, "one train of ten wagons, in front were eleven yoke of oxen and dragging after them four large wagons all heavily laden. Two other teams of seven yoke each drawing three wagons followed. The train carried from 2500 to 3000 hides." During August about 200,000 hides were sold in Griffin. The next year, in January, 1878, there was a four-acre yard in Fort Griffin covered solidly with skins. It was estimated that 200,000 buffalo were being killed each season. In Rath's camp it was estimated that a million hides had passed from the hunter's hands to the trader. By the fall of 1879 the southern herd had been finished. The buffalo hunters scattered to the four winds, their ruthless killing finished, the buffalo gone, and the Indians with their larder depleted relegated to life on the reservations. Behind the buffalo runners came the rancher and the farmer who pastured the rolling plains with cows and turned the virgin sod with plow and sweat. It was the end of one era, the commencement of another.

15

SAM BASS

Joel Collins was a Texas cowboy who had a good reputation. He was not a gunfighter, did not headquarter in the saloons and gambling hells, and the most of his friends were ranchers and their hands. When Collins was in off the range he was usually found in San Antonio. Here he met Sam Bass. The two immediately took a liking to each other, and when Collins, who had been up the trail with a series of cattle herds, decided to gather his own bunch and move them to northern markets, he asked Bass to ride with him. Sam agreed.

The ordinary herd would number from fifteen hundred to as many as three thousand cows. Seldom did one rancher have this many marketable animals on hand. He would throw his saleable stock in with others of his neighbors. The combined drive would be put in the charge of a reputable foreman who in addition to running the stock northward would accept payment at the railhead, return to Texas, and pay off the several owners. This was what Joel Collins did. He had a reputation for being a hardworking, thoroughly reputable young man, and when he approached a number of friends they were all agreeable to throwing their cow brutes into the Collins herd.

The drive had ten cowboys, a cook, a cook's helper, and a fifteen-year-old boy, Tom Langhorn, who sometimes helped the cook, other times rode night herd, and was general handy man about the camp. The drive crossed the Red River, wended its way up through the Nations, and finally reached Abilene. Here, normally, it would have been sold by Collins. But something had happened to the normally upright, straightforward Joel on the long ninety-three-day trek from Uvalde to Abilene. He was not the honest lad who had talked so earnestly to friends and neighbors in Texas. He had a plan. He loaded his twenty-seven hundred beeves on the train and shipped them to Sidney, Nebraska. Here the cattle were off-loaded, and with a new string of cowboys, he went on northward. His plan was to disappear with cows and money, and for many months his supporters in Texas were wholly in the dark as to just where he was. They were not sure what he had done. The beef had simply evaporated.

Collins' destination was Deadwood where gold had been found. He sold his cattle there and paid off his hands. He and Sam Bass by this time were bosom amigos, and Sam was quite aware of the skulduggery which Collins had perpetrated. He was in full accord, and apparently Joel split at least a part of his sales profits with his partner. Collins believed that the defrauded Texans could not find him in the Dakotas. He and Bass bought wagons and teams and went into the freighting business. When the chill of winter settled on the land they found this was a bit too strenuous for them, and so they sold out and bought a bawdy house. Both were in their middle twenties, and this was a much more pleasant way to sit out the snowy winter. The combined whorehouse and saloon failed, and the partners found themselves dangerously near to being broke.

What to do? Collins watched the comings and goings of the daily stage, and he persuaded Bass, who it seems was pretty easily talked into doing whatever Joel suggested, into robbing the stage. They held up the carriage seven or eight times. By this time they had gotten a couple of other drifting cowpokes to throw in with them. These were Jack Davis, a fellow Texan just out of California, and Norm Nixon, who may have been a Canadian.

Sticking up the stage was not too profitable. It kept the partners in whisky money but mighty little more. Davis opened up the prospect of bigger things. He said a lot of gold was being shipped over the Union Pacific Railroad to the east and that something ought to be done about it. Collins, who by this time had forgotten his uprightness, had spent all his cattle money and was determined upon a life of crime, planned the train robbery. With him besides Jack Davis and Norm Nixon he had Bill Heffridge, who had come up the trail with him, and another drifter, Jim Berry, from somewhere in Missouri.

At ten o'clock on the night of September 19, 1877, the band climbed aboard the eastbound passenger train, as it stopped to take water at Big Spring, Nebraska. Forty minutes later they waved the engineer on his way. They had just gathered up three thousand brand new twenty-dollar gold pieces. This gold had been minted at San Francisco, and each coin bore the 1877 date. It was the only gold minted in the west that year, and so the money when it was put in circulation was easily identified.

The gang split into three pairs, each pair taking $20,000 with them. Collins and Bill Heffridge elected to ride toward Texas. Just why the gang leader in view of his wanted status in his home state would turn southward is unknown. Possibly he had some idea of returning and repaying those ranchers who had trusted him. We will never be sure. Norm Nixon headed for Chicago and may have ducked back into Canada. Jim Berry returned to Missouri with his $10,000 where he was captured after a gun fight. He had less than $3,000 when a load of buckshot dropped him in an alley in Mexico, Missouri.

Sam Bass and Jack Davis also headed southward. They rode for three days and then swapped their horses and saddles for a light spring wagon and a team of horses. They threw the $20,000 in gold under their feet and rode merrily on their way. Every day they were accosted by roving bands of possemen who were out to get the express company reward money for the robbers. They fell in with a detachment of cavalry, and when they persuaded the lieutenant in charge that they were just simple busted farmers traveling across Nebraska to find another likely farming site the troopers asked them to camp the night and eat their victuals. They did.

Joel Collins and Bill Heffridge did not fare so well. They elected to ride out of the scene of the holdup and had packed their share of the loot on a packhorse. When they got to Buffalo Station, a watering stop on the Kansas Pacific Railroad, they were going into camp when Sheriff Fred Bardsley and ten cavalrymen rode up. The sheriff was suspicious, and when he demanded that Collins unpack the horse and display the contents of the panniers, Joel went for his six-shooter. It was a fatal mistake. The troopers shot him to doll rags. And Bill Heffridge who, the story goes, had not made a move toward his gun, was shot down too.

Sam Bass was bound for Denton, Texas, where he had lived before he went up the trail with the Collins drive. Sam had arrived in Texas when he was seventeen and had gone to work for Dad Egan who was the local sheriff. Not as a deputy but as a handyman. He had worked for the sheriff for a year and somehow acquired a race mare. He ran her around the country, and as she was a fast horse he won more races than he lost. Sam drifted from running horses to playing cards, and by the time he had reached his majority was a professional gambler. He interspersed his gambling with some cowpunching and had a good many friends not only among the people of Denton but among the cowboys on the surrounding ranches. Bass was a likeable, even merry, individual who was good natured and happy-go-lucky. The fact that he had drifted into stage and train robbery was undoubtedly due to the influence of Joel Collins. Now he was going to go back to his old stamping grounds and show off his wealth. He'd buy another race horse, maybe invest in a saloon, and be a big man around town. When the money ran low he'd just plan another train robbery. Life looked pretty simple to this simple young man.

Jack Davis was not from Denton, and he did not propose to go along with Sam. When the pair struck Waco, Davis kept right on riding south. It is rumored that he journeyed to New Orleans and thence entered Central America where he was killed in one of the banana revolutions. Bass continued to Denton, but instead of going boldly into town he prudently made camp in the river bottoms and thickets about the town and only went into the village after dark.

This was opportunity enough to skylark and to toss about the twenty-dollar gold pieces. Each with its telltale date of 1877 to identify it as booty from the Union Pacific episode. Sam was lionized by the wild young riders who flocked about him. He set up round after round of drinks, took the boys to the bawdy houses, and was a veritable "hail fellow well met." As his pile of gold commenced to shrink he looked about for a replenisher of the supply.

As a result of his nightly visitations to the honkytonks of Denton, he had picked up a coterie of followers who when he told them he planned to stick up a train were ready to go along. These cohorts included Seaborn Barnes, Tom Spotswood, Al Herndon, Arkansas Johnson, Henry Underwood, and Sam Pipes. The gang, with Sam leading, held up the Texas Central at Allen Station on the night of the eighteenth of February. They went back a month later and robbed the same train at Hutchins. At Eagle Ford on the fourth of April the Texas & Pacific was held up and at Mesquite on the tenth of the month it was again hijacked. This was all within a few miles of Dallas, and the excitement was intense. It was the biggest story in the local news sheets, and the railroad law enforcement people, U.S. marshals, the sheriffs of the local and adjoining counties, policemen, and detectives were all literally stumbling over each other in pursuit or supposed pursuit of the robbers.

Sam Bass by this time was established as the gang leader, and a big reward was on his head. Lesser lights like "Sebe" Barnes were also known, and rewards were offered for him. After each daring foray Bass would lead his outlaws back to the river bottom and the dense thickets near Denton, and there they would hole up, making occasional forays into the town to laugh, drink, play poker, and live it up. None of the train holdups netted anything like the bonanza struck in Nebraska when the Union Pacific had been tapped for the $60,000. As a matter of fact the four train jobs were worth only $2,000 altogether. As presumably Bass split the take with his partners this made each man only a few hundred dollars. It was enough to keep Sam happy. In those days it was not difficult to go about unidentified, and Sam frequently rode boldly into towns about Dallas and was not picked up. He stopped at many ranches and was not recognized. The country was rather amused that the robbers always operated against the big corporations—the railroads—and there was no little sympathy and admiration for the outlaw band.

You would have thought with all the excitement, newspaper

notoriety, and speculation that the Bass gang had kicked up that the Rangers would have gotten into the picture. Actually the force did not take the trail until after the train robbery at Mesquite on April 10. Then the adjutant general ordered Major John B. Jones, who commanded the Frontier Battalion, to Dallas to take charge of the hunt. There were no Rangers either in the city or thereabouts. The Frontier Battalion was operating in west Texas, and it was considered best to recruit a detachment of Rangers for this special assignment. Major Jones after considering various prospects selected June Peak who was a former deputy sheriff, city marshal, and who had background in law enforcement. Peak, after he was designated, was authorized to enlist seventeen Rangers.

Dallas was thoroughly enjoying the limelight. The town had been made the focal point of the activities and held William Pinkerton of that famous agency together with a dozen of his detectives. The U.S. marshal, S. H. Russell, had eighteen deputies with him and along with these forces, the railroads and the express companies had their operatives in the field. It got so it was dangerous to get out and beat the thickets for fear of shooting each other up. Sam and his boys meanwhile played it cool, stayed in hiding, and planned the next robbery.

June Peak, once he had selected his men, took the field. This detachment was not up to par so far as the usual Ranger performance was concerned. They had been hastily recruited, and a good many of them had scanty law enforcement backgrounds. They were none too effective. Nonetheless they got on the trail of the outlaws after the Mesquite robbery and captured Al Pipes and Hank Herndon. They were locked up in Tyler. A month after the holdup, Peak's detachment and a sheriff's posse ran onto Sam and his boys at Salt Creek in Wise County. A gunfight developed, and Arkansas Johnson was killed. The Rangers captured all the outlaws' horses and set them afoot. Accomplished horse thieves, the band was soon remounted and rode back into the river bottoms outside Denton.

There were a lot of sympathizers for Bass and his bully boys among the settlers. These people ofttimes fed the gang when they rode through, provided horses, feed for the animals, and above everything else gave all the information they could on the whereabouts and the activities of the officers. Some of these people were so bold they were arrested, jailed, and tried for harboring the criminals. Among these were Henderson Murphy and his son Jim. The latter was suspected of being one of Bass' gang but it could not be proven.

While on trial in Tyler, Jim Murphy asked to talk to Major Jones, and during this conversation he proposed that he be released. He said he would go and join Sam and his riders and would then endeavor to lead them into a trap so that the Rangers could capture or kill the leader and his followers. Major Jones considered this proposition and agreed to it. Murphy was turned loose, and his father was also released.

It was true that Jim Murphy had ridden with Bass, and he had a cousin, Frank Jackson, who was a regular gang member. Murphy rode away from Tyler and commenced to try to make contact with Sam. It took him ten days but he finally succeeded. He got back with Bass and the remnants of his party after the fight at Salt Creek. He was immediately suspected of being a spy. Sam and Sebe Barnes pulled their pistols on him and threatened to kill him. Only the intervention of Frank Jackson, the cousin, saved his life. Murphy swore that he was loyal and offered to go first into any robberies they might stage. This got him off the hook temporarily, but both Bass and Barnes watched him like a hawk. He was never permitted to ride off alone, and when he asked to return home to see his father he was told to stick around or he would be gunned down. From June 11 until July 13, Murphy had no opportunity to send Major Jones any word. By that time the outlaws had relaxed their vigilance a bit, having decided that the story they had heard that Murphy was a traitor was probably erroneous.

In Denton during a nighttime carouse, Murphy had the opportunity to smuggle a letter out to Sheriff Jennings Everhard, who was privy to the plan. In this note Murphy stated that the gang was going to clear out and ride to Mexico. En route they planned to rob the bank at Round Rock. The next morning the party saddled up and rode south.

At Georgetown Murphy managed to disappear for minutes

without arousing suspicion, and here he got off a letter to Major Jones, who had returned to Austin, stating in substance the same information he had passed along to the sheriff in Denton. There were in the group by this time, Bass, Seaborn Barnes, Frank Jackson, and Jim Murphy.

While Sam was quitting his old stomping grounds at Denton, he rode away as lightheartedly as he had ridden into Denton when he returned from the sortie against the Union Pacific in Nebraska. He was happy and gay, and there was the usual cowboy banter as they jogged down the trail quite oblivious to the hazards of such travel. The bushes were literally alive with professionals and amateurs, each equally anxious to hang Bass' scalp to his belt. The outlaws rode openly into Waco, put up their jaded horses at a handy livery stable, strode into the Longhorn Hotel where they got rooms, and then went to the bar. There Sam tossed his last double eagle on the scarred surface. "There goes my last '77 gold piece," Bass said, "an' it's done me mighty little good." It was a sort of left-handed admission that the life of crime did not pay.

The outlaws rode on toward Round Rock. Meanwhile Major Jones had left Austin and was in Tyler to sit in on the trial of Pipes and Herndon. Murphy's letter was sent forward to him, and he lost no time in getting off a wire to the headquarters company in Austin. He directed that Corporal Vernon Wilson ride to San Saba with all speed and convey Jones' orders to Lieutenant N. O. Reynolds of Company E to gather a suitable detail and ride into Round Rock for the forthcoming holdup. Jones had few Rangers in Austin. It was closer by a great many miles for the force to send a detachment from the capital, but Jones was fearful that Bass might actually try to heist the state treasury if he knew all the Ranger force had been dispatched to Round Rock. Despite these hazards the doughty little battalion commander further ordered Dick Ware, Chris Connor, and George Harrell to Round Rock. Then he loaded up in his own rig and departed for the scene of the Bass & Company visit.

Corporal Wilson rode at a trot and a gallop for sixty-five miles to Lampasas. He was riding a fine little mare that had been standing in the ranger barns for months and was far too fat for a hard ride. The sixty-five-mile ride made in twelve hours killed the gallant little horse. Wilson left her and caught the morning stage for San Saba, still some fifty-five miles beyond. He got to Reynolds' bivouac after dark on the eighteenth. He had then been traveling for twenty-four hours without rest or food.

Lieutenant Reynolds was seriously ill. He was too sick to ride, but he got up off his sick bed and ordered eight of his men —those with the best horses—to be ready in thirty minutes to ride to Round Rock. For himself he put a pallet of saddle blankets in the back of a buckboard and told Corporal Wilson to drive a pair of pack mules that were harnessed for the first time. The Rangers rode at a trot and a gallop all night and by morning were at the crossing on the San Gabriel River. They had covered sixty-five miles, still had forty-five miles to go. Reynolds from his bed in the buckboard gave the party thirty minutes in which to cook breakfast, feed the horses, and be again on the trail. It was the morning of July 19; Bass had planned the robbery for the next day. There was yet time. It was a hot summer day; July in central Texas is notable for 100-degree temperatures. This day was no exception. Not a man or a horse faltered, and indeed neither did the indomitable Reynolds who was suffering stomach pains and in agony every minute from the bouncing and bumping of the springless buckboard.

While all this was going on, the outlaws reached Old Round Rock and went into camp near the cemetery. It was July 18. Sam had deliberately ridden down early so they could scout the town of New Round Rock and most especially look over the bank and the getaway route. Quite unknown to him and the others was the fact that the Rangers dispatched by Major Jones, Ware, Connor, and Harrell, were in town and so was their leader, Jones himself. All were keeping out of sight, except for a conversation between the major and Morris Moore, who was a Travis County deputy sheriff, and two other deputy sheriffs, Ellis Grimes of Williamson County and Al Highsmith. Jones explained to them what was shaping up and asked them to lay low and let the Rangers handle the situation. All promised to keep hands off and to take no action unless Major Jones requested it.

On the morn of the nineteenth, Sam decided they would ride

into Round Rock and buy some tobacco, meanwhile scouting the bank and the likely escape roads out of town. Their route took them through Old Round Rock, and somehow Jim Murphy managed to persuade Sam that he would drop out and buy some corn for the horses. Why Bass was not suspicious of this Judas who was under the watchful eyes of both himself and Sebe Barnes is not understood. Of course the robbery was not planned until the day following, and as Murphy had been threatened and had assured Bass and Barnes that he would be first into the bank, and since, too, Sam probably was wholly unaware that a trap was even then laid for him, he permitted Murphy to drop out and go to a local feed store. The others—there were three of them including Frank Jackson, Murphy's cousin—rode on into New Round Rock. They did not push their mounts down the main street but took a side road which led them behind Kopperel's Store. This was a general merchandise emporium, the biggest in the little town, and at that sleepy hour in the afternoon was presided over by a single clerk, Simon Jude.

The outlaws tied their horses behind the store and went in a side entrance. Their going was witnessed by Ellis Grimes and Morris Moore, the two deputies. Grimes looked at Moore and read plainly what the other was thinking. "One of them fellers was packing a six-shooter under his coat," Grimes said. They both headed for the store. This despite the fact that they had just given their assurances to Major Jones that they would take no action if they saw the outlaws come to town.

The two walked up to the robbers who were busy in conversation with the store clerk, Jude. Grimes took hold of Seaborn Barnes' left arm and spun him around, saying, "You packin' a gun?" Those were his last words. Barnes instantly drew, as did Bass and Jackson. All three of them shot Grimes who died instantly. They then turned on Morris, who had drawn his gun and had fired one shot. He was shot through the upper chest, the bullet going completely through him. Just who did the execution was lost in the swirl of gunsmoke. The outlaws then made a run for the back door and their mounts.

They got to their horses, flung themselves into the saddles, and made tracks. Their route took them down a side street past the town's only barbershop. In the shop and getting a shave was Ranger Dick Ware. When he heard the firing he guessed what had happened and dashed into the street, the barber's apron and lather still upon him. Just at that instant the outlaws came galloping by. Dick Ware took his .45 six-shooter in both hands and commenced shooting. At about the time he opened up, George Harrell and Chris Connor rounded the corner at the Kopperel Store, and they also commenced firing. Major Jones, who was a bit farther down the side street but in position to intercept the riders, pulled a little .41 Lightning model six-shooter out of his holster and loped up to get in on the firing.

Dick Ware hit Sam with his first shot. The bullet struck from the side and went through the outlaw from right to left. It was a fatal wound. It knocked the robber almost out of the saddle, but he caught the horn and rode on. One of the Rangers shot Seaborn Barnes through the head and he fell from his horse dead. Bass, after rocketing along for another two hundred yards, also fell into the dust of the street. Frank Jackson upon seeing this reined in his horse and, despite the concerted fire of the four Rangers plus a scattering of local citizens anxious to get in on any scrap, lifted Bass and put him astraddle his own horse. Then at a walk, with his hand steadying the outlaw leader, they rode out of town. There was no pursuit. The four Rangers had their horses in a secret camp outside Round Rock and had to go to camp to get them. At about this time Lieutenant Reynolds and his party of Rangers rode into Round Rock. Had they been ten minutes earlier they would have gotten into the very middle of the melee. It was by this time growing dusk. Pursuit of the wounded Bass was given up until the morrow.

Jim Murphy, who had betrayed his fellows to Major Jones, rode into Round Rock quite boldly and identified himself to the Ranger leader. He looked down on Sebe Barnes and said he was indeed the outlaw. He was asked how he was so sure, and he told the officers that Barnes had three bullet holes in his right leg and one in his left. When the body was examined this was found to be true. The crowd was all for throwing Murphy in jail until Jones interfered and took the man away with him.

The next morning, the detachment of Lieutenant Reynolds,

they and their horses now rested, began the search for Bass and
Jackson. On the outskirts of Old Round Rock near the cemetery
where Sam had made camp they found the dying outlaw. Jackson
had placed him under a pin oak and had halted long enough to
tear up Bass' shirt and bind the big abdominal wound with it.
When the Rangers approached, Bass held up his right hand
which had been hit by a Grimes bullet in Kopperel's Store, and
said, "Don't shoot. I'm Bass. I'm dying, get me to a doctor."

Major Jones called for a rig, and Sam was laid on a pallet in
the back and taken into Round Rock. Here Dr. Edward Cochran
examined the wound, cleaned and bandaged it, and got Jim
Chatman as a nurse. He shook his head as to the prognosis; the
bullet had wrecked the kidneys and it was only a question of a
little time. Shot on Friday, Bass lingered until Sunday when he
died. He talked freely to Major Jones and remained lucid to
the very end. His last words as he died were, "The world is
bobbing around."

He was buried in Round Rock with his lieutenant Sebe Barnes.
Frank Jackson never looked back. He rode into New Mexico,
and rumor had it he was deeply mixed up with Billy the Kid in
the Lincoln County War. Whether this is true or not is problematical. At least nothing definite was ever afterward heard of this
compatriot of the merry outlaw, Sam Bass. Jim Murphy was
quickly branded as a traitor, a disloyal comrade in arms who
had sold out his fellows for a mess of pottage. He was scorned,
shunned, and criticized wherever he went. He returned to Denton, his home, safe from prosecution through the understanding
with Major Jones. Within a year he took a dose of poison and
killed himself.

Depending on the historian it has always been a moot question
whether Bass was gunned down by Dick Ware or George Harrell.
Jim Gillett who was with Lieutenant Reynolds on the hundred-
mile ride from San Saba said he went carefully over the ground
and he listened to Major Jones question Sam on his death bed.
Said the outlaw, "That hombre with the lather on his face was the
one who shot me." Certainly, it seems, Bass should have known
who pulled the trigger.

16

FEUDS AND FIGHTS

What caused the bad blood between Pink Higgins and the Horrell boys will probably never be known. Higgins had enlisted in Terry's Texas Ranger Brigade when the Civil War got under way, and all three of the Horrels, Tom, Mart, and Sam, were in the same company. During a patrol action in the forward years of the war, Tom and Mart fired at Higgins and slightly wounded him. They claimed it was a case of mistaken identity, they thought Pink was a Union soldier. Higgins had different ideas about the wounding and he nursed a grudge toward all the Horrells. In 1865, just weeks before the war ended, he got his chance and wounded Sam Horrell. It was bare-faced bushwhacking, and the company commander recognized it as such. He would have tried Higgins but discipline was fast breaking down and nothing was done about it. Then the war ended and the Texans found their way home.

Their home was the country around Lampasas where both had ranches. It seems strange that they did not know each other before they enlisted with Brigadier Terry and his Texas volunteers. Most likely they were acquainted, and it is probable there was bad blood between them before it erupted in the private feud which they waged during the years of the North-South struggle.

There is still another story that the Higginses and Horrells truly did not know each other during the war and there was no conflict between them until after 1870 when both ranchers commenced to boot long lines of cattle up the trail to Abilene. Higgins was the bigger of the two ranchers and he took three thou-

169

sand head of mixed stock to the railhead in 1872. The drive included not only his own stock but that of various neighbors including the Horrell brothers. Tom went along on the drive to see that all went well with the steers he had to sell. In Abilene, the drive finished and the money paid over for the cattle, a big poker game was commenced in the gambling hall next to the Longhorn Saloon. After a day and a night, Pink Higgins and his partner, Rex Mitchell, had all of Tom Horrell's money. All of Tom's money and that of his brothers as well. Cleaned out, Horrell shoved back his chair, leaped to his feet, and went for his gun, claiming he had been tricked and cheated by Pink and Rex Mitchell.

Horrell went for his gun but not fast enough. He was covered by Higgins who was no slouch on the draw himself and who had been expecting just such a reaction. Right there bad feelings were stirred and when Tom Horrell got back to his Lampasas headquarters empty-handed his brothers believed his story and swore vengeance against the Higgins faction. From then on the shootings commenced and killings were commonplace. These bits of gunplay sometimes came off when members of either clan met at waterholes, crossroads, in town, and around at the various social events which were seldom free of gun swinging.

These were the years of the Reconstruction government in Texas. It was a time of carpetbagger rule; the citizens of the Lone Star State could not vote but had an appointed legislature and a carpetbagger governor. This governor, a man named Davis, refused to reorganize the Rangers and instead had a state police. This was an inefficient body, politics ridden and thoroughly despised by all Texans. In 1873, the last year of the Davis reign, he sent a state police captain, Tom Williams, and two other officers to Lampasas to arrest Clint Barkley, wanted for murder. Now Barkley was a cowboy on the Horrell rancho and was well thought of by the brothers. At the same time Captain Tom Williams was a son-in-law of Pink Higgins, and even though Higgins didn't care a hoot for either Governor Davis or his state police he did have considerable regard for his son-in-law, Williams.

The trio rode into Lampasas and put their horses up at the

local livery stable. They went over to the Antlers Hotel and got rooms. They then went to see the local sheriff to ask him the whereabouts of the man Barkley. The sheriff was friendly to the Horrells, and he passed word along to them as fast as a deputy could saddle and ride out to the Horrell headquarters. Meanwhile he refused to give the state policemen any information or assistance.

The officers stayed in Lampasas for three days, and in no time at all everyone knew they were there to arrest a Horrell cowboy. Of course Pink Higgins and Rex Mitchell were abreast of the visit and knew that trouble was going to pop when Captain Williams made his play. It all came to a head in the Matador Saloon late in the evening on the nineteenth of March.

Word was passed to Williams that he could find Clint Barkley in the bar but that he was surrounded by Horrell cowboys and would take some doing to place him under arrest. Tom Williams was no coward. Like McNelly, who was also a state policeman and afterward became one of the most outstanding Rangers, Williams was a fearless and upstanding officer. He had arrived in Lampasas to arrest this murderer, and he intended to do it. He strode into the Matador bar with his deputies on either side.

It was getting dark, and within the saloon it was even more gloomy. The bartender had wanted to light up his coal-oil lamps, and Tom Horrell who was on hand had forbidden it. When Williams and his men entered from the street they could scarcely distinguish one man from the other of the considerable number lined up at the bar. In the gaggle at the scarred and battered old bar was not only the man they were seeking, Clint Barkley, but also both Tom and Mart Horrell. Sam may also have been on hand. Altogether there were ten hands from the Horrell Ranch ready to defend their fellow 'puncher from the state policemen.

Scarcely had the officers cleared the swinging doors of the bistro, when the Horrell faction opened up on them with six-shooters and Winchesters. It is believed that Barkley (who sometimes called himself Bowen) had a Model 73. There were seven empty .44-40 cases on the floor after the shooting. Tom Williams was hit eight times, and his deputies were riddled. But not before Williams had shot both the Horrell boys. Tom was shot in the neck and Sam had a bullet hole through a wrist. Tom was later arrested for the killings, was tried, and promptly acquitted. He claimed the state policemen shot first. He had all the witnesses to back up this contention. The death of his son-in-law enraged Pink Higgins. It was murder, he stated, and the Horrells would have to pay.

Higgins, riding his range one day, came upon Zeke Terrell, who was identified as a Horrell cohort. Old Pink hauled out his Winchester and from about ninety yards shot the cowboy out of the saddle. On riding closer he found the man had shot a Higgins cow and was busy butchering her. Pink got down off his horse, opened up the cow's belly, unloaded the intestines, and proceeded to stuff and cram the dead man within. When he had the grisly job completed, he cut some strips of leather from the flanks of the dead bovine and did a rough job of sewing up the belly. He then rode into Lampasas and gave the sheriff explicit directions as to where he could find one of Nature's greater miracles—a cow giving birth to a man!

On another *paseo* across his broad acres he was confronted by a gent whom the Horrells had imported from Abilene. He was Ike Lantier, a Quantrell raider, buffalo runner, and gunfighter. They hired him to kill Higgins, and Lantier with admirable forthrightness immediately rode out to do the job. He came onto Pink at a spring where the two factions watered their stock. Higgins, fortunately for him, saw the stranger riding into the willows about the waterhole and sagaciously pulled his Model 73 from the scabbard beneath his knee. When Ike rode into the little clearing beside the spring, he knew this was his man. He went for his belt weapon but Pink had him cold. He shot within an inch of the ornate beltbuckle which held up the six-shooter. The shot cut the gunfighter's spine in two.

When Tom and Mart Horrell came up for trial for the shooting of the state policemen, they were ambushed about five miles out of Lampasas and both were wounded. This unquestionably was Pink Higgins' answer for the death of his son-in-law. No one had the temerity to arrest any of the Higgins-Mitchell clan for this bushwhack attempt. This was in March, and by June the feud had really heated up.

During that month the two parties had a series of gun battles. One, the first, occurred at a line camp manned by Higgins. He kept two cowboys in this camp and on going to the shack one morning he found that the Horrells had laid in wait for the 'punchers and as they emerged at daylight to cook their morning meal had shot both of them down with Winchesters from the vicinity of the corrals, a distance of about thirty yards. One man was dead and the other was shot through the lungs with a .44-40 slug. He lived to be returned to Higgins' headquarters place but died after three days. Pink and Rex Mitchell called in all their hands and armed the crowd—there were fourteen cowboys —with the new Model 73 rifles and plenty of ammunition, and they rode off toward the Horrell domain.

They surrounded the Horrell main house and corrals and stayed in place for forty-eight hours, keeping up a steady rat-tat-tat against the big house and the bunkhouse. It was a poor show. Only two Horrell hands were hit and these only superficially wounded. Higgins had sent back to his headquarters for rations after the first day but when cartridges commenced to run low he called off his stalwarts and they rode away home.

On July 25, Pink sent a trusted lieutenant, Carson Graham, into Lampasas to buy tobacco, whisky, and cartridges. Three miles from the ranch he was bushwhacked and killed. In the dust beside the body, where it had tumbled from the horse, was a neatly drawn Horrell brand. Higgins and Mitchell needed no such marking to identify the killers.

About this time there rode into Lampasas a slight little man with the very ordinary name of John Jones. He was the commanding officer of the Ranger Frontier Battalion. Major Jones had fought with Terry's Texas Rangers during the Civil War and had been promoted from private to major before the show was all washed up. Once Texas overthrew the Reconstruction government and ousted Davis the carpetbagger governor, the incoming and duly elected governor, Richard Coke, lost no time in disbanding the notorious state police and organizing the Rangers. In southwestern Texas he had his Special Force, led by Captain L. H. McNelly of whom we have already heard. Across all the western end of the state, stretching for six hundred miles, he had the Frontier Battalion. He gave the command of this force to Major John B. Jones. This remarkable man has been largely neglected by the chroniclers. He was one of the outstanding law enforcement officers of the turbulent seventies, and his successes as the leader of the Frontier Battalion were monumental.

John Jones was a halfpint, about five feet, seven inches tall and weighing not more than 135 pounds. He was dark skinned, black enough to look like a Mexican, with a shock of raven hair and piercing black eyes. He was almost forty years of age when he assumed command of the five companies which comprised the battalion. He handled this far-flung force like a general officer, not like a local commander. He located the companies at strategic spots across his lengthy battle line and kept in touch with his company commanders through a constant flow of dispatches, some by courier, others by mail and wire. As for himself he took about thirty Rangers and a light wagon called in those days an ambulance, and was constantly on the move from one group to the next.

In 1874 when the Frontier Battalion was organized, the principal problem had been the Indians. Within a couple of years the depredations of the savages had been pretty well contained, and now Jones and his hard-riding fellows turned to white outlaws. It was this shift in emphasis which brought the tough little leader and seven of his Rangers to Lampasas right after Carson Graham had been gunned down. Jones had been informed of the Higgins-Horrell feud, and he determined to ride into the midst of the gunplay and put a stop to it.

On July 28, only three days after Graham had met his end, Jones rode up to the Horrell headquarters, got down off his horse, his men remaining in the saddle, walked into the house, and announced that all the Horrells along with eleven of their cowboys who were in the bunkhouse were under arrest. Not a gun was drawn, not a shot was fired. The feudists had been told by the obliging Lampasas sheriff that the Rangers were in town. They knew very well why the officers were there. It is indicative of the formidable reputation the lawmen held that the Horrell coterie made no fight.

After a parley he released all the 'punchers, but took the Horrell boys into camp with him, under arrest. He would not trust them to the Lampasas jail because of the questionable sheriff so he held them in his Ranger encampment. There was talk going around quite freely that not even the formidable Rangers could hold the Horrells long in detention. Too, it was spoken that the Higgins-Mitchell faction would get to them and wipe them out now it was known where they were. This did not perturb the little terrier Jones who proceeded within a span of two days to arrest Pink Higgins, Rex Mitchell, and a third confederate, Woodrow "Woody" Wren. He had by this time called in reinforcements and had the most of Company B on hand. The combatants were held in separate camps only a few hundred yards apart.

Major Jones was a highly intelligent man, remarkably well educated for his day, and he had a most persuasive way about him. He could argue a point, gain his argument, and do it so smoothly and so amiably that the other fellow would still like him. His approach was always a considerate and friendly one, and even though he could be as stern as an executioner, he believed in moderation and consideration in everything he did and said. Once he had the principals in the bloody feud in his camp, he commenced to arbitrate their differences. Instead of threatening both sides with court trial and a proper hanging for their killings he proposed that they declare an armistice and thereafter make serious effort to avoid each other and a resumption of hostilities. This plea fell on exceedingly deaf ears. Men had been killed, and the leaders were determined on blood revenge. Major Jones persisted and in his arguments declared that he would keep his Rangers in Lampasas and vicinity indefinitely to see that no injustices were done by one side to the other.

Finally after three days of almost steady powwow the logic, diplomacy, and persuasiveness of the diminutive Ranger leader accomplished his ends. Both sides agreed to a truce. It was a signed peace treaty and is remarkable for its context. Both sides drew up their own agreements, and both were witnessed and signed by Major Jones. These documents are in the Ranger archives in Austin to this day. The first of these statements took the form of a letter which was addressed to Pink Higgins and

Rex Mitchell and was signed by all the Horrell brothers. These were rough, ignorant cowmen, unlettered and little schooled and in reading the two documents it is pretty apparent that Major Jones, an educated and cultured man, must have had a big hand in fashioning both. The Horrell declaration reads as follows:

Pinckney Higgins, Rex Mitchell and Woodrow Wren

Gentlemen:

From this standpoint, looking back over the past with its terrible experiences both to ourselves and to you, and to the suffering which has been entailed upon both of our families and our friends by the quarrel in which we have been involved with its repeated fatal consequences, and looking to a termination of the same, and a peaceful, honorable and happy adjustment of our difficulties which shall leave both ourselves and you, all our self respect and sense of unimpaired honor, we have determined to take the initiatory in a move for reconciliation. Therefore we present this paper in which we hold ourselves in honor bound to lay down our arms and to end the strife in which we have been engaged against you and exert our utmost efforts to entirely eradicate all enmity from the minds of our friends who have taken sides with us in the feud hereinbefore alluded to.

And we promise furthermore to abstain from insulting or injuring you and your friends, to bury the bitter past forever, and join you as good citizens in undoing the evil which has resulted from our quarrel, and to leave nothing undone which we can effect to bring about a complete consumption of the purpose to which we have committed ourselves.

Provided:

That you shall on your part take upon yourselves a similar obligation as respects our friends and us, and shall address a paper to us with your signatures thereon, such a paper as this which we freely offer you. Hoping this may bring about the happy result which it aims at we remain

Yours respectfully

Witness   Thomas Horrell
John B. Jones   Samuel Horrell
Maj. Frontier Battalion   Martin Horrell

This was an earth shattering document, and Pink Higgins and Rex Mitchell had to read and reread it to believe what was before them. It had been carried over by Major Jones, and he meticulously explained the document word by word and line for line. It finally satisfied Higgins and Mitchell that the offer was a genuine one, and it then fell upon Major Jones to influence the pair to make a proper return.

They labored over their reply for three days. It was not until August 2 that it was delivered to the Horrell boys. It shows the fine hand of Jones throughout. The excellent selection of words, the terminology, and the very evident refinement of the writer were quite at variance with the characters of the signers. While the writing is not in Major Jones' hand, the phraseology must undoubtedly be his. This letter reads:

Martin, Thomas and Samuel Horrell

Gentlemen:

Your favor dated the 30th ult. was handed us by Maj Jones. We have carefully noted its contents and approve most sincerely the spirit of the communication. It would be difficult for us to express in words the mental disturbance to ourselves which the sad quarrel with its fatal consequences, alluded to in your letter occasioned. And now with passions cooled we look back sorrowfully to the past, and promise with you to commence at once and instantly the task of repairing the injuries resulting from the difficulty as far as our power extends to do.

Certainly we will make every effort to restore good feeling with those who armed themselves in our quarrel, and on our part we lay down our weapons with the honest purpose to regard the feud which has existed between you and us as a by gone thing to be remembered only to bewail. Furthermore as you say we shall abstain from offering insult or injury to you or yours and will seek to bring our friends to a complete conformity with the agreements herein expressed by us.

As we hope for future peace and happiness for ourselves and for those who look to us for guidance and protection and as we desire to take position as good law-abiding citizens and preservers of peace and order we subscribe ourselves

Respectfully yours

Witness   J. P. Higgins
John B. Jones   R. A. Mitchell
Maj. Frontier Bn   W. R. Wren

This served to keep the peace for ninety days. Then the feud got under way again. It was only ended by the decision of Pink Higgins to move out of the country. This he did, removing to a far distant range which overlapped into New Mexico. Rex Mitchell dropped from sight, and it was rumored that he ended his days in New Mexico. Woody Wren was a hired gunfighter, and when peace was declared he soon drifted on never to be heard from again. The Horrells, a quarrelsome crew, were over the years reduced to only Martin. Tom and Sam were killed in gunfights, not with the Higgins faction but with other gun slingers who resented their blustering ways and shot it out with them.

17

SKULDUGGERY AND GUNSMOKE

Texas, a vast state, has a corner which has never known exactly to whom it does belong. This is El Paso, the farthermost city of the Lone Star, and a town and country around that might well belong to either Chihuahua or New Mexico. It is six hundred miles from El Paso to the state capital at Austin and nine hundred miles to the Louisiana border. Directly after the Civil War El Paso was called Franklin and had less than a hundred citizens of Texan blood. There were thousands of Mexicans, and across the Rio Grande in Juarez there were other thousands of latinos. Down river a dozen miles was Ysleta, the oldest settlement in the state. It was the county seat, and like El Paso, or Franklin, if you will, it held a handful of Americans and several thousand Mexicanos.

The country might technically be a part of Texas, but the inhabitants were sympathetic to Mexico. They crossed the sluggish boundary waters at will, trading sometimes in Chihuahua, other times on this side, claimed relatives on either bank, attended fiestas, cock fights, and bull baitings on either side, and if they had been asked their allegiance would have proudly stated they were allied with the Land of Mañana.

There was a trifling amount of farming in the valley of the Rio Grande. Its waters were tapped and diverted, and this nurtured small plots of corn, beans, and chili. Some years the river ran dry, and when this occurred the crops were scanty indeed. The population in the little pueblos of Ysleta, Socorro, San Elizario, Loma Colorado, San Ignàcio, and the others had difficulty in existing during the lean years. During the years of the Great War some venturesome Mexican discovered the Salt Lakes or salt flats. These natural salt deposits lie 112 miles east of El Paso. The salt was relatively free of dirt and other minerals and could be hauled away and with a minimum of screening and other refining could be utilized by both humans and animals. The Mexican who discovered the deposits called the place the Lagos de Guadalupe or Guadalupe Lakes, but this name did not stick. The place, of considerable area and covered during the infrequent rains by a shallow stand of water, came to be known as the Salt Lakes.

Within a few years the valley Mexicans, who had depended for their precarious living on the irrigation waters of the undependable Rio Grande, found if they hauled the salt back to their villages they could carry on a lively and profitable barter trade with Mexicans in the interior of Chihuahua. This then grew into a considerable industry and soon attracted more than local attention.

By the end of the Civil War news of the salt deposits had penetrated as far as Austin and San Antonio. Men could by application to the state government secure land certificates which permitted them to acquire title to state lands without ever having actually set foot on the site. Sam Maverick of San Anonio directly after the war acquired such a land title, and it included a sizeable piece of the Salt Lakes. This was only a beginning, and in a little while there was a company organized in El Paso to claim the remaining areas of the lakes and to exploit the salt. Directly there was another faction in El Paso, headed by Albert Fountain, who also tried to gain title to the lakes but this time the effort was made not for personal gain but to hold title to the deposits in the name of the people of El Paso County.

These beginnings boded the Mexican population no good. Heretofore the little man had needed nothing more than a two-wheeled cart and a yoke of strong oxen to make the two-hundred-mile trip to the Salt Lakes and return with a load of the highly tradeable mineral. Now the gringos, as the Americans were called, were making trouble. It was the aim of the various groups to seize the deposits and thereafter levy tribute on every ox cart load of salt that was hauled away. The Mexicans outnumbered the Americans by a hundred to one, and it took no little perception to see that trouble was going to ensue. This was encouraged by two leaders among the brown-skinned population—a local priest at Socorro and San Elizario, Antonio Borajo, and a politician, Luis Cardis. This pair, while leaders of the Mexican majority and publicly announced as in favor of free access to the Salt Lakes for everyone, secretly plotted to gain control of the beds and divert the revenue thus attained to their own pockets.

About this time there appeared on the scene, moving into El Paso from New Mexico, a man who was destined to play a big part in the maneuverings and warfare which broke out over utilization of the saline deposits. This adventurer was Charles H. Howard, an announced lawyer and politician, and a fellow who could bend people to his will through the force of his personality and persuasion. Within the year this forceful individual had made a prominent place for himself in El Paso. He got into the good graces of both Padre Borajo and Luis Cardis and through them gained the backing of the Mexican populace. In the succeeding year he ran for office and through the support of the Barajo-Cardis combine as well as the confidence of the latinos was elected district judge. At the same time, and trading on his new ascendancy, he was instrumental in getting Cardis elected to the state legislature.

The trio entered into an agreement about the distribution of the salt and proceeded to charge an established fee for each litre of the mineral that was hauled. After a time Howard threw over his partners and claimed the lakes as his own. This turned Padre Borajo and Cardis against him and along with them the Mexicans who had supposed that with the beds in the hands of these operators they could expect to visit the deposits and come away with their ox carts loaded. And all for free.

Howard gathered a survey party about him and started for the flats. En route he stopped off at Quitman where Cardis had a stage station. Finding the owner on the premises, Howard proceeded to thoroughly thrash him. It was the second time he had beaten his erstwhile partner. When he returned from the Salt Lakes he posted notices in all the pueblos up and down the Rio

Grande stating that anyone who hauled salt from the lakes would
have to pay the requisite fee. There was only one trail which ran
from Ysleta to the salt beds. He posted lookouts to collect his
due and in no time at all had collared a pair of oxen drivers with
heavy loads of salt. He seized them and hauled the pair into the
Ysleta court of Justice of the Peace Garcia.

The Mexican settlers had a speedy word-of-mouth telegraph
which kept them abreast of all the machinations of the gringos.
Word sped rapidly through the pueblos that two of the salt
haulers had been arrested and were even then in court. A crowd
—an angry mob—gathered speedily. This gathering was armed
and in a venomous mood. They marched into the offices of the
justice of the peace and there seized the judge, Gregorio Garcia,
Howard, and his road guards. The group was thrown into jail
and to gain their release the Mexicans stated that Howard would
have to relinquish all claim to the Salt Lakes, would have to post
a $12,000 bond to insure that he would depart El Paso County
and never return. The mob was controlled, and the terms were
drawn up by Luis Cardis.

These were hard terms, but after several days' consideration,
Howard agreed to them. He wanted to escape the confines of
the local *juzgado* and felt if he once got ·ee he could again
gain the ascendancy in his battle with Cardis. Jason Ellis and
John Atkinson along with Manuel Tober and Jesus Garcia
signed the bond. Howard at once departed for Mesilla Park
which is about thirty-five miles above El Paso in New Mexico.

The success of the Mexicans in ridding their country of Howard and gaining free access again to their precious salt em-
boldened them to make threats against all the gringos. Instead
of disbanding after the confrontation at the Ysleta jail they kept
their guns handy and met in a series of counsels during which
they sometimes listened to Luis Cardis and other times gathered
about a new bravo, a self-appointed *jefe,* Chico Barela. This
Mexican lived in Mexico, although he had relatives in Socorro
and San Elizario, and was a border bandit and badman. His
harangues before the highly volatile audience did a great deal to
keep them at a fever pitch to wipe out all the Americans and
plunder their homes.

Charley Howard had reached Mesilla Park on the sixth of October; by the tenth he was back in El Paso again. He had planned to return and he was gunning for his enemy, Luis Cardis. He found the Mexican leader in the general store of Ernest Schutz on Overland Street. Cardis saw him coming, and since the American had a 10-gauge Greener in his hands he knew he had to fight. He sprang behind an old roll-top desk and whipped out his six-shooter. Howard saw the move and turned loose the left barrel of the Greener on the widespread legs of his adversary discernible beneath the desk. The charge of buckshot brought Cardis to the floor, his pistol unfired. As he slumped behind the desk, Howard loosened the right barrel of the 10-gauge into his body. He died within the hour.

Howard strode behind the desk, reloading as he went. He peered down at his erstwhile enemy, rolled him over with his foot, and noted that the man was dying. His six-shooter, cocked, lay beneath him. The killer then strode to the door and crossed the street to the Custom House. He felt he would be safe inside. Mayor Magoffin went to him and told him that when news of the shooting swept down the river the Mexicans would storm into town and most certainly would break into the Custom House and lynch Howard. After a discussion, the duellist decided that the mayor was probably right. He went to his rig and climbed aboard and returned to Mesilla Park.

Mayor Magoffin, realizing the murderous mood of the lower valley Mexicans, got off a hurried telegram to the state capital asking the governor for immediate protection. The nearest Ranger force was almost five hundred miles distant. To get them to El Paso would have required not less than three weeks of the hardest riding. In the town at the time was a handful of soldiers. But the military had been admonished from taking any action in purely local civil strife.

Despite the fact that it would require several weeks to move a company of Rangers into the area, Governor Hubbard ordered Major Jones, commander of the Frontier Battalion, to proceed at once to El Paso and take every action he thought advisable to bring peace to the community. Jones went at once to El Paso, but instead of pausing there he proceeded to Mesilla Park where he sat down in powwow with Charles Howard and Fountain.

Meanwhile the San Elizario mob had not been idle. Joined by a hundred Mexicans from out of Chihuahua, the band had surrounded Howard's bondsmen and had them bottled up in Atkinson's store. These beleaguered members included Ellis, Tomas Garcia, Gregorio Garcia, Cobos, Ball, and Atkinson. The entrapped group managed to get a messenger out of the pueblo, and he carried a plea to El Paso for rescue. The sheriff, Charlie Kerber, could not raise a posse of gringos big enough to stand off the mob which now numbered in the hundreds. Jones determined to recruit a Ranger company right on the spot, since he could not hope to get any of his regularly organized companies from the Frontier Battalion into the fray in time to be effective. He looked around for a likely company commander and settled on John B. Tays.

Tays had a rather poor background for the command of a Ranger company. He had never been a peace officer, was a veteran of the Civil War, had run buffalo in a desultory fashion, was a muleskinner, a sometime cowboy, and was tending bar when Major Jones appointed him a lieutenant in Company C of the Frontier Battalion. It was largely left up to Tays to select his own people to fill out the detachment. Jones interviewed each man but in somewhat sketchy fashion. The whole operation was of an emergency nature, and each individual including John Tays was enlisted for only ninety days.

Meanwhile Major Jones journeyed down to San Elizario to treat with the Mexican mob leaders. He told them to disband and to let the law take its course. They, in turn, contended that when Charles Howard returned to El Paso he broke his bond and that they intended to collect it. They had the bondsmen bottled up in Atkinson's store and intended to hold them there until the $12,000 was paid over. Further than this they were enraged that Major Jones was recruiting a company of Rangers to be used against them.

Jones returned to El Paso and after some time agreed with Charles Howard that he could return to El Paso from his place of refuge at Mesilla Park and make bond in the killing of Luis Cardis. This Howard did and was immediately freed upon posting the necessary monies. He then proceeded about his duties as district judge not forgetting for a single instant that he had a vital interest in the salt 112 miles to the east. Meanwhile the siege had been lifted at San Elizario, and the beleaguered gringos who had spent two weeks cooped up in Atkinson's store were free to return to their homes.

Chico Barela was busy meanwhile and soon organized an ox cart convoy to visit the salt flats and fetch back a cargo of mineral. The party set forth and was accompanied by an armed guard intent on shooting it out if Howard attempted to intercept the wagons upon their return.

When the district judge heard about this expedition he waited until it had returned to San Elizario, and he then went to Lieutenant Tays, Major Jones having returned to Austin, and demanded an escort to San Elizario where he intended to place all the drivers and teamsters under arrest. Tays had established a detachment of his new Rangers in San Elizario and Howard with his four-man escort went to this headquarters. The place was immediately surrounded by the Mexican mob. Word was gotten out to the military in El Paso to effect a rescue. The soldiers were only a platoon in strength and were commanded by Captain Blair. This officer and fourteen of his infantry made the march from El Paso, but when they drew near the pueblo, they were intercepted by the Mexicans. After a parley Blair turned his troopers about and returned to El Paso. The Mexicans accepted this as a signal that the army would take no action to rescue Howard and his people.

The party was divided between Ranger headquarters and Ellis' store, the two adobe buildings standing side by side. The mob closed in about these two strongpoints and commenced a heavy fire at all the doors and windows. Within were not only such Rangers as had been stationed at San Elizario by Lieutenant Tays but also all of Howard's bondsmen, together with a half dozen or so Americans who lived in the pueblo. Without were several hundred Mexicans, fully a third of them from across the Rio Grande but intent on adding their guns and hatred to the battle.

The fighting went on intermittently for three days and nights.

It was obvious that there could be no rescue. As Charlie Kerber had wired the governor, he could not raise enough dependable forces to effect a rescue and the few remaining Rangers who were in El Paso had no stomach for the scrap. The odds were fearful, some three or four hundred armed Mexicans to less than twenty surrounded gringos.

Jason Ellis, in whose store a segment of the besieged was holding out, was captured by the mob and brutally killed. He was stabbed in the heart, his throat was slashed, and his beard, ears, eyebrows, and nose were cut off. The body with its grisly remains was dumped in front of his store by the Mexicans. Sergeant Conrad Mortimer, of the new Ranger detachment, attempted a dash from the Ranger headquarters to the store and was shot down. He was rescued by Lieutenant Tays under a hurricane of fire. About this time John Atkinson, one of Howard's bondsmen, turned up with $11,000. He had dug the money up, all in gold coin, from beneath his store. It was believed that if the mob was paid off the amount of Howard's bond they would withdraw and permit the surrounded men to return to El Paso peacefully.

The fighting continued for another two days and nights. Finally Tays held a parley with Barela, and he agreed to pay over to the Mexican leader the $11,000 in gold if all would be given safe escort back to El Paso. Chico went back to discuss the matter with his cohorts and evening came on. That night the Mexicans did very little shooting but at a second powwow at daylight the next morning they informed Tays that they had mined the Ranger house and the Ellis store and would blow up everyone inside unless Howard was surrendered to them.

Tays and Howard walked out to the mob leaders, but since neither could speak Spanish they sent back for John Atkinson. This man could speak fluent Spanish, and he informed those other Mexicans who were on hand that if all could go free they would pay over the $11,000. During the discussion Atkinson returned to the store and ordered all the besieged party to turn in their arms and to stop all resistance. The group was disarmed and herded into a single small room and there held under guard.

The Mexicans having gotten their hands on the gold were not ready to desist until blood was spilled. Their most important captive was the hated Judge Howard. They jerked and kicked him up before an adobe wall and lined up before him at distance of six paces. Charles Howard was no coward. He threw his head back, lifted his chest, and clenched his fists. "Fire!" he commanded. Although the command was given in English, the mob understood. He fell under a ragged volley, struck down by twenty bullets. Despite his many wounds he thrashed about on the ground not yet dead. Juan Telles, a member of the mob, ran forward and with up-swung machete took a cut at Howard's head. He missed and cut off two of his own toes.

McBride, who had long been Howard's agent, was next placed against the adobe wall. He had nothing to say. The mob fired and he fell pierced by many bullets. There was a surge forward, and he was hacked and stabbed until the body was badly mutilated.

The third victim, John Atkinson, whose crimes were that he had been a bondsman for Howard and had paid over the eleven thousand in gold, was pushed forward. He strode up to the wall, removed his coat, tore open his shirt, and in perfect Spanish told the mob, "When I give the command, fire at my heart— *Fuego!*" He was hit by a dozen bullets, but none reached his heart. He fell but was still perfectly conscious. He got back to his knees and shouted, *"Mas arriba, cabrones!*—higher you sonsofbitches!" Another round of shots was fired, but still he was not dead. He propped himself up on the ground and pointed at his head. Apolinar Apodaca came forward and put his pistol at the valiant man's temple and pulled the trigger. The bodies were dragged by saddle horn a half-mile, stripped of clothing, and dumped into an abandoned cistern.

Having shot those they considered primary enemies, the mob then thirsted for the remainder of the prisoners. Shouts were raised to kill all of them. Chico Barela, the Mexican jefe, stood between the captives and the mob. He would not permit any more killings, and the next morning having been held in the stifling room all night, the Rangers and others were permitted to depart for El Paso.

There was wild excitement in the town when the survivors straggled in. The sheriff hustled about to rearm the Rangers. He sent word to Mesilla Park that Howard was killed and the town needed help. Fifty questionable characters rode down out of New Mexico and announced they would ride to San Elizario and shoot all the Mexicans they could find. After several days' delay, Lieutenant Tays led a group back to the scene of the battle. En route a number of Mexicans were killed, including Juan Telles who had cut off two of his toes in trying to decapitate Howard. The group found that most of the Mexicans had fled and there was no resistance. The bodies were recovered from the cistern, and Atkinson and McBride were buried in Socorro. Howard's body was returned to El Paso and buried.

San Elizario remained a trouble spot for another half century. It harbored bad Mexicans who jumped back and forth across the Rio Grande, sometimes dodging the Rangers, other times keeping out of the way of the dread *rurales* of President Porfirio Diaz. It had long been a favorite crossing place for smugglers, and the Prohibition Act gave new life to the settlement. The Border Patron had many firefights with descendants of Chico Barela and his cohorts. Sometimes the *contrabandista* were bested in these fights, and occasionally the Border Patrol suffered casualties. To this very day the valley from Ysleta to well below San Elizario is good country to stir up a gunfight.

18

HARDRIDING JOHN HUGHES

The six riders sticking loosely to the Chisholm Trail were a hard lot. They had all ridden into Abilene separately, three of them with cow herds, the others drifters down out of Nebraska and the badlands of the Dakotas. In Abilene their money had gone quickly for dice and booze and women. Now, headed back down the longhorn route for Texas, they had talked of holding up a train or a bank or working together a herd of cattle and shagging the stolen steers into Wyoming where they could be sold.

Toward nightfall on the tenth day of their ride out of Abilene they made camp in a deserted shanty hard by a stand of cottonwoods. Within the boundary of the clump of trees was a strong spring. It was an ideal place to stop. Having shot and butchered out the loins of a yearling steer that afternoon and with nothing else for food, they barbecued the steaks over a fire at the door of the tumbled-down shanty. They had been living on a strictly beef diet and despite the succulent goodness of the meat, all groused about its sameness. That night, just as darkness crowded in upon them, horses commenced to crowd in upon the spring. There were ponies by the score. Good horses many of them and others only scrubs. Rustled beef had to be driven to market, but horses could be sold anywhere. It was not necessary to reach the railhead to peddle a stolen caballo. Everywhere there was a demand. And here was the supply!

The riders lay about the spring all the next day and hatched a plan. When the herds approached the water the next evening, they would be ready for them. Mounted and saddled.

The spring and its clump of trees were surrounded by a rickety corral. The hidden riders let the corral fill with the range stock, and then they flung the crude gate, contrived during the day, shut on the band. There were seventy-three mares, colts, and stallions within the enclosure. They held the stock in the corral for three days and nights without feed and with only the spring to provide water. On the morning of the fourth day they let the band slowly trickle out of the enclosure. The riders were ready, and as the horses commenced to feed they were slowly nudged westward. It was the beginning of a long trek for men and horses.

Three days later John Hughes, a rancher and owner of eighteen of the horses in the rustled band, rode up to the shack and its nearby spring. The whole story was written plainly in the dirt of the corral. He could see that the riders had camped at the shack, had held the remuda for some days in the corral, and had then gently eased the famished livestock out of the trap and hazed them toward the west. It was a plain case of thievery, for Hughes knew his neighbors, who owned their share of the filched animals, and he was aware that none of them would do these things.

He did not take the trail as he wanted to do. He was a cow rancher and he had to think about his ranch, his cattle, and the other horses remaining to him. He rode back to his headquarters, a modest shack some eight miles to the south. There he gathered up a frying pan, a coffee pot, some bacon and flour, tied extra .44-40 Winchester cartridges on his saddle, and rode off in the darkness to see his neighbors. There were three of them, all of whom ran their stock over the same range. All had undoubtedly lost horses in the raid at the cottonwood spring. In the night he talked to one after the other of his fellow ranchers, and he struck a bargain with them. If they would look after his outfit, branding his calves and colts and holding them within the range they all called their own, he, in turn, would take the trail of the horse thieves. The bargain was made. And without turning homeward again, Hughes swung off toward the cottonwood spring where just as day was tingeing the eastern sky he picked up the old trail of his missing horseflesh.

John Hughes was twenty-seven years of age, the year was 1884, and the country was central Texas, north of what is now Mason, Texas. Our rider was a typical cowboy. He had ridden out of Illinois when only fourteen, had drifted into the Indian Territory where he had been involved in a gun battle with whisky runners when but seventeen years of age. A .45 slug had cut through his right arm above the elbow and crippled the member so badly that ever thereafter Hughes had to do his shooting with his left hand. He had practiced with the left until few knew but what he was naturally a southpaw. Despite the handicap of the right arm he could still hold a rifle in it and fire from the left shoulder. He drove several herds upon the trail to Kansas railheads and finally in 1878 had decided to go to ranching on his own. He owned a sprinkling of cows but most of his effort was devoted to raising horses.

Had Hughes happened to note the day, which he did not, it was the first of May. Spring was upon the land, and grass was newly sprung from the earth and offered good feed everywhere the rustlers pushed their herd. They had no reason to hurry. The country was unsettled, not traveled, and after a week at the cottonwood spring where they had not seen any riders they had no reason to be alarmed of pursuit. They had decided to push their stolen ponies slowly across Central Texas, thence into the Panhandle and finally into New Mexico where they believed they could sell to Chisum, the big New Mexico rancher. They would avoid the towns, ride around such scattered ranches as might lie athwart their path, and thus avoid detection. At the same time their horses could fatten on the new spring grass.

This was a good plan except for one thing. That was the nemesis back behind who was now hard on their trail. It had not rained, and the sign lay plain upon the prairie. The passage of seventy-six horses leaves a considerable trail. John Hughes, the Winchester Model 73 beneath his knee and his old single action six-shooter at his hip, did not count the odds of six to one against him. He was intent on getting back his livestock.

On the sixth day he sighted the herd ahead, rolling along at a mile-per-hour gait, the mares and stallions browsing, the colts making play. That night Hughes struck the camp. The rustlers, despite their seeming lack of caution, had a night guard holding the herd from wandering. He saw Hughes approaching down an arroyo and fired at him. This set off the others and while two of them engaged the redoubtable pursuer, the others rounded up the horses and took off in a gallop toward the West. One of the last shots fired killed Hughes' horse. He was left afoot, thirty miles from the nearest ranch. He limped in after fifteen hours and told his story. The rancher, sympathetic with his cause, promptly outfitted him with a second horse, and the chase was on again. Hughes rode his borrowed horse back to pick up his saddle and the trail.

He followed the sign to the Canadian, across the river, and up into the Panhandle of what later became the State of Oklahoma. The rustlers then turned back southward in a great meandering loop, and Hughes lost the trail. He spent anxious days and weeks searching for the men and his horses. Weeks stretched into months, and he kept relentlessly on. He wore down a succession of horses, but all he had to do was to pull into a ranch and explain to the owner what he was doing and a fresh mount was instantly forthcoming. Ofttimes these ranchers would send their cowboys to ride with the dauntless tracker.

The rustlers were now on the alert. Twice they laid traps for the lone rider who dogged their steps. And twice Hughes shot his way out of ambushes. The thieves were now afraid to try to sell the herd but were unwilling to give them up. One of the cowboys dropped out and rode into Fort Griffin. The remaining five commenced to edge the band of stolen animals toward the New Mexico line. Their plan still to move into the adjoining state and thus be out of the jurisdiction of Texas lawmen and also to sell to whoever would accept the rustled stock.

It was here that John Hughes finally ran them to earth. The riders had thrown the remuda into a box canyon, and they camped in the mouth of the draw to prevent any of the stock from drifting out. Hughes rode into the canyon before dawn and waited in the rocks above the tiny spark of the campfire for day to come. When it was first light he called out to the sleepers about the fire.

Sleeping on their rifles they came up shooting. Three were killed by the deadly Winchester and the other two threw up their hands and begged for mercy. Hughes buried the three rustlers and bound the others to trees while he gathered his stock. He then tied his prisoners on their horses and rode for twenty-four hours until he could turn them over to the sheriff at Fort Griffin. He then rode on home. He had been on the trail a full year lacking only fifteen days! He came back with sixty-seven horses, some having died but others with brand new colts. He had ridden, he conservatively estimated, twelve hundred miles, had ridden down nine horses, had left home with forty-two dollars, and had returned with seventy-six cents. But he had taught the rustlers a lesson, had vindicated the faith his neighbors reposed in him, and more than that had evidenced a tenacity of purpose which was an integral part of the man.

Times were lively, and Hughes had no sooner gotten back to his neglected ranch when a Ranger rode in on the trail of a murderer. Hughes offered to give a hand, and the pair after two days of hard riding cornered the outlaw near the town of Menard. In the ensuing gun battle the gunman was killed. Hughes became a marked man in the country and rode through two bushwhacking attempts, in one of which he was slightly wounded and the other he lost a horse. As he told a neighbor, "If I am going to be bumping up against these outlaws all the time I might as well get some official status." He enlisted in the Texas Rangers. It was August 10, 1887.

For the next twenty-eight years our trail rider wore the badge of the Ranger force. He became a captain, one of the best known and most famous, he fought innumerable gun battles and brought to justice literally hundreds of criminals. He commanded Company D of the Frontier Battalion, and he led his outfit up and down the Rio Grande, familiar with every crook and turn in the meandering stream. His service in the Rangers is one of the longest and his reputation for a fearless and hard-riding lawman one of the very greatest.

Hughes enlisted in the Rangers at Georgetown and was then

compelled to ride seven hundred miles to join his assigned company. The following winter he rode on one scout after another
out of the company headquarters at Rio Grande City. Brushes
with rustlers and other chocolate-colored outlaws who rode up
out of Mexico were commonplace. Hughes, a big man, with dark
hair, a bristling mustache, brown eyes, and a poker face, fast
gained the confidence of not only his fellow Rangers but the law
violators as well. Never quick to shoot, he was always ready if
the opposition elected to make a scrap of it.

In 1889 the company was moved northward along the Rio
Grande to the vicinity of Shafter where a lively silver mining
operation was under way. The owners complained that high-grade
ore was disappearing. Hughes went into the mine, under cover,
and after some weeks of quiet sleuthing discovered who was
highgrading the silver. He fetched in another Ranger, and the
two laid a trap for the thieves. Actually there was one shift boss
who was diverting all the choice ore. Then a burro train would
cross the nearby Rio Grande, load the ore into panniers, and
scoot for the Mexican side. Hughes and his partner met the
train on the trail to the river.

When the robbers were ordered to halt, the shooting started.
All were armed with rifles, and they laid down a hot barrage.
The shooting lasted for more than an hour. When it was over,
there were three dead bandits and two wounded burros. The shift
boss was apprehended the next morning. Hughes, who was by
this time a Ranger corporal, buried the thieves under shining
white crosses on the hill overlooking the river crossing. A warning to others that the same fate awaited them if they sought any
more of the Shafter silver.

Company D was moved to Ysleta and along went John Hughes.
By 1893 he was made a sergeant. The company was under the
command of Captain Jones, not to be confused with Major John
Jones who commanded the Frontier Battalion. In June of 1893
Jones and five of his Rangers were below San Elizario hunting
cow thieves. This is the same area that figured so largely in the
Salt War. The Ranger detachment rode a trail which sometimes
followed the south bank of the Rio Grande. That is, it placed
the lawmen on the Mexican side of the border.

Jones and his fellows bumped into the rustlers and shots were exchanged. The bandits retreated to Tres Jacales and holed up in the adobe houses of the settlement. A gunfight built up and Captain Jones was fatally wounded. The other Rangers were forced to pull back to the river because of the numbers of Mexicans who had rushed in to the rescue of their fellows. Jones' body was left where it fell.

Representations were made to the Mexican government for the return of the Ranger's body and for the arrest of the killers. The rustlers were arrested and placed in the carcel in nearby Juarez. Captain Jones' body was duly returned across the international bridge. The murderers did not long remain in jail. They were released within the week. Then strangely, one after the other (there were four altogether) was found killed. Two were shot and a third was discovered along the trail mysteriously hanged. The fourth decamped for the interior of Chihuahua and was no longer seen around familiar haunts. Who accounted for these outlaws is unknown to this day. Suffice it to speculate, however, that Captain Jones was exceedingly popular with his men and very probably some of them took on the chore of rubbing out the killers as a small extracurricular duty.

With a vacancy for the commanding officer created in Company D, John Hughes stepped into the boots of the commander. A sergeant at the time, he skipped the usual grade of lieutenant and was made a captain. Certainly the new commanding officer was no swivel-chair leader. During the first two years after he assumed the captaincy of Company D, reports in the adjutant general's office at Austin show that the Rangers rode 26,000 miles. This included 142 scouting parties. Hughes rode his full share of these forays. Just how many gunfights he had during his three decades as a member of the famous Ranger force will never be known. He was not the kind of a man who talked about his battles nor yet the men he had been forced to gun down. There are old timers who speculate that Hughes may have had more gunfights than any Ranger. Be that as it may, the life he led was a hard one.

It was no career for the home-loving married man. John Hughes never took a wife and undoubtedly his years in the

Rangers persuaded him that he had little to offer a mate. He was so constantly in the saddle, so busily engaged in following out the trails of cattle rustlers, bandit raiders, killers, and badmen that he had no home he could call his own. His home was the Chisos Mountains, the sky, and the stars overhead, and a saddle blanket for a covering. He one time said he quit a cattle drive to Fort Dodge because the boss insisted he sleep under the chuck wagon. "It was too confining," the big Ranger afterward confided to a friend. And so was the thought of a home and a bride. Hughes remained a bachelor all his days.

Company D was stationed at Ysleta, living under canvas in the bosque some three miles from the pueblo. The company could be reached from Austin via telegraph, and when things were urgent this was the usual means of passing along orders. From the capital to Ysleta was almost six hundred miles and this journey by horseback took fifteen hard days. There was a good deal of latitude permitted the Ranger commander as to how he handled his men, his country, and his lawbreakers. Captain Hughes, accustomed to making his own decisions, liked it that way.

Miguel de la Torre, an early day Pancho Villa, operated in the Big Bend country. Sometimes on the Mexican side of the Rio Grande, other times on the Texas shore, he drove off horses and cows, raided isolated ranches, shot up outlying stores and small hamlets, and after a half dozen killings of badly out-numbered ranchers, he dodged over into Coahuila. His crimes were considerable even on the Mex side of the frontier and the rurales were soon on his track. During an ambush layed by these dread riders, Miguel de la Torre had seven of his buckos killed and escaped himself with a bullet in the leg. He thought it wise to convalesce on the Texas side of the river.

John Hughes had a system of spies who relayed word to him in distant Ysleta that Miguel was in Bajitas, a tiny *pueblito,* hard by the Rio Grande, a settlement which contained nobody save confederates of de la Torre. Down went Hughes, taking only three Rangers with him to gather up this murderer. Now from Ysleta to the Big Bend is—as distances usually are in Texas— a long way. Almost three hundred miles. Hughes wisely loaded men and horses in a freight car and the day following unloaded at Marfa and from there rode off into the vastness that is the Big Bend. Three days later he and his Rangers rode boldly into the dusty main street of Bajitas and up to the only *cantina* in the settlement. There under an arbor made of mesquite was a group of twenty bravos surrounding a scar-faced squatty Mexican who leaned heavily on a cane. Hughes and his men, Winchesters across the pommel of each saddle, covered the dangerous ones.

The Mexicans were all armed, some with two six-shooters, but so taken by surprise were the outlaws that none made a first move to start shooting. Hughes, always capable of forseeing the moves of his enemy, had thoughtfully fetched along a saddled horse. He dropped out of the saddle, covered by his steely-eyed comrades, and without a moment's hesitation, strode over to Miguel, who he accurately guessed was the man with the cane, caught him by the arm, and hustled him over to the waiting mount. By this time the bandits were aware of the game. They commenced to mill about, and one of them drew a pistol. A Ranger shot him through the chest. The others stood hitched. Hughes, a big powerful man, literally tossed the Mex outlaw into the saddle. He handcuffed him through the tree fork and not bothering to tie feet to stirrups, swung into the saddle, and with a lead rope to the horse carrying de la Torre commenced a slow retreat down the dust-choked calle. The party had scarcely gotten fifty yards before the bandits opened up. But their aim was bad. The Rangers halted in the middle of the tiny street, swung their horses broadside and returned the fire. Three outlaws dropped in as many shots, struck by the .44-40 slugs from the 73s. That broke up the battle. The survivors raced for the protection of the adobe cantina. The Rangers turned and rode out of Bajitas. Three days later Miguel de la Torre was delivered to the jail in Marfa. Hughes and his men loaded their horses back aboard the Southern Pacific and rode in style back to camp at Ysleta.

This swing into the Big Bend was accomplished in March, 1896. The Ranger force was armed with the Winchester Model 1873 carbine .44-40 caliber. Some Rangers elected to choose the 73 rifle, but the majority preferred the short and handy carbine. Company D of the Hughes command had the Model 73. It was a standard item of issue and a new Ranger received the Winchester and one hundred cartridges when he went on duty. These hundred cartridges represented an annual issue, and if he fired them in a gun fight, practice, or hunting, he was compelled to replenish his stock from his own pocket.

Directly after the Civil War when the Rangers were again organized, the standard rifle was the old single shot Sharps. This was a sorry weapon for a fighting force and many officers bought at their own expense the Henry rifle which was the forerunner of the Winchester Model 66. Others bought the Model 66, and when the Model 73 was announced, a good many more paid the fifty dollars which the rifle commanded. The monthly pay of the Ranger private in those days was $40. Despite the high cost of the Model 73, a great many Rangers saw the worthwhile advantage of this quick firing lever gun and invested in it. They then swapped off the .45 single action for a .44-40 and thus carried only one cartridge for both handgun and carbine.

The State of Texas was slow in arming its frontier force with the Model 73 Winchester. It was not until pressure was brought to bear on the governor by a great many legislators that a purchase of Model 73, consisting of two hundred carbines and fifty rifles, was made in 1881. When these were issued, the Ranger was charged with the rifle and payment was taken from his first pay. When he quit the force he took the rifle with him.

Despite the fact that the infinitely better Model 94 rifle in .30-.30 caliber came out in 1894, the adjutant general, although under compulsion to purchase new rifles, did nothing about it. Individual Rangers, just as they had done when the 73 appeared, commenced to arm themselves with the greatly improved Model 94 and its modern cartridge. The majority of the Ranger companies, however, had the older and lighter .44-40. It was the rifle John Hughes had taken into the Great Bend in pursuit of Miguel de la Torre. It was also the principal arm when he again went south, this time after horse thieves near Alpine.

The introduction of the Model 1876 Winchester had not gone unnoticed by the Rangers. It was chambered for the .45-75 cartridge, a round twice as powerful as the .44-40. A sprinkling of these big rifles was seen in all the companies, most especially in the Frontier Battalion where long-range battles with both Indians and outlaws made it highly prized. Likewise when the fine Model 1886 appeared it was eagerly purchased by many Rangers who liked the big cartridges, the greater power, and the good accuracy. The most popular calibers were the .45-70 and the .45-90.

While it was apparent to everyone in the field that the Model 73 was long obsolete and that Rangers in pitched gun battles were more often than not outgunned when they matched the peewee .44-40 against the guns of the outlaws, the state still delayed the day when a new rifle would be purchased. This situation went on until 1897 when a new adjutant general and a new governor made an initial purchase of one hundred of the new Winchester Model 1895 rifles, .30-40 caliber. These rifles were made with 22-inch round barrels and were hailed with delight by the Rangers. Subsequently, additional purchases were made until not only did all the force have the new Model 95 but there were spares with the headquarters company. It was a highly desirable switch from the older weapons and one that met with great enthusiasm from the Rangers in the field.

We have diverged from our story of Captain Hughes and his adventures along the Rio Grande—

Word came to him via the telegraph that he was needed in the Marfa-Alpine country to take the trail against a gang of horse rustlers. These night riders made a specialty of stealing only quality livestock—race horses. Now the ordinary cow-horse is not specially prized, but when the thief comes into the home corral and rustles a top running horse, that is another thing! Two of the ranchers who had lost fine stallions were waiting for Hughes when his freight car was shunted onto the side track at Marfa and he commenced to unload men, horses, and gear.

Before John Hughes and his party had arrived on the scene, Jim Gillett, previously mentioned in these pages and now a successful rancher in the area, had taken the trail of the rustlers. Gillett was no longer a law officer. After his six-year stint with the Rangers he had settled at Valentine and had been elected sheriff of Brewster County. Now, although no longer the sheriff, he was approached in town by rancher neighbors who pleaded with him to take the trail of the outlaws. He agreed.

After a day and a night on the trail following a plain sign which angled off toward Fort Stockton, Gillett and his posse turned back. It was then that they met Hughes and his Rangers. The doughty captain had been reinforced by various ranchers and cowboys who had lost prized stock to the raiders.

Jim Gillett had carried a Model 73 during his six years with the Ranger force. He had bought the carbine out of his own pocket, and he kept it to his dying day. However on this chase he was packing a brand new Model 1886 rifle. It was a .45-90, and Gillett had a full cartridge belt of the big rounds. Jim Stroud, a neighbor of Gillett and one of the losers of two fine quarter horses, borrowed the Model 86 from Gillett.

Although they were twenty hours behind the outlaws, the Rangers pushed on at a steady trot. Just before nightfall they came upon the campfire of the horse thieves, made twenty-four hours before. An examination showed the riders were living on a straight diet of beef. There were no signs of bread making, no coffee grounds, or other evidence of a varied diet. John Hughes decided the trio would ride into an isolated ranch, probably McCutcheon's, and try to beg or buy some flour and coffee. He headed in that direction.

It was a poor guess. The raiders did not approach the head-quarters. The country is mountainous, and a passage through it is next to impossible unless you ride the passes. Hughes split his party and detailed Thalis Cook, Jim Stroud, and Beau McCutcheon to take the Nogalitos Pass while he and the others rode off on the flank, aiming for Ojo Azul.

The outlaws had killed off their horses by too much hard riding. The animals had gone lame and badly needed a rest. The threesome stopped in the very top of Nogalitos and hobbled their worn-out mounts. They saw the little posse long before the lawmen had any idea they had caught up with their prey.

The outlaws were well armed. Each of them had a Model 94 carbine and plenty of .30-30 cartridges. When the three-man posse was a good three hundred yards distant they opened up. Only Thalis Cook had a rifle. He had insisted that Jim Stroud give him the Model 86 rifle of Jim Gillett. Stroud had the old Model 73 carbine handed him by Cook, and McCutcheon was armed only with a six-shooter. When the firing became general the outlaws advanced on the officers, realizing that they had the better fire power. When the distance had been chopped to 150 yards, Cook opened up with the .45-90 and held them off.

Hughes and his possemen heard the firing from a long distance, and knowing full well that the outlaws had been cornered, turned and galloped toward the sound of the shooting. The captain, an old hand at border skirmishing, came in on the battle off the left flank. He pulled the horses down at a couple of hundred yards, dropped to the ground, and commenced a bold advance without any heed for cover or the bullets which splashed the rocks about him. Jake Combs who was at Hughes' shoulder got an earlobe shot away. Jubel Friar, one of the outlaws, rose up behind a rock and triggered off two quick shots at the advancing Hughes. Thalis Cook shot him in the head with the big Winchester.

The pair of outlaws ran up the mountain, attempting to reach their hobbled horses. Ease Bixler got to a horse, cut the hobbles, and bareback rode out of the fight. Art Friar, brother of the man just killed by Cook, threw up his hands. "I quit," he yelled, "don't shoot no more."

Captain Hughes and Cook closed in on him. When he did not put up his hands at the command, the lawmen separated and moved in at a trot. When at a distance of thirty feet, Art Friar suddenly whipped his hand around behind his back and drew a six-shooter he had rammed into the pants belt. Both Hughes and Cook fired and both hit him. He was killed instantly. The third rustler was picked up two days later trying to steal a saddle.

The dead outlaws were roped on their own horses and hauled out to Alpine. The arrest warrant, issued by Judge Van Sickle of Alpine, had somehow gotten saturated with blood. It was returned to the good judge in that condition. Mute evidence that it had been served.

Captain John Hughes went on to serve the Rangers until 1915, a tenure of twenty-eight years. He was a Ranger captain from 1893 until his resignation. His service is one of the longest of any officer the force has ever claimed. How many gun battles he fought, how many outlaws felt the bite of his lead, how many miles he rode and how many arrests he made are things of which the still-faced Ranger would never speak. In his early years he had been punching cows in the Indian Territory, and there in a brush with outlaws he was shot in the right arm. The bullet did such extensive injury that Hughes was compelled to change his six-shooter to the left hip and do all his shooting from the left side. That he was not naturally left-handed was a fact few of even his intimate acquaintances were aware. That the change-over affected his performance when lead was flying was never in evidence.

John Hughes lived to be eighty-six years old. Finally, filled to the brim with a life which had grown stale and humdrum, his lively past long behind him, he shot himself.

MELISSA LEITH '81

19

THE LONG RIDE

By the late 1870s more than twenty different tribes of Indians had been shunted into the Indian Territory, reservations had been designated for them, agencies had been established with an Indian Agent, together with traders and their trading stores, and the red man had found that many of the promises made him by the Great White Father in Washington were hocum. Worst of these was the matter of rations. The allowance made the Indian Service by the Congress was simply not enough to feed the tribes. As a matter of fact the Indian was starving. He was issued a ration of barest essentials at monthly intervals, and this, besides such staples as cornmeal, coffee, and salt, was supposed to include fresh meat. The latter was sometimes missing altogether, and if a cow was butchered it did not provide enough cuts to last more than a day or two.

The army was on hand to see that the corraled braves did not stray from the reservation. But army commanders were aware that the situation was a critical one, and when little parties of braves slipped away from the tribal confines on hunting expeditions it was winked at. If these parties sometimes raided isolated ranches, killed a settler or two, and ran off his horses and cattle, the effort made to find and punish the guilty was never very energetically accomplished. The most of the hunting parties drifted westward, going beyond the borders of the Territory and hunting in the Texas Panhandle. There buffalo could be found in numbers, and here the Kickapoo, the Comanche, and the Cheyenne could kill and jerk the meat and thus get home with

203

enough food to care for his family. The practice became so general that it was finally realized as an accepted fact, and instead of blinking their eyes at the absent parties, troop commanders sent along an escort of ten soldiers under a sergeant who actually kept an eye on the braves and saw to it that no raiding was done. The Indians did not object to the escort so long as the soldiers did not interfere with the buffalo running. It was a good workable solution and undoubtedly kept many an erstwhile savage and his family from starving.

This was all well and good except that by 1878 the Panhandle of Texas had commenced to sprout no inconsiderable number of settlers. These were ranchers for the most part, but some farmers had moved into that great sweep of high windy plains and were attempting to dry-farm. Along with these some miniscule villages were springing up and freighters were beating out trails from Dodge, Fort Griffin, and even far-away Fort Worth. The regular forays of the Indians, even though accompanied by cavalry escort, was bitterly resented by the Texans. There were just enough hunting parties that managed to slip their shackles and come into the area so that with regularity a ranch house was burned, a cowboy was scalped, and horses were stolen. Strong measures were demanded of the state governor to do something about it.

Into the Panhandle rode George W. Arrington. He was in command of Company C of the Frontier Battalion. The records in the office of the adjutant general in Austin do not indicate that the Rangers were dispatched to the Panhandle explicitly to take care of the Indian problem, but there seems little doubt that pressure on the state governor was behind the assignment.

Arrington, in his early thirties, was a hard man. He had cut his teeth on fighting when in his teens under the famous Confederate raider Mosby. After the war he had gone to Mexico to fight for Maximilian, and when that fizzled he had journeyed on to South America. By 1875 he was returned to Texas and was punching cows when Major Jones, organizing the Frontier Battalion, urged him to join. Arrington signed on. Within a space of three years he had through hard riding, a rough but willing hand, and a coolness when bullets were flying that was noted by his superiors, climbed from private to sergeant, lieutenant, and to captain and the command of Company C.

A hard-driving man who insisted on instant obedience to his orders, Arrington was never liked by his men. Respected he was but there existed no warmth between the commander of C Company and his fellows. When a pair of Rangers went into Fort Griffin and got drunk, Arrington clapped both of them in jail. After they spent three days in the town lockup, he fired them from the force. Before riding into the Panhandle to exert pressure on the marauding Indians, he took ten men and rode into San Saba to break up a mob then ready to storm the county courthouse and hang an attorney who had killed a saloon man. Arrington camped in the courthouse, and the mob soon thought better of its lynching mood. Later, it was 1878, he rode into Fort Griffin there to arrest John Larn and Old John Selman, who were stealing cows, holding up the stage, and killing isolated travelers. Beofre Arrington arrived on the scene local citizens captured Larn and hanged him. Selman decamped for El Paso where years later he shot John Wesley Hardin in the back of the head, and was killed himself by George Scarbrough.

The men of Company C were armed with a miscellany of rifles. Despite the fact that the Model 73 Winchester had then been in production for five years, only five of the Rangers possessed the rifle. These had been purchased by them. Captain Arrington was one of these. The others had old Model 66 Winchesters and the state-issue rifle, the single-shot .50 caliber Sharps. The state would not provide ammunition for the privately owned rifles within the company, and these Rangers had to carefully husband their ammunition not only because of its cost on their modest salary but also because they were seldom in a town where the .44-40 cartridges could be purchased.

In December, 1878, Arrington was camped outside Fort Griffin. By the first of the year, with snow falling and the bitter winds of the high plains sweeping down upon him, he was scouting northward on the lookout for reservation Indians who were rumored moving into the Panhandle for a late winter hunt after the remnants of the southern buffalo herd.

After a week-long sweep the force struck the trail of about thirty Indians and after hard riding for a dozen miles caught up with the raiders. In the ensuing fight, a running battle on horseback, they killed a member of the hunting party. Keeping on, they rode over a long crest and down into a cluster of cottonwoods along a meandering little creek and here found the Indian camp. There were eighteen lodges, and the Indians were holding close herded more than a hundred ponies. Horses with Texas brands on them. About that time a detachment of the 10th Cavalry rode up. The lieutenant informed the Rangers that they were acting as an escort for the red huntsmen. Reluctantly the Rangers broke off with the appearance of the yellow-legs.

The Rangers withdrew but not before Arrington informed the lieutenant that only his timely arrival had spared the Indians a fight. He threatened to remain in the vicinity and watch every move of the hunters unless they moved back into the Indian Territory. As good as his word, and despite a foot of snow on the ground, the Rangers went into camp barely a mile above the lodges. Within forty-eight hours the cavalry had hustled the hunting party back toward the Texas boundary. Arrington, upon seeing this, turned back toward Fort Griffin.

During the summer of the next year, with a rising crescendo of reports reaching both Arrington and Major Jones about the Indians who were spilling over into the Panhandle from reservations in the Territory, Company C took to the saddle. Pack mules were loaded with enough rations and extra ammunition for a thirty-day "scout." After a long hard march to the northward the force went into camp in newly formed Wheeler County, near the military outpost Fort Elliott. That the Ranger commander elected to set up a base camp hard by the cavalry encampment can hardly be accepted as happenchance. He knew that the army condoned the Indian hunting parties in the Panhandle, provided escort for the red men, and stood between them and any retaliation by the Texan settlers. It is likely that Arrington intended to spy on the post and when he noted Indian parties leaving with the cavalry detachments that he would intercept them.

The newly established post was under the command of Lieutenant Colonel J. W. Davidson, breveted a brigadier general, and his troops consisted of two troops of the 10th Cavalry. When Colonel Davidson heard that the Rangers were camped within a couple of miles of the post, he flew into a rage, called up his ambulance—a sort of light buckboard—and with a suitable escort, drove to the Ranger encampment. There in an exceedingly bad humor he wanted to know if Arrington had orders to kill those Indians he found in the Panhandle. Never a man to mince words, the Ranger commander informed him that if he found armed bands roaming through his territory he would fire on them. This concluded the brief powwow. The post commander climbed back aboard his ambulance and rode off to Fort Elliott. There he announced that if the Rangers attempted to kill any Indians who had the tacit permission of both the Indian Service and the army to hunt over the Texas Panhandle, he would order his troopers to fire on the lawmen.

When Davidson's remarks were brought to Captain Arrington, he sat down and addressed a letter to the post commander, sending a copy of his note directly to the adjutant general of Texas. Arrington wrote: "A clerk in the post trader's store has informed me that you have stated if I or my men fire on any of the Indians now in the Panhandle that you will order your troops to fire on us or to arrest us and put us in chains. This man, Donnelly, who you used as a messenger upon my arrival here has passed along this information. I desire to know whether this man Donnelly has accurately stated your intentions or not. I would like a statement from you not because I have any alarm about your proposals but simply that I may lay the entire matter before the Governor of this State."

Needless to say Colonel Davidson did not reply to Captain Arrington's letter. He did get hold of his messenger, Donnelly, and forced out of him a signed statement to the effect that he had misquoted the Tenth Cavalry commander. He then sent a letter to Governor Roberts, together with a copy of the Arrington message and with the statement which he had wrung out of the loquacious Donnelly. Nothing more came of the affair, although Arrington gained considerable stature in the eyes of the governor as well as the adjutant general by his open challenge of not only the authority of the army but the federal government as well who acquiesed in the hunting activities of its red charges.

When it seemed the Indians were avoiding Fort Elliott, undoubtedly as a result of advice received from Colonel Davidson, Arrington gathered up his little force, and they marched completely across the Panhandle to the Goodnight Ranch. They then turned southward and rode for 150 miles through Briscoe, Motley, and Floyd Counties. The force then turned eastward again and returned to their original base at Fort Griffin. Everywhere they rode they heard complaints from the ranchers that the Indians we.e in greater force. These renegades were cleaning up the last remnants of the buffalo but were also wont to butcher cows, sheep, and pigs, would run off horses, and would occasionally rob and sometimes murder isolated families.

It appeared to Arrington that his Rangers were not situated where they could respond with promptness to the predations of the marauding bands. He recommended that Company C be stationed farther westward, over near the Texas-New Mexico boundary. This recommendation was looked upon with favor, and early in the fall of 1879 he gathered up all his men and rode westward for eight days, finally winding up at a spot which was named after a famous Ranger, Roberts. Camp Roberts was in Crosby County some ten miles from Blanco Canyon. Here the Rangers built corrals to hold their livestock, dug into the sides of the canyon on Catfish Creek, and prepared to winter there.

Catfish Creek was a strong stream, and it supported a fringe of cottonwoods and willows. The side draws and arroyos which ran into the main stream held cedar and brush. Turkey abounded and out of the breaks were an abundance of pronghorn antelope. There remained some scattered small herds of the southern Buffalo, and Arrington divided his force and put a detail of six men to doing nothing but shoot and jerk meat for the forthcoming winter. This group included all the owners of the excellent Model 73 rifles, and it was their job day after day to work up and down the creek shooting. The game once brought to bag was fetched to camp, and there it was jerked and put out in the dry autumn sun to cure. Once sun-dried it was cached like cordwood in a high, dry cave dug into the creek bank.

Scouting parties made great meandering sweeps about the headquarters camp, and in surprisingly little time word on the exact location of the rangers had gotten not only to the reservations in the Indian Territory but had also penetrated westward to the Indians in New Mexico. Arrington noted time after time that trails struck by his scout parties found the tracks of the marauding huntsmen turned westward.

Through the long rides made during October and November the Rangers found all the lakes within a radius of a hundred miles. These included the Double Lakes, Silver Lake, Cedar Lake, and Rich Lake. But on westward there was rumored to be a chain of lakes used by the Indians but unknown to the white men. It was Arrington's belief if he could find these lost lakes he would sit on the crossroads of all the red man's migrations, both west and east, as well, very likely, as those going north and south. The only problem was the great distance involved to reach the country of these lost lakes. The country was a barren waste and to ride into it invited disaster. Both horses and men could very well perish for a lack of water and food. Despite the hazards of an exploration into this forbidden land, he determined to find the lost lakes and to camp there until he intercepted some of the Indian bands which traveled through the section.

From the headquarters camp on Catfish Creek, Arrington marched fifteen of his Rangers to Double Lakes where John Causey, a buffalo runner, was camped in the caves there. Here, the Ranger leader lashed four ten-gallon kegs on two of his pack mules. These he filled with water, and then leaving behind five of his officers, he pushed off in a southwesterly direction. It was his plan to march for twelve to sixteen hours daily. If after two days he had not found the lost lakes, he would then water his live stock, fill his canteens, and turn back. He believed that somewhere during this trek, which would take them very close to a hundred miles, he would strike an Indian trail which would guide them into the lost lakes.

Horses on a long sustained march must be grain-fed to give them the strength and endurance to bear a rider through a long day and keep it up day after day. These Ranger mounts never saw any grain. They were loose herded about the Ranger camp, and all they had to sustain them was grama and buffalo grass. It was the usual thing on far-ranging scouts to ride for two days and then make camp in a likely meadow and permit the horses to rest and graze for a day. In this way the strength of the animals was sustained. If this was not done, in a very little while the mount grew thin and weak and could be killed with continued riding. Arrington knew the condition of his horses and just how much steady riding they could withstand.

Traveling by compass the Rangers rode for forty miles when they noticed that the country was rapidly changing. Where they had crossed over a high, level tableland, cut here and there with washes, the country now grew more rolling with sandhills continually blocking the way. The ground beneath the horses' feet had lost its covering of grass and was now sparse with weeds and low brush. There were no trees and the brush was creosote and mesquite. The total lack of water was an alarming indication that the tiny supply carried by the pack animals would have to sustain both man and animal.

As the party pressed onward the country steadily worsened. The weed growth grew even more sparse, the mesquite and chaparral thinned noticeably, and the sand became loose and the tired horses plunged into it with a lagging gait. The days were clear and cloudless, and the sun even in midwinter cast up a heat mirage which at times provided a fantasy. A mirage which inevitably portrayed the lost lakes which the group was seeking.

Although he had decided to turn back at the end of the second day, the determined Ranger kept on into the night after two days and with a full moon shining down on the vastness, the party rode up on one of the innumerable sandhills, and there looked down on a series of dry sinks. Skirting these dry lakes they eventually came upon a brackish spring. Camp was made at midnight, and the horses were staked out on the sparse salt grass about the tiny oasis. The Rangers, despite the cold wind which whistled across the desert, slept until daylight.

The next morning they scouted the country about the spring and found a profusion of Indian sign. But all of it was old. This, Arrington assured himself, was not the lost lakes he was seeking. These must be even beyond, and after resting men and horses for a day and a night the party saddled up, and with the ten-gallon kegs filled with the brackish water, they again rode southwestward. After a ride of twenty miles they came to a series of five lakes. These were in a chain running generally from northeast to southwest. Here was a lot of Indian sign and around the principal lake, sitting at the north end of the chain, were the carcasses of horses killed and butchered by the Indians. The Indian, given a choice, much preferred horse meat to beef. Arrington determined to camp on the lakes and await the return of roving bands which he believed would pass this way when the moon was full.

He surveyed the chain of lakes, which he felt sure was the fabled Lost Lakes, rode back to the spring and the little lake beside it, and carefully summed up all the evidence of the Indian usage. As a result of this study he decided that actually more of the marauders were using the spring—which his men had named Ranger Spring—than were coming in to Lost Lakes. As a result of this decision, he moved his force after a couple of days of rest back to Ranger Spring. Here he made a camp well back from the water, threw all the horses into a box draw where by erecting a brush fence they could be held to graze. After that he dispatched two riders, one to John Causey's camp to get extra rations and another to Camp Roberts to bring up the five Rangers left there. He then settled down, his officers deployed about the waterhole, to await the arrival of the hunting bands.

For sixteen long days the Rangers guarded the waterhole. The full moon came and went, and still no roving bands came in to the spring. The force had not planned to remain so long afield. The swing had been planned for only four days, two outward bound and two to return. From eating half rations the members of Company C were reduced to quarter-rations and finally to only a handful of cracked corn daily. There were antelope coming to the water every day but Arrington, ever the iron disciplinarian, would not permit a shot to be fired. It might be heard by the Indians, he insisted, and now with this long wait he could not frustrate the ambuscade by a chance rifle shot.

Finally after the seventeenth day had passed and all the food was gone and no raiders had appeared, the commander gave the signal to break camp. It was the first of February, the dead of winter, in a country noted for zero temperatures, piercingly chill winds, and frequent snow blizzards. The first day, the horses rested by the fortnight of grass and leisure, the party forged ahead. A pronghorn was shot and cooked and eaten where it fell. The party rode into the night, making at least fifty miles although the horses, filled with the sorry grass, were trying to stop and lie down before a halt was called.

The next morn the force awoke to a chilling sight. A snow blizzard had broken with all its devastating force. There was no breakfast, and indeed there was no food. Horses were saddled and the men mounted, visibility reduced to a few hundred yards and landmarks obliterated. Captain Arrington took the lead, compass in hand, and with his men strung out behind him knew that he had fifty or sixty miles to ride to get to Causey's buffalo camp at Double Lakes. If he should miss the camp the death of the entire party was entirely probable. In this storm and with temperatures near zero their fate would be sealed.

The horses, ridden too hard the day before and close hobbled during the night for fear they would stray, were played out. Despite their lack of strength the animals were the only salvation of the humans. The men, gaunt, worn, and weak after two-and-a half weeks of starvation diet, were hardly strong enough to pull themselves into the saddle. All realized the seriousness of their plight and without any discussion looked to the indomitable Arrington with his compass to fetch them into Double Lakes and the warmth and protection of the Causey camp.

The group had scarcely ridden out of their overnight bivouac when Dub Elton announced that his horse had given out. And it was true, the animal, an old horse with bad teeth, had not fared well on the salt grass about Ranger Spring. He had steadily lost weight and now he was done for. His head down, front legs widespread, breathing heavily, it was evident he could not go on. During the sojourn at Ranger Spring an Indian horse, abandoned by some passing band because he was played out, had come in for water. Arrington had roped the paint and turned him in with the Ranger mounts. This horse, a young animal, had prospered on the pasturage. The captain had had the fore-sight to fetch him along. Elton swapped his saddle from his own horse to the Indian pony. The march went on.

All day it snowed, and the horses were plunging through a covering which came up to their hocks. By nightfall the snow had slackened somewhat and by eight of that evening it had stopped. The clouds cleared, and the stars commenced to blaze out one by one. The doughty commander held his course, guided by the tiny pocket compass, and by ten of the night the little band fell off into the canyon near the Yellow Caves. Here they found a series of caves and with a roaring mesquite fire spent the remainder of the night.

The next morning two Rangers with the strongest horses, to-gether with a pack mule, were dispatched on ahead to Causey's buffalo camp and there secured rations. Without pausing the pair lashed on the food and turned back for the Yellow Caves. By this time some of the Rangers were so weak they could no longer stand and had to be fed slowly and carefully as they recovered from their long ordeal. After resting for two days the force again took to the saddle and rode in to Camp Roberts after two days of marching. It was the sixth of February. The company had been forty days away from camp and had covered, they estimated, more than eight hundred miles.

Captain Arrington believed that Ranger Spring and the Lost Lakes were in Gaines County, Texas. Later on it was discovered that he had actually ridden into New Mexico. When news of his long ride became generally known, the army wanted to know more about the lakes and stated that it had known of their existence for a long time but could not reach them because of the lack of water. The Comanches who ranged through the country had been unaware of the lakes until told by the Apaches. After that both tribes when on raiding forays would pass by, and it was these Indians who had left signs of their comings and goings which were found by Arrington and his Rangers.

20

HIRED GUNS

The advertisement in the Fort Worth *Star Telegram* for the 23rd of March, 1892, was quite specific.

It read: "Will hire 25 gunfighters for a special job in Wyoming. If you apply bring your own guns and expect a fight. Cattle rustlers, brand blotters, and night riders are the game. Apply Drovers' Hotel. Ask for Major Frank Wolcott."

It was significant that these gunmen were recruited in Texas. The Lone Star state was filled with hardcase, quick-on-the-draw renegades who lived more outside the law than within. Sometimes cowboys, other times rustlers, not adverse to running a herd of longhorns across the Red River, or shooting up a Southern Pacific train when it paused for water at Van Horn, the two dozen gun swingers were signed on during the first 24-hour period.

Most of the aggregation were cowboys looking for excitement and the $5 per day pay which was five times the puncher's usual stipend. But there were also some really dangerous hombres in the platoon.

There was Terry Southwick, thrice tried for murder and as many times acquitted; and Harry Longbow, who was out on bail for a double killing in San Antonio; and Ed McCracken, erstwhile Texas Ranger, deputy sheriff, town marshal and probably the meanest gent in the whole crew—a scorpion, a rattlesnake, a ringtailed tooter.

"He's bad all the way through," was the way John Hughes, old time Texas Ranger, described him.

The honest-to-god bad men in the gathering tended to band together, ignoring the ragtag and bobtail element who made up the rest of the mercenaries. While Major Wolcott, a Wyoming rancher (and a big one), had journeyed down to Fort Worth to recruit his killers, he bowed out in favor of his foreman, an unsavory character named Tom Smith. This individual, well padded with the coin of the realm, payed his hit men a half-month's salary, bought 25 horses, three Studebaker wagons, army tents, cots, and bedrolls for every man-jack. Those adventurers who did not have a rifle were presented with brand new Winchester Model 1876's chambered for the .45-75 cartridge and with special 22-inch carbine barrels. Every "soldier" was handed 100 rounds of ammo with the admonition from Tom Smith, "Fer every rustler you git with thim shells we're gonna pay yah a hundred bucks."

The organizer and captain of the force was prepared to buy just as many .45 Colt Frontier sixshooters but his Tejanos all professed more confidence in the guns they packed. For all that, Smith bought five Colt Model 1873 .45's, each with 7½-inch barrels—("Jist in case som'buddy loses his gun," he explained to Ranch Wolcott.) The old James Prescott Hardware and Feed Store, according to their invoice, provided not only the armament but the cartridges as well.

The destination of this unsavory band was Johnson County, Wyoming, where the big ranchers had declared war on the nesters. Now a nester was a small operator who might have a section of land and 25 cows. These homesteaders, all of whom were well within the law by settling on the public domain and claiming their 640 acres, were a thorn in the side of the big cattlemen. These latter had been there first and had claimed thousands of acres. The "nesters" usually settled at a spring or permanent waterhole and while the big stockman's cattle could still water there, a few settlers, out of pure obstinancy, fenced the water off and this inevitably raised a row.

Too, there were more than a few nesters who set out to build up their herd at the expense of the land baron. An owner, who might be 25 miles away, and even with a dozen cowboys, could not ride very close herd on his thousands of cattle. The little operator with a sticky loop slapped his brand on many a calf and when the round-up came in the fall he blandly claimed those calves still plainly running with cows that carried the big man's brand. This sort of thing got so bad that large ranch owners got together and decided to clean out the rustlers. All were known, a hit list was made up, and Frank Wolcott was dispatched to Texas to enlist not less than 25 gunmen to put a stop to the depredations.

With plenty of money and no small amount of prestige, the lethal Mr. Tom Smith, laid on a passenger coach, a baggage car, a flat car and two cattle cars and into this melange he loaded two dozen of very probably the most dangerous hombres in the whole state of Texas. There was not a man who had not killed his man, not an individual who was not wanted by a sheriff somewhere, not a man who had not busted the law—and some of them very recently. Had the Texas governor known that these 25 tough customers had been persuaded to leave the state it is probable he would have declared a statewide holiday!

The story has it that this crew rode the train into Denver and changed there for Cheyenne but this is inaccurate. In the first place there was no railroad between Fort Worth and Denver and in the second place the Atchinson, Topeka and Santa Fe hitched on the passenger car, the baggage car, the flat car and the two cattle cars behind a freight train. The ensemble took three days and nights to reach Chicago where it was switched during dead of night to the Union Pacific and after another two days and nights pulled into Cheyenne, Wyoming.

By this time tempers were short, beards were long and the continual poker game had resulted in one exceedingly lethal gunplay. Long John Armitage was gunned down in the aisle by Ad Jason. According to witnesses, Long John played an ace when all the aces were out. Ad Jason was losing steadily and when he saw that ace he whipped out his slip gun and bored his poker playing companero spang through the brisket.

"What'll we do with him?" Ace Schneider asked Tom Smith. The foreman pondered that one a minute and said, "Take off his sixshooter and dump him out the door." And that was why the section gang working between Kirksville and Keokuk found a dead man along the right-of-way next day.

Finally arriving in Cheyenne, where Major Wolcott had a special train standing by, the entourage rattled away northward. At Casper, 120 miles south of the town of Buffalo, county seat of Johnson County, the travel weary badmen debarked. The horses were jumped off the cattle cars, the Studebaker wagons were loaded with tents, grub and bedrolls, the somewhat sullen crew (three gamblers in the crowd had by this time gotten all the money) saddled up and in the dead of night commenced the long ride northward.

"If'n anybody asks we're a gang of surveyors makin' for Bald Mountain," Tom Smith warned. Nobody asked.

An hour after good light one of the riders chanced to glance back over his shoulder and was startled to see another sizeable bunch of riders trailing along behind. He spurred up to the head of the column and said to Tom Smith, "Who is this bunch a-trailing us?"

"Don't you never mind, Will," spoke the leader, "them's some of our people." The ranchers, busy in Casper, had recruited another 25 riders from among local cowboys, drifters, range detectives and others and this group, aware of the bad hombres fetched up from Texas, had wisely elected to tag along but keep their distance.

The bad feeling which had generated the Texas invasion was not wholly on the side of the cattle tycoons. The nesters, small ranchers, dry-land farmers and even the local townsfolk were mad too. Jim Averill, a saloon-keeper and store owner, who had a little place a few miles outside the town of Buffalo, had a girl friend, Ella Watson, sometimes called "Cattle Kate," who owned a few cows. It was alleged that Ella sometimes traded a night in bed with a rustler who had a calf or two and thus built up her herd. Be that as it may, the cattlemen sent over a cowboy, Dude Schmmel, to warn Averill and his inamorata to get the hell out of the country. This they both ignored until early one evening when a sizeable crew of cowboys descended on the saloon-trading post and hauled Jim and Ella out to a nearby cottonwood and hanged them.

A while after that Tom Waggoner, a typical nester with a small place (by small I mean to say the usual 640 acre spread, with 18 head of cows, one rangy bull and a dozen calves) was jumped out at midnight, escorted with a rope around his neck to a cottonwood near his waterhole and there hanged. His reputation as an honest man was generally known in the neighborhood.

The settlers, alarmed and thoroughly angry, waylaid Orley Jones, sometimes called "Ranger," and shot him out of his buckboard just as he pulled up the bank out of Big Muddy Creek. He was shot at exceedingly close range with a charge of 00 buckshot.

In retaliation, it would seem, John Tisdale, who had been a cowboy for Teddy Roosevelt, was returning home from Buffalo with rations for his family and Christmas presents for his family when he was shot off the seat of his spring wagon in midstream of the Powder River. So close to home was he that his wife heard the single shot. Tisdale was identified with the small settlers.

A few months later a gang of cowboys surrounded Ross Gilbertson and Nate Champion while they were in a line cabin west of Saddlestring. These two were no strangers to shoot-out situations, and the duo proceeded to kill three horses, while shooting one of the cowpunchers through the thigh. The raid fizzled out very shortly after that.

Probably, very probably, the cowman's posse in this case was on the hot scent of a pair of real rascals. Neither Gilbertson nor Champion had any visible means of support and yet both seemed to live well. "They throw a mighty sticky loop," one cowman was heard to comment.

The situation was building toward a showdown. Both sides were fighting mad and, with the approach of the 50-odd gunfighters, the fuse was aglow. After riding hard half the night and all the day following, the ragtag cavalry pulled into the Boxed W Ranch on the South Fork of Powder River just as the shadows lengthened. Unknown to them at least three nesters had spotted the dust clouds stirred up by the passage of so many horses and, riding in relays, had gotten word to the town of Buffalo, and to Sheriff Duke Angus. Angus was in none too much of a hurry to go out and brace 50 heavily armed riders.

"Les' see what they aim to do," he told one of the hard riding informers. "Maybe they're a survey crew," he continued lamely. Duke had been put in office by the cowmen.

Meanwhile during the night, Mike Shonsey, who was a top

hand for the Running M outfit, rode in and said that he had passed Nick Ray and Nate Champion at the KC Ranch and it looked to him like they were camped there. No one had anything in particular against Nick but Champion was No. 1 on the hit list. The guerrilla troop was on the trail an hour before the coming of day. The KC Ranch, belonging to Charley Nolan, was a two-bit outfit, rumored as a way station in the movement of rustled stock. It was 14 miles on up the trail.

It was barely sunup when the cavalcade reined in their horses in the coulee behind the corrals. There was a wisp of smoke trailing dejectedly out of the stovepipe over the leanto kitchen.

"They're in thar alright," Tom Smith ejaculated to no one in particular, "Shonsey knew what he was talkin' about."

The coulee held a piddling small spring and this water spilled over into a corner of the corrals. Still, it offered water for the 3-room log cabin when it held riders. In no time at all Jimmie Fergus, a trapper, together with Simon LePage, came meandering down to the spring, a water pail in the hands of each man. Half asleep and wholly unprepared for danger, the frontiersmen did not look off toward the corrals where the gunmen stood.

"Come over hyar," Tom Smith commanded. There were 20 guns trained on them. They obeyed, hands in the air.

"Whose in tha shack?" the leader demanded. He recognized Fergus and could tell from the buckskins of the second man that he was most likely a trapper. "Nate and Nick Ray," Jimmie Fergus replied. "You ain't gonna kill us 'er ye, Tom?" he inquired anxiously.

Smith did not bother to reply. "Take 'em," he motioned to Brian Dudley, "an' tie em up on the far side of the brandin' chute. Iff'en they're lyin' we'll deal with 'em later." Then on second thought he stopped the cowboy, "No, I gotta better idee," he held up his hand. "Go back thar to tha shack an' tell Nate Champion we got tha' place surrounded. Iff'en he'll come out with his hands up we'll let 'im go," he winked ponderously at those riders who crowded in close.

Fergus nodded and started toward the shack but when he got at the near corner of the 3-room cabin he suddenly whipped around the corner and legged it for the nearest coulee. Tom Smith laughed, "Let 'im go," he commanded. "We don't want 'im nohow."

A council of war was held. With a sweep of his hand he spoke to Ed McCracken, the real curly wolf from Texas, "Ed, take a dozen boys and work yer way 'round to the fur side. Don' shoot 'till I open up." Harry Longbow was given another 10 riders and he swung off to the other side. The remainder took up positions along the corral and down the coulee which held the spring.

The leader cautioned, "No shootin' 'till I let's go."

Simon LePage, as scared as a man could get after watching his trapline partner duck out, was motioned forward. "Go tell Champion he'd better surrender. We've got 'im cold turkey. An' let me tell yah som'thin', Trapper-boy, iff'en you tries to dodge aroun' any corners ahm gonna have a dozen rifles on yah."

LePage nodded miserably and commenced a slow cautious approach to the blanket which hung over the back door.

The fracas a-building is best told from here on by Nate Champion, who remarkably kept a diary of his last hours on earth.

"Me and Nick was just getting breakfast when we saw all them horses in the coulee behind the corrals. We knowed something was up."

The arrival of Simon LePage, who burst through the ragged blanket at the back door, almost getting himself killed, but bringing with him Tom Smith's ultimatum, left no doubt in the minds of Champion and Ray as to where they stood.

"We ain't giving up." Champion wrote in the log.

LePage found a dirty dishrag and after tying it to a broom handle essayed a cautious exit. Three shots were fired at him but all missed. He continued to sidle off toward the trail to Buffalo and finally broke into a run.

Nick Ray for whatever reason will never be known, tried the same tactic. He was hit by a dozen guns before he had run 20 feet. Champion broke into the open firing his .45 Peacemaker wildly. He holstered the gun, lead cutting the ground all around him, and catching Ray beneath the arms dragged him back into the shack.

"Nick ain't dead," he noted in his diary, "but I reckon he ain't long for this world," Ray lived for five hours.

The firing became general, from all sides, the bullets digging into the walls made of cottonwood which withstood the big 300-grain .45 caliber bullets surprisingly well.

Nate noted in his book, "I only got 17 cartridges. I'm going to have to be sparing with them."

Jim Fergus, only 19 at the time, and a typical frontiersman, broke into a fast trot and barreled off toward Buffalo. By mid-morning he overtook Harley Hammer, a nester in a buckboard, and told him what was taking place at the KC Ranch. They whipped up the team for Buffalo.

About 3 of the afternoon, Ollie Flagg and his stepson, Alonzo Taylor, came down the road from Buffalo and were fired on by the strung-out posse. They had heard the shooting for some time as they approached and knowing that Nate Champion usually hung out around the KC, they had little doubt that he was besieged. By whom they knew not but the rumor of a big cattle-man's strike force had been bandied about long before.

"I reckon them cowboys have got ol' Nate cornered in thar," Flagg said to his son. "Maybe we'd better git back to Buffalo an' tell the shur'ff," he said as they whirled their horses and galloped back the way that had come.

Despite 50 guns yammering away at the log cabin, Champion hung on. Once every quarter-hour he let drive at any ranny fool-ish enough to stick his head up over the banks of the coulee.

Behind the corral was a stock of last year's hay, cut from the low ground along Powder River. Too, there were running gears of a wagon and, turned on its side, a hayrack.

"Set the hayrack back on the runnin' gears," Tom Smith directed. "Ah got an idee."

The hayrack was loaded with hay and with a dozen men behind was shoved up to a little incline on the blind side of the cabin.

"Now set the hay afire," Smith chuckled.

The fire wagon rolled off the little hill and, gathering speed, crashed into the back side of the cabin. The impact shook half the load of hay off the rack and it fell against the cottonwood walls of the shack. These commenced to burn strongly. Nate Champion knew they had him. He made his last entry in his diary, a book which did not burn because the fire snuffed itself out before the building was consumed.

"Just to let 'em know I'm still alive and fighting," he wrote in his diary.

Nate wrote, "The cabin is on fire. I reckon they've got me."

His .44-40 ammo all consumed, the redoubtable Texan-fled-to-Wyoming, a suspicious character, probably more scoundrel than anything else but full of fight to the end, came charging out of the back door with his old Colt blazing. He was struck by 28 bullets.

The cattlemen, through a series of riders, were keeping pretty close tabs not only on the fight at the KC Ranch but also the goings-on in Buffalo. And when they were aware of the boiling anger of the nesters and the townspeople they got word to Tom Smith to pull out and fort up at the TA Ranch on Crazy Woman Creek.

This was a big place, belonging to Doc Jerome Harris, a big-time rancher. Not only was the house a big one, built of hewn logs, but the barn was just as sturdily put together. The troopers turned their horses into the horse trap and all moved into the headquarters and the sizeable barn.

Meanwhile word had gotten to the town of Buffalo that Nate Champion and Nick Ray were dead and that the invaders were at the TA Ranch. Without waiting for Sheriff Angus, Bob Foote, who owned the biggest store, a sort of frontier trading post where you could lay in a six-month supply of rations or buy enough rifles to stand off the whole Oglala Sioux tribe, handed out Model 73 Winchesters and box after box of 44's. Arapahoe Brown, part Indian and a nester as well as the owner-operator of a feed store, organized a force of 49 well-armed and mounted cavalry and with a series of informers who rode in almost hourly, the force bore down on the cattlemen's army.

From somewhere, from this time and distance a bit hazy to decide, Duke Angus showed up in Buffalo and had no trouble at all in recruiting another 40 angry homesteaders. He set out in trail behind the Arapahoe Brown war party.

The battle was joined. For two days it consisted of a desultory exchange of long-range rifle fire. The nesters rode in from as far away as Greybull and Ten Sleep, a hundred miles to the west, and finally there were better than 300 vengeful homesteaders ringed around the Doc Harris place. Doc, let it be noted, was not on the premises!

When the cowman's troop left off the killing ground at the KC
Ranch, they brought with them the Studebaker wagons (one of
which was loaded with 540 pounds of dynamite, together with
plenty of fuse and caps) and a powder man who was supposed
to blow up nester shacks. With the riders in the house and barn,
their horses had been shunted into a horse trap, and the wagons
were left standing behind the barn. This proved something of a
tactical error.

The second night of the attack, a dozen resolute homesteaders
moved stealthily through the shadows and quietly wheeled off
the Studebaker loaded with a quarter-ton of explosives. The next
morning, under the direction of Arapahoe Brown, a fuse and
primer was attached to the powder, the wagon was wheeled into
position behind a huge, clumsy barricade. This buffer was
mounted on the running gears from the other two Studebakers.
The assembled infernal machine was hauled, pushed and shoved
to within 20 feet of the north walls of the TA Ranch headquarters.

"Hey, Tom Smith," shouted Arapahoe Brown, "come out or
we'll blow the whole bastardly lot of you to hell. We've got all
your powder up against the side of the house and I'm fixin' to
light the fuse." There was no reply from Tom Smith.

About that time up galloped Col. James J. Van Horn and
three troops of U.S. Cavalry. It was just in the nick of time. Ob-
servers on the ground said that old Arapahoe had out a box of
kitchen matches and was just on the point of lighting the fuse
which ran back 300 feet behind a slight rise.

The big ranchers, kept in almost hourly advice about their
stalwarts in the TA headquarters, had gotten off a series of
frantic telegrams to the governor—a governor who up until then
had ordered his adjutant general not to honor any requests to
send any national guardsmen to Johnson County. Now with the
pleas coming from the big stockholders, the governor got off
urgent messages to both senators, to Brig. Gen. John R. Brooke,
who commanded the region, and even routed President Benjamin
Harrison out of bed begging for succor.

The President got in touch with the War Department and in
turn Col. Van Horn and his troopers were ordered to depart

forthwith from Fort McKinney. That they arrived not a minute too soon is a matter of recorded history.

The prisoners (three had gone over the hill during the two nights the TA headquarters was besieged) were escorted by the cavalry to Fort Fettermen and then loaded aboard a special train bound for Cheyenne. On the outskirts of the capital was Fort D. A. Russell and here they were incarcerated—not, let it be realized, without a considerable amount of liberty. The big ranchers had not lost any influence with either the local or state officials nor, it seems, with the military. Most of the renegades could be found in the town's bistros.

The fight at the TA Ranch had occurred during the shank end of April 1892. The invaders were not fetched to trial until the 21st of January, 1893. By this time, and quite amazingly, all the hardbit cases from Texas had strangely evaporated. Not a single man-jack answered the call of the bailiff when court convened that stormy Monday morning in 1893. Those 25-odd Wyoming cowboys, drifters, stock detectives, and roustabouts who had made up the local contingent all stood trial and all were just as promptly acquitted for lack of evidence. The star witnesses, those trappers, Jimmie Fergus and Simon LeLage, were missing—bought off, it is said, by rancher checks which later bounced.

21 BARBWIRE AND SQUATTERS

When barbed wire was invented in 1873 no one in Texas thought much about it. Before the advent of the prickly wire, fences had been built of sturdy posts set side-by-side as when constructing a strong corral, and there were fences of poles, brush, and piled stone. A new kind of fencing, with barbs which cruelly cut cows and horses and was strong enough to turn an entire herd, was little imagined.

By 1880 the picture had changed considerably. During the short space of seven years barbed wire in the hands of farmers, small stockmen, vegetable growers, and even in some cases the bigger ranchers had made tremendous inroads on the free, open range of Texas. Longhorn herds, hurrahed up the Chisholm Trail to railheads in Kansas, now were continually pestered by the nuisance of the barbed wire fencing. Where one season the trail would be free and unhampered, by the following spring the trail boss would be constantly scouting ahead to cut away the wire before the herd leaders approached.

The rancher did not like the wire. He was accustomed to grazing his cattle just as far as he pleased, and if his stock intermingled with his neighbors, they were sorted out, cows, calves and saleable steers, at the round-up. Best of all when a series of rains touched down in a valley some eight or ten miles distant producing the magic bounty of the God-given moisture, he could shag his herds into that greenery and leave them there to fill up on the succulent new grass, as did his neighbors. There was room and range for all. That is, before the fences came.

227

Nothing was more irritating to the big cattleman than to find water holes fenced by incoming nesters. The cowman, first upon the scene, looked upon the springs that dotted the range as his by inalienable right. When such watering places were homesteaded by latecomers, and with the advantage of the newly developed barbed wire, hemmed in so that his stock could not water where it had always gone, he was infuriated. He promptly got down off his horse and cut the wire, and if the nester remonstrated he was offtimes burned out. The rancher looked on him as a johnny-come-lately, an upstart with no real title to the land, much less to the water.

One of the greatest irritants was the railroad which insisted on fencing its right-of-way. This was a nuisance to the cowman who owned pasturage on either side of the rails. It was a real problem when the good range was on the south side of the tracks and all the water on the north. For the herder who had to move a thousand head of spooky steers to market, bumping against the twin fences was especially maddening. And even the cowboy riding 'cross country hated the sight of the railway with its strongly barricaded lines. He got down, as did the cowman, and simply cut the fence. The railroads maintained repair gangs, called section gangs, at intervals along the rails. It was the job of these little crews to keep the tracks in shape. During the two decades from 1880 to 1900, one of the biggest chores done by the section gangs was to mend fence.

During the eighties the bigger ranchers came to accept fences as a necessary evil and even commenced to see the advantages of the hemmed-in pasture. It, for one thing, reduced the man-power needed to manage the cattle. When a herd was turned out in a ten-thousand-acre pasture which had a fence on all four sides, it not only kept the animals from drifting on to distant ranges, but it also reduced the number of cowboys needed to watch over them. Along with this it kept the cows from mixing with the herds of neighboring ranchers and thus made it easier at round-up time to separate the cows and calves from those of other owners. Finally it reduced rustling, for the cow-thief did not particularly like to operate inside a barbed wire enclosure. As these advantages became more and more apparent the big cow men of Texas became more or less reconciled to the fencing of the range.

This is not to say that all Texas stockmen agreed. A great many of the smaller fry, the fellows with perhaps no more than ten thousand acres or so, did not like it. What the fence did was to restrict him narrowly to his own acres. These would be insufficient to run his cattle profitably, and to graze his stock he had always been accustomed to let them range freely. Most of the time off his own ranch and onto his neighbors. The same was true of water. His stock would drift off the home ranch, and after months of feeding afield would go into water where it was easiest found. The extensive fencing of the range stopped all of this. Now, instead of grazing across three ranches and watering at a spring some ten miles from the home ranch, the cows would be fetched up short against a series of barbed wire fences.

Texas in the eighties and nineties was filled with a lot of hard customers who seldom hesitated to resort to Winchester and six-shooter to gain their own ends. The advent of barbed wire was the signal for a lot of gunplay, generally along the fence lines and around the waterholes. And most of the shooting was done by the small stockman who hotly resented the loss of free range. When shooting did not solve the impasse he took to carrying a pair of fencing pliers, with a big wire cutting edge on them, on his saddle. When he came to a barbed wire barrier he simply got down off his horse and snipped his way through.

Not all the nesters took the fence cutting lying down. Ofttimes, when a homesteader had built a fence about a waterhole, he lay near the hole with his Winchester cradled in his arm and fought off the rancher and his men who came to cut their way in to the precious water. Such a nester had to be tough because he was invariably badly outnumbered and even though he might stand off the raiders today the next week they'd return and burn him out and sometimes gun him down if he again offered resistance.

By 1885 the fence cutting had resolved itself into a war generally between the bigger ranchers and the smaller ones. By this time the large spreads had found that the fenced pasture was an advantage. The smaller cowman had likewise learned that he was shut off from both extended range and water. The latter took exception to this, and he organized into gangs that rode out after nightfall and cut his big neighbor's wire. This was done systematically and ofttimes on large scale. The raiders would commence on a fence that was perhaps ten miles in length and would in a single night sever every panel of the barbed strands for three miles or so. In the Nueces Country, Frank Smith fenced a pasture with a four-strand fence. It had scarcely been strung when the fence cutters, working at night, cut all four strands along one entire side of the pasture. It was replaced and within two weeks had been cut again. For the third time it was replaced, and despite the fact that Smith put riders out to guard the wire it was again destroyed.

The depredations of the fence cutters got so bad that the state governor finally took a hand. The legislature passed a law making the cutting of a fence a felony. This was intended to throw fear into the night riders, but if anything it had the effect of encouraging them to greater destruction. The Rangers were called into the picture and were put to work.

The Rangers have an outstanding reputation for doing a job. When cattle are stolen, or contraband is smuggled, when killers are on the loose, or banks are robbed the hard-riding, fast-shooting lawmen invariably get their man. It may take many days of strenuous effort, days filled with rough going and danger, but the outlaw who escapes the Ranger nemesis is indeed rare. That is, all but the fence busters.

When the governor insisted that the state legislature make it a felony to cut a barbed wire fence and thereafter put the rangers on the job of apprehending the wrong-doers he thought he had solved the problem. Between the gravity of the offense plus the reputation of his elite force he believed that no more fences would be breeched. He could not have been more mistaken.

The adjutant general sent his officers into the field in pairs. They were disguised as ordinary cowboys, farm laborers, door-to-door peddlers, and one pair ran a medicine show! But the successes of these undercover agents was small indeed! They found they could get into the area where fences were chopped up almost every night, and could become acquainted with numbers of the fence cutters, but to penetrate these gangs—usually numbering only three or four—was next to impossible. The night riders would talk about their depredations, even brag about them, but when it came to taking along a newcomer to the neighborhood that was something else again. He was mistrusted even though he had a good cover story, and for that very reason the Rangers were more often than not frustrated.

When they did get the goods on a fence cutter and he was brought to trial it was found that on almost every jury there were one or two members who secretly sympathized with the defendant, and these jurymen voted for acquittal, thus neatly hanging the jury. It was a trying time in the cow country.

Captain John Hughes, it will be remembered, had D Company of the Rangers. His first sergeant was Ira Aten. Now Aten had been in the force for seven years, and he was a ring-tailed tooter. He had been through a score of gunfights and seemed to have a penchant for breeding shooting scrapes. He liked to do gun battle, he had more than once confessed, and it may have been this enjoyment of the fight that saw him so continually embroiled. Aten remained in the Rangers for eight years and then got into the cow business in the Texas Panhandle. Here he prospered, and after a number of years he migrated to California where he was quite successful in the construction trades, in banking, and other enterprise. He died a wealthy man. His son Ira, Jr. stuck with the cow business, and for many years he managed one of the biggest ranches in New Mexico, the Vermejo.

Anyway, when it fell to the lot of the Rangers to do something about the fence busting, the adjutant general selected, among others, the first sergeant of Hughes' company, Ira Aten. Along with Aten he also sent Jim King, another member of D Company. These worthies were to go into Navarro County, and working under cover, were to learn the identities of the principal depreda-tors, worm into their confidences, accompany them on their fence cutting parties, and thereafter swear out warrants for their arrest. Navarro County had a bad reputation not only for the amount of wire that was destroyed but also as the home ground of large numbers of exceedingly bad citizens. Outlaws who had prices on their heads, gunfighters and killers who did not stop at simple fence destruction but also stuck up lone travelers, burned homesteads, sometimes shot the occupants, rustled horses, cows, pigs, and goats, and shot it out with the sheriff and his deputies. Into this hotbed one day rode a pair of young fellows who looked like they were just out of Arkansas. Their team was a horse and a mule, both poor and fleabitten, the harness a patchwork of worn leather and rope lines, the wagon a rickety Indian wagon about to fall apart. In the bed was a sketchy cooking outfit, a tarp-enshrouded bedroll, an old Winchester rifle, some odds and ends of clothing, and a half-sack of corn. The men looked more like farmers than cowboys, and indeed with battered straw hats and ill-fitting brogans, raised no suspicions at all. Actually here were Iran Aten and Jim King. They went into camp near Mexia and commenced to get acquainted in a cautious, farmer-boy way.

This pause gained them little. After a few days they moved on to Richland, and there King went to work in a cotton gin and Aten agreed to pick thirty-five acres of cotton. They had no trouble in making the acquaintance of some of the better known fence cutters in the area, but these fellows were rightfully suspicious of newcomers. The sheriff, who had not been advised that the Rangers were on hand, let drop the word that he had heard from Austin that detectives were in the country on the lookout for fence-choppers and cow rustlers. This made the job of our pair of lawmen all the more difficult.

The officers had no better success in Richland and finally moved to the Love Ranch where they went to work as cowboys. The owners, a partnership, had suffered a lot of fence loss and were heartily in sympathy with the activities of the Rangers. Aten told them who they were. Having given up worming their way into the confidence of the fence gang, Aten and King took to laying out at night at a common fence corner, the juncture of four pastures, and here they would listen for sabotage along the barbed wire. Aten had his Model 73 and King had a double-barreled 10-gauge. According to letter reports sent at irregular intervals to Austin, Aten was dead set on killing a fence buster or two. He simply ached to come down on a crew while it was busy at its nefarious play. Finally one night he and King heard the unmistakable sounds of the big pliers. Barbed wire is stretched with a set of mechanical stretchers until it is so taut it will hum like a violin string when struck. When the big fencing pliers sever the strands it gives off a musical note which will carry for hundreds of yards. The sounds which reached the ears of the alert Rangers were those of a considerable gang.

Not bothering to catch up their horses the Rangers ran down the fence, the Winchester in Aten's hands held at the ready, and Jim King with the old double-10 swinging along at the high port. The fence destroyers were so involved that Aten and King were among them before they knew they had company. On the command "Hands up" all hell broke loose!

The gang consisted of five members, and all were dismounted and busy with the pliers. While one man chopped the wire in a panel, the others hurried ahead of him, each taking a panel which is normally about thirty-two feet of fencing. As a result of this the gang was scattered, and Aten and King corralled only three. The others took to their heels, and when they reached the first rise, commenced to shoot back into the darkness, unmindful that they might hit their compatriots. The Rangers did not bother to return the fire. They handcuffed their prisoners together, inquired the whereabouts of their horses, gathered up all animals, leaving the two missing members on the range afoot, and moved all night to lodge their law-breakers in the county jail by sunup. The cat was out of the bag then. Word spread like wildfire that the fence busters had been caught redhanded by a pair of Rangers who were working in the country under cover. Aten and King had to move on. Once their identity was known, their further worth at least in Navarro County was dubious. Aten had vowed to the adjutant general that he was going to kill a fence cutter, but when the opportunity presented itself he had held his fire.

Over a period of months the pair were again assigned to an area in another part of the state where fences were continually destroyed. By this time the pair and most especially Aten had grown heartily sick of the long interminable nights of lying along the fence waiting for the cutters who never came. He wrote the adjutant general and told him he had a belly full of the business. He would rather, he wrote, be in Austin on a private's pay of $30 monthly than out here on the fence detail at $50. If he was not pulled off the detail pretty soon, he was going to dump six-shooter and Winchester in the campfire and ride away to a quiet little nester's shack he had in the Panhandle and call it quits. These dire threats had utterly no effect on headquarters. Aten and King were left on the job and despite the monotony of the task they stuck with it.

Then Aten thought of a new tack. He wrote in his next rambling letter-form report that he had invented a dynamite bomb which he was going to attach to the fences and when the cutters passed that way they would be smeared all over that end of Texas. In his first report he alluded to this dynamite bomb but did not explain how it was designed nor how it would function. In a subsequent memo he went into more detail.

He had gotten an old double-barreled shotgun and into either tube he had affixed a dynamite cap. Just ahead of the cap he had stuffed the bores with dynamite. The weapon was then set up in a box and box and gun buried beneath the wire. To the trigger he fastened a string which in turn was tied to a loose post. When the wire was cut the post would tumble over and this would pull the triggers on the gun which in turn would permit the hammers to fall, the firing pins striking the dynamite caps in turn would set off the explosive. It is pretty doubtful if Aten ever ran a field test of his infernal machine. The chances are that the whole thing was the result of too much brooding during the long night watches on some rancher's fence line. At any rate when the second report reached the adjutant general about the dynamite bomb, as Aten referred to his device, he was admonished by telegram to take up any such bombs he might have planted and not to set any regardless of the situation and his own feelings. Shortly thereafter Aten and King were withdrawn from the fence busting detail. They never returned to the job, giving over all their information, their contacts, and their list of suspects to an incoming pair.

The problem of fence cutting went on until the turn of the century. By that time all the better cow range had been put under wire. It was the new order of things, and despite the turbulence of the era and the resolve of a lot of exceedingly tough customers to prevent grass and water from being claimed by a few to the exclusion of the many, it came to pass. That the Rangers had but small success in their attempts to protect the pastures and their enclosures can be attributed to the circumstances of the situation. There were literally thousands upon thousands of miles of fences; there were but a few hundred Rangers. The physical impossibility of patrolling the limitless strands of barbed lines made their job a herculean one even from the beginning. The fence-cutting war was one of those affrays in which the Rangers came off second best.

22

LOS BANDIDOS

That sizeable strip of Texas real estate, with all its mesquite, greasewood, and cactus, that is flanked on the north by the Nueces and on the south by the Rio Grande has always been a battleground. It was settled by a breed of latino who outnumbered the gringos by a majority of at least ten to one, who spoke an alien tongue, and who held allegiance to a foreign power. These dark-hued riders called their land "Medio Mejico"—"Half Mexico." Their hatred of the *Tejanos,* the native Texans, was the shooting kind.

Since the inconclusive finish of the United States–Mexican War, the enmity between the two peoples had been a brittle thing, fanned by literally hundreds of fights and killings. The Mexicans rustled cattle, horses, and other livestock, and the Texans in riding after them shot and hanged those they caught. Riders along the turbulent Rio Grande, on either side of the boundary stream, were bushwhacked and shot simply because they represented the enemy. From the death of Porfirio Diaz, Mexican president and strong man who ruled the country with an iron hand for thirty years, there occurred one revolution after another. Throughout the years from the turn of the century until the late 1920s, Mexico was in a turmoil. This unrest spawned banditry, looting, and murder, and a great deal of this marauding occurred along the Rio Grande, especially in that before-mentioned strip which lies south of the Nueces River—Medio Mejico, where the sympathies of the residents were written large in gunsmoke and a bullet awaited the unwary Tejano.

237

Pancho Villa kicked things off when he raided Columbus, New Mexico, in 1916. The raid was a long way removed from our particular part of Texas, but the foray into sleepy Columbus, the subsequent bombardment of Vera Cruz by our warships, and the landing of bluejackets and marines together with the punitive invasion by General Pershing in search of Villa all kindled fires of animosity and revenge in the hearts of many coffee-colored inhabitants of not only Medio Mejico but the principal land as well. Raids across the Rio Grande grew in numbers and intensity. Americans resident of the Land of Mañana had to abandon homes and business and scurry across the frontier, and relations between the two countries and most especially betwixt the hot-headed Texans and the equally brash Mexicanos were tense indeed.

The first great World War got off to a bloody beginning, and the Germans, with an intuitive understanding of where the sympathies of the United States would lie, had infiltrated Mexico with large numbers of espionage agents. These hearties worked their way up to the border and endeavored to create an atmosphere of tension and distrust between the two countries. About this time, a Mexican by the name of Basilio Ramos was arrested. A resident of the Medio Mejico strip, this worthy was a first-water scoundrel. He dodged back and forth between Mexico and Texas, was twice arrested by the Mexican authorities and unceremoniously booted back into Texas. In January, 1915, he was hauled off to jail by Tom Mayfield, an ex-Ranger who at the time of the arrest was a deputy sheriff in Hidalgo County. On Ramos was found the Plan of San Diego.

The Plan of San Diego, written in Spanish and signed by eight Mexicans, all of them residents of this side of the Rio Grande, provided that on February 20, 1915, the Mexicans would rise in arms and slay all the hated gringos. After this had been cleaned up they would declare the independence of Texas, California, Arizona, New Mexico, and Colorado. Their army would be the Military Forces of Races and Peoples and would sport a red flag with the words "Equality and Independence" emblazoned upon it. Monies to support the army would come from arbitrary levies placed upon the cities and states. No one was to be enrolled as a volunteer in the liberation forces except Mexicans, Negroes, and Indians. The Indians were to be given back all their lands.

The five states were to be annexed to Mexico, and once consolidated the forces would then go on to capture six more states. These would be Oklahoma, Utah, Wyoming, Kansas, Nebraska, and South Dakota. These were to be handed over to the Negroes who had by this time joined the liberation forces, and they would be encouraged to organize a nation which would serve as a buffer between the United States and the new republic.

While relations between the United States and Mexico were strained as a result of the Villa raid and the resulting actions of our government, there was no indication that the Plan of San Diego had any official backing by the Mexican government. It had been conceived in Medio Mejico and was simply another indication of the bad blood and strained relations which existed between the latinos who resided there and the Texans.

By the late spring of 1915, bands of raiding bandits, numbering from a score to as many as 150 riders were daily fording the Rio Grande and openly rustling cows, horses, pigs, mules, and goats. Isolated stores and ranch houses were looted and burned, cowboys caught out alone were shot or hanged. Of the two principal gangs one was headed by Luis de la Rosa and the other by Aniceto Pizaña; both had the title of "General" and both claimed they were furthering the Plan de San Diego.

During July a cowpuncher riding fence was captured by the Pizaña bandits and summarily executed. The same gang, about forty of them, all mounted, rode into the Los Indios Ranch and shot the foreman. He was suspected of informing the Rangers of the activities of the bandits. One of the gangs apparently planned to rob the train, for a railroad trestle was burned near the little pueblo of San Sebastian.

Word got to the Rangers that Luis de la Rosa was shacked up at a ranch some four miles from Paso Real in the Arroyo Colorado. A posse consisting of Cameron County deputies, Rangers and cowboys rode down on the place, and when they were fired upon charged the main headquarters. Two bandits were killed, and when the officers broke into the 'dobe building there was a gunfight with Desederio Flores, a lieutenant of Luis de la Rosa. He was killed.

During mid-August about twenty heavily armed bandits rode into San Sebastian and robbed the only store. There was a feed mill in the pueblo, and they rode over to it and fed their horses. Two small ranchers, Albert Austin and his teen-age son, Charley, were there grinding feed. When Elmer Millard drove up in a wagon the Mexicans forced the Austins into the wagon, drove out to a stand of cottonwoods on the edge of the town, and there hanged them both. Millard went free. As the Texans swung beneath the cottonwood their bodies were riddled with bullets.

An old Dodge touring car driven by Art Pollard was approaching Los Fresnos, and bandits lying in the mesquite alongside the road fired into the car and wounded the driver. The nightwatchman at Lyford, Abe Wilson, was slugged and shot as he sprawled on the ground.

One of the divisions of the mammoth King Ranch is Las Norias. A bandit troop of more than fifty riders rode into Los Cerritos, southeast of the Las Norias headquarters. Here they captured three of the King Ranch cowboys. One of the cowboys, Pedro Longorio, counted the bandits and found there were fifty-two of them. He looked over their armament and reported afterward they were armed with the Winchester Model 94, the Model 92, and the remainder had the 7mm. Mauser Model 92 as made in Spain. The raiders had struck El Cerritos at 2:00 A.M. After watering their horses they rode on toward Las Norias.

At the Las Norias headquarters were Mark Hines, Porter Gay, Joe Taylor, George Forbes, Frank Martin, Lauro Cavazos, Albert Edmonds, the Negro cook, together with a squad of eight soldiers under the command of Corporal Watson Adams. There were several women in the big rambling two-story house, and in the workers' shacks against the railroad were a half dozen Mexican laborers and their families. During the subsequent fight a bandit bullet whistled through the thin walls of a jacal and killed a woman.

At Las Norias the day before had been Ranger captains Henry

Ransom and Monroe Fox, each with portions of their companies. On the day of the gun battle, both officers had taken their detachments and left the headquarters on an extended scout for the bandits. The outlaws saw Ransom and his fellows at a distance of a mile and hid in a motte until the Rangers passed. They then moved in on Las Norias.

It was eight o'clock in the morning, and everyone had breakfasted. The soldiers, encamped near the corrals, were first to see the approaching horsemen, and on the command of Corporal Adams they gathered up their Springfields and took cover in a deployed formation against the railroad embankment. The cowboys at the main house took stations both upstairs and down, and the firing became general. The Mexicans were under the command of Tony Rocha and Desidario Morado. The vaqueros captured at Los Cerritos and strangely enough released said that the pair quarreled almost continuously. During the course of the attack on Las Norias, Morado in a foolhardy act of *machismo* galloped up to the main corrals and was shot and killed by the defenders.

The bandits believed they would surprise the people at the headquarters and attempted to ride into the place without firing a shot. This failed because of the alertness of the squad of soldiers who shot them down as they galloped forward and as they turned and beat a hasty and unseemly retreat. After that the bandits dismounted and tried to infiltrate the corrals. The ground about Las Norias is flat, and the only cover is from the railroad embankment. While some of the raiders did reach the corrals and managed to shoot George Forbes and Frank Martin as well as two of the infantrymen, they were beaten back with losses. The battle went on for two hours when it ended quite as suddenly as it had begun. The Mexicans had a bugler; he sounded recall whereupon the entire band faded into the mesquite.

The defenders had killed ten of the bandits and wounded a number of others. The only person killed of the Las Norias contingent was a noncombatant, Manuela Flores, wife of a railroad laborer. Among the defenders there were mostly Winchester Model 95 .30-30 rifles, but there were also three Model 95 rifles in .30-40 caliber. The Rangers had by this time almost entirely abandoned the .30-30 in favor of the Model 95 in carbine length.

The widespread depredations of the bandits, most of the bands crossing out of Mexico but sometimes joined by outlaws from Medio Mejico, had the entire Texan population very much on edge. A good many ranchers, who knew they could not hope to hold off the marauders who would outnumber them by twenty to one, moved into the small towns and abandoned their ranches. Others simply moved in together and planned to shoot it out. When they had to work cattle or repair fence or windmill, they rode together. The army had patrols constantly moving up and down the Rio Grande, but because of the espionage system working for the bandits it was simple to keep them informed by agents on either side of the river and thus avoid the military. The Rangers were in the area in numbers, but the country was large and their numbers comparatively small. It was easy to dodge the officers just as the gangs evaded the soldiers.

Directly after the scrap at Las Norias a band of thirty raiders hit the pueblo called Ojo de Agua. They looted the only store in town and on riding away set it on fire. Instead of riding for the Rio Grande they commenced a long looping return, and before they could turn back they were followed by a detachment of cavalry under Captain Frank McCoy. With the soldiers was a posse under the charge of Sheriff A. Y. Baker. The pursuers rode hard and hit the bandits at Los Cavazos, a crossing much favored by the long riders. A running battle ensued and the Mexicans lost twelve killed. A number were wounded, but just how many was never determined. When the bandits got safely on the far bank they took cover and continued the fight. The Americans held up at the banks of the Rio Grande; they were forbidden by the state department to pursue their adversaries into the Land of Mañana.

During the latter stages of the fight, Captain McCoy caught the reflection of some bright object in a tree several hundred yards behind the entrenched bandits. He studied the tree for a long time with his binoculars and finally determined that it was a man with field glasses. He was not firing, so McCoy decided he was selecting targets for his bully boys on the ground below. In the Third Cavalry detachment was Paul Schaeffer, a sergeant who was the cavalry rifle champion at the time. "Schaeffer," commanded the captain, "there is a man in that big tree over there. He is in the first big fork. Give him a try." Schaeffer, who was armed with the 1903 Springfield, guessed the range at 600 yards, adjusted his sight, got into his sling, and in the prone position fired three fast shots at the observer. On the third round the bandit was seen to tumble out of the tree. The next day the military commander at Reynosa, on the Mexican side, complained to the U.S. Consul that one of his officers had been killed while peacefully strolling along the Rio Grande near Los Cavazos.

Bill Sterling, a rancher in the area, and afterward a Ranger for more than thirty years, had this to say about the firearms used by these border raiders:

The revolutionists were armed with a wide variety of guns. These had been acquired by purchase, capture or theft, as the opportunity presented. Their most popular rifle was the light handy .30-30 Winchester carbine. It was designed strictly for sporting purposes and would quickly overheat from rapid fire. Many bandits used the Mauser which was the standard rifle of the Mexican army. One of the bandits had come into possession of a .405 Winchester designed especially to kill elephants. On one occasion the Rangers were in a fight and were lying under the partial shelter of a river bank. Bullets from across the river were flying overhead. Ranger Joe Davenport declared that each bullet sang its own song. He explained, "When a bullet from that old .405 elephant gun goes over it moans in deep bass tones *C-u-i-d-a-d-o* (Look Out!) and the pointed Mauser whines *G-r-i-n-g-o!*"

Down toward San Juanito, in Hidalgo County, Jason McAllen had a ranch. It was not a big outfit, and he was in the habit of staying a few days on the place and then going back into town to remain with his family. He had two cowboys, but he kept them in line camps and was most of the time at the headquarters place by himself. That is, all alone except for an elderly Mexican woman, Maria de Agras. Now Maria was a sturdy character. She was Mexican born and raised and had been a *soldadera*—a woman soldier—in the Madero revolution. One day she had full opportunity to recall former experiences.

Jason McAllen was at the headquarters place. It was midafternoon and after the fashion of a good many west Texan ranchers he was taking a siesta. Maria was busy in the kitchen and hard at work when she heard sounds of creaking saddle leather in the front yard. She went to the door, and there stood a bandit and behind him were twenty leering followers. The bandido *jefe* asked for the *patron*—for the owner. Maria knew they would shoot down the gringo if he were so foolish as to come to the entrance. She excused herself and scurried back to the bedroom, grabbing up an old Winchester Model 1897 pump repeating shotgun which rested behind the door. She shook her patron awake, hurriedly babbled the nature and intent of the callers in the front yard, and pressed the scattergun into the hands of McAllen.

The Texan strode to the door, threw it open and fired five charges of double-ought buckshot into the midst of the marauders. The first blast killed Gregorio Aleman, the bandit leader, and the remaining blue whistlers so grievously wounded two others of the gang that they succumbed that night. The volley scattered the riders like quail.

McAllen slammed and bolted the door and went to the nearest window. The Mexicans took cover behind the outbuildings which scattered about the main house. They commenced to fire on the house. Maria de Agras dragged up three Model 94 .30-30 rifles, and as Jason McAllen answered the fire, she kept the rifles loaded. After fifteen minutes of hot battle the rancher turned a rifle over to his valiant cook, and he went to the phone to see if the line was cut. By a stupid oversight the bandits had not bothered to sever the wires. He called his neighbor Sam Lane and told him to get in touch with the Rangers. "I'd call 'em myself, Sam," he explained, "but these cholos are a-keepin' me too busy." Sam agreed to round up a relief force.

After a couple of hours of give-and-take firing the bandits melted into the brush. The Rangers and the local sheriff arrived by late evening. The rancher had killed another bandit near his corrals. The band when riding off left both their dead where they fell. A horse was also shot, and it lay in the front yard. From cartridges found on the bodies both were armed with the Model 92 Winchester .44-40 caliber. The raiders had carried away the rifles before they departed.

The foray against the McAllen ranch came in September. During October the raiders came within six miles of the city of Brownsville and there pulled a rail on the St. Louis, Brownsville, and Mexico Railroad and wrecked the train. It was near the Olmitos switch. The locomotive overturned, killing the engineer and badly injuring the fireman. The bandits, once they had halted the train, climbed aboard and went through the passenger cars robbing the passengers. They found four soldiers aboard who were returning from furlough. They shot the soldiers leaving all of them for dead. Only one was actually killed; the others, although seriously wounded, survived. Several civilians were also shot. Dr. E. S. McClain was killed, and Jack Klieber and Harry Wallis, the latter a former Ranger, were wounded. The remarkable thing about the raid was that no one among the passengers was armed. The bandits departed leisurely.

The Rangers rode onto the scene that same night and commenced to investigate. They found that various Mexicans on this side of the Rio Grande were implicated. Three were found holed up in a jacal (shanty) only a few miles from the scene of the wreck and were all summarily shot down. Informers told Captain Ransom of the Rangers that there had been sixty bandits in the raid and they were led by Luis de la Rosa and Aniceto Pizaña, already mentioned in these pages.

Later that month an outpost of the Third Cavalry was hit at Ojo de Agua. With the troopers was a detachment of the Signal Company of the regiment. When the bandits swept into the outpost the first thing they did was to put the telegraph line running back to G Troop headquarters at Mission out of order. There was another cavalry outpost only two miles away. Hearing the firing these troopers, twelve of them under the command of Captain W. J. Scott, saddled up and rode over. By the time they arrived the Mexicans had ridden off for the Rio Grande. Of the fifteen men in the outpost three had been killed and eight wounded. The bandits left seven dead, and rumor had it that seven wounded were carted away by their fellows.

The winter that followed was a chaotic period for the Texans along the lower Rio Grande. Isolated ranches were raided, small towns were not safe, the railroad operated on a hit-or-miss time table never certain when a trestle would be burned or rails pried up. The more timid of the outlying people moved into the bigger towns and abandoned their holdings. The Rangers were reinforced and rode continuously. The cavalry put out extensive patrols, and these were doubled as the depredations became more severe. During the spring of 1916, the army put Brigadier General James Parker in command of the Brownsville District. Not a young man, this officer had fought the Indians and he knew something about guerrilla fighting. After riding out all the territory comprising Medio Mejico, Parker was ready to act. The first thing he did was to saddle up and with a proper escort he jogged over the international bridge at Brownsville and made a call on the Mexican commandant in Matamoros. This man, General Alfredo Ricaut, knew all about the activities of the numerous roving bands of renegades but he professed not to be able to do anything about their activities.

General Parker informed him what he intended to do. He said that despite the objections of the Secretary of State, William Jennings Bryan, the next time word reached him that a Mexican bandit gang entered the United States, he would start off in pursuit of them and he would not stop at the Rio Grande but would run them to earth even though they might flee a hundred miles into the interior of Mexico. To this the Mexican raised his eyebrows and said nothing.

During June, as if to test the intentions of the American commander, a band of fifty-odd raiders forded the Rio Grande about twelve miles above Brownsville at a favorite crossing called El Ranchito. They struck off toward the interior of the country and by daylight ran spang into a detachment of Parker's cavalry under Lieutenant Art Newman. A fight developed, and a bandit was killed by the cavalrymen. The remainder of the band turned back, slowly, toward the river.

Newman relayed word of the battle and the direction of the retreat to General Parker. Back came the order to pursue the bandits and punish them. If they first gained the Rio Grande the Third Cavalrymen were to press on across the river until they caught the raiders. This Lieutenant Newman and his troopers did. They found the Mexicans in camp at Los Pedernales, a ranch some twenty-five miles below the border. In the fight which developed the bandits lost two more men killed. The cavalry suffered no casualties.

Before Newman and his troopers could pull back from Los Pedernales, General Parker sent reinforcements. These were considerable and consisted of a full squadron of cavalry, elements of the Fourth Infantry, and bits and pieces of support units, to include a signal detachment, quartermaster, and engineer elements. This force crossed about a dozen miles up river from Fort Brown and proceeded toward Las Pasculas, a notorious ranch hangout of the raiders. It was evident to Mexican outposts that the sizeable American force was headed for Matamoros and would ride into that city on the morrow.

During the crossing, Mexican soldiers under the revolutionary president, Carranza, fired on the rear guard of the cavalry. Orders were given to charge the Carranzistas and this was done. The Mexicans took to their heels at once, and the cavalry had a long stern chase on their hands. Despite the speed of the retreat and the fact that the cavalry had to fire at the gallop two Carranzistas were killed. The Americans lost not a man.

The Third Cavalry was recalled by the War Department. Not, however, until it had occupied Mexican soil for twenty-four hours. The cheerful willingness of General Parker to ride into the sister republic in pursuit of bandit raiders had a most salubrious effect all up and down the Rio Grande. Raids tapered off and life, over a period of months, commenced to return to some semblance of normality. It required a couple of years to see a full termination of the bandit forays but these gradually pinched out. Relations between the residents of the two countries did not improve materially, and it took a full generation from the hectic days of 1915–16 before a man riding his back pasture could be sure when he saw riders approaching him that he was entirely safe. To this very day the trusty Winchester rides under the saddle fender or hung on the rack in the back of the pickup truck just to be sure that the odds are kept reasonably even.

23

CHASING VILLA

When Pancho Villa, the Mexican revolutionary, guerrilla and bandit leader, sacked Columbus, New Mexico, the "El Paso Times" said there were 1,500 Villista troops involved. The U.S. Army had a troop from the 13th Cavalry Regiment guarding the town. Now a full troop numbered 160 men but actually there were only 62 troopers present and this included both men and officers.

But while we are getting down to cases, the Mexicans actually numbered only 185 and Villa was nowhere around. He had elected to send his raiders under his righthand bower, Col. Julian Cardenas, a trusted member who usually had command of the "Dorados," the palace guard.

It was the 9th of March, 1916, and the attackers moved up under the cover of a raging sandstorm. They had encamped scant miles below Palomas, the Mexican pueblo below Columbus, and, with darkness to hide them and the few scant lights of the settlement to guide on, moved to within a couple of miles of the border. Here Cardenas divided his forces. He took a hundred riders and the single Chauchat 8mm light machine gun; the remaining 85 bravos he tolled off to Col. Candelario Cervantes with orders to come onto the town from the left flank. For himself and most of the raiders, he moved off to the right flank where a low hill offered a site for the machine gun.

Sgt. Ellery Waters, "C" Troop, the 13th, was sergeant of the guard that night. He had five posts and had just completed an inspection of the last of his pickets when the Villistas struck.

Unbelievably the Americans had all their arms locked in the orderly room. With tension at white hot heat it is inconceivable how any commander would have insisted his troopers lock up their rifles.

Sgt. Waters, armed with the .45 M1911 service pistol, ran for the orderly room for he had the keys. He unlocked the place as Mexican riders spewed into the company street. Waters stood in the doorway and banged off all 21 rounds he had been issued. Troopers trickled in and caught up their rifles, but not before 1st Sgt. Norwell Burns unlocked the circular steel racks which held the rifles.

The 13th Cavalry still could not go into action because the ammunition was locked in the supply room and only the supply sergeant, Hampton Armitage, had the key. Sgt. Armitage was nowhere to be found. He turned up next morning with the story that he had been kidnapped. Actually he was hiding under the Southern Pacific water tank.

The 1st Sergeant and the sergeant of the guard, Waters, broke down the door and issued bandoleers of .30-06 cartridges to those troopers who answered the assembly call. The truth is not a Villista was killed by the U.S. Army during the raid. For all that eight troopers were killed and 14 were wounded. Civilian casualties were even higher, nine killed. The raiders burned three buildings in the tiny village, looted three stores, and held sway for almost two hours. Then they faded across the international boundary.

Francisco "Pancho" Villa nee Doroteo Arango, bandit, terrorist and revolutionary had his sights set of the presidency of Mexico. He was from Chihuahua, the largest state and the northernmost and he very well controlled that part of Mexico. But the southern portions were under the grip of another revolutionary, Venustiano Carranza. When the United States elected to recognize Carranza as the provisional president, Villa was deeply angered and he determined to create tension between the two countries by committing his soldiery to a raid across the U.S.-Mexico frontier. The strike at Columbus, small, unimportant, and isolated was the result. Columbus had little reason for existing. It was a port of entry, 30 miles south of the larger town of Deming, and a hundred miles north of the sizeable town of Casas Grandes, Chihuahua; the population at the time of the blood-spilling was 276 souls.

This was not the bandit chieftan's first effort at inciting the United States to armed intervention. The 13th of January, barely two months before the raid at Columbus, Villa's Dorados—the Golden Ones—had flagged the Noreste de Mexico passenger train to a halt near Santa Isabela, scant miles north of Chihuahua City, searched the train and hustled 17 Americans off the train. These bewildered and complaining prisoners were marched into a nearby arroya and all were summarily executed. One man feigned death and subsequently walked away from the death site. This wanton act of cold-blooded murder on the part of the revolutionary leader incited the United States and there was open talk of war. The Carranza Government profusely apologized and promised to run the gangsters to earth. The Wilson administration accepted the apologies and the promises and any plans for a march into the land of manana was held in abeyance.

Now the Columbus incident was the proper spark to prod President Wilson and his pacifist secretary of war, Newton D. Baker, to action. A cable to the Southern Department, Fort Sam Houston, Texas, directed Maj. Gen. Fred Funston, to take immediate and energetic action. Funston, a going-hell-for-leather sort, ordered Brig. Gen. John Pershing, commanding officer at Fort Bliss, Texas (and nearest Columbus) to proceed at once to the town and assume the direction of the punitive expedition. It was determined that American forces would pursue Villa into Mexico and continue that pursuit until the terrorist leader was brought to bay.

General Funston designated elements of the 13th, 7th and 10th Cavalry Regiments to compose a part of the expeditionary force and as well there was the 6th and 16th Infantry Regiments together with two batteries of field artillery, both from the 6th Field. As well, an entire battalion of the 4th Field Artillery was named as a part of the task force.

For the first time in American military history the 1st Aero Squadron with a total of eight aircraft was designated to report to Pershing at Columbus. In command of Capt. Benjamin D. Foulois, a pioneer pilot with the rickety and untested Jennies,

Foulois was assigned to the Signal Corps and was on hand to act as an observer, liaison link between the commander and his forward elements, and to convey messages. The fragile little ships, underpowered and undependable, were soon reduced to two flyable machines. But it was a beginning for the future American air force, even though, possibly, hardly an auspicious one.

Whether Fred Funston's plan or that of the commander-on-the-ground, Pershing, the invasion force was divided into two elements: an Eastern column and a Western column, the two separated by 60 miles. The Western force was to push off from the Culberson Ranch in the Hachita Block, and the Eastern, of course, from Columbus.

The Eastern contingent managed to walk into the land of manana on the 14th of the month, some five days after the attack. During the interim, President Wilson had wrung out an agreement with the provisional president of strife-torn Mexico, to permit the Pershing forces to pursue the renegade Villa. President Carranza had stipulated when agreeing that the Americans would not enter any towns; neither could the forces utilize the existing Mexican railnet. A copy of the agreement was carried by the commanders of all major units in the Pershing expedition. For all that when the 950-man force, consisting of cavalry, followed by two packtrains and a troop of mountain artillery, rode up to the pipsqueak pueblo of Palomas, some six miles below the border, the Carranzista commandante with a rag-tag platoon of infantry blocked the way.

A display of the agreement between the countries meant nothing to him. He couldn't read anyway. Instead of brushing him aside, a proper gesture, Pershing took the time to wire Funston back at Fort Sam Houston. The Funston reply, in effect said, "Full steam ahead and to hell with the torpedos." The Mexican soldiery, all barefoot, ragged and tattered, armed with Mausers, Winchesters, Henrys and Lebels stood aside in surly silence as the cavalry pushed on toward Casas Grandes.

The Western group commenced its march at 12:30 p.m. on the 16th. There was no opposition on the part of the Carranza forces. For some reason, possibly to see that the force from Columbus met no opposition from the Mexicans, Pershing held up his departure from Columbus until these troops were on their way. He then drove by Dodge motor car to the Culberson Ranch and made the entry into Chihuahua with this contingent. This was the larger force. It included both the 7th and 10th Cavalry along with a battery of the 6th Field. Pershing had commanded the 10th (the only negro cavalry in the Army) and it may have been that he wanted to be closer to his old command.

The plan was for the two columns to converge at Ascension but word reached the commander that Villa had even then passed Casas Grandes. It was immediately decided that Col. Jim Erwin, who was regimental commander of the 7th, would split off two squadrons and with a total of 657 men and 32 officers attempt to cut Villa off from a retreat into Sonora over the Sierra Madre Mountains.

There followed several days of futile will-of-the-wisp chases by the American forces. The 7th Cavalry found their forced march to block Villa's entry into Sonora a failure. Col. George Dodd, who relieved Erwin, met Col. Umberto Salas with a force of 200 Carranzistas and this worthy informed him that he had skirmished with Villa on the 19th at Namiquipa. The 7th at once turned southward and after fording the Santa Maria River camped near Namiquipa. Intelligence was skimpy and untrustworthy. The entire Mexican nation was hostile toward the gringos and, while there was reason to want Villa captured, the Mexicans, to include the president, wanted to do it themselves.

Meanwhile Villa retreated briskly. Below Namiquipa he suddenly wheeled and with 400 troops against 200 of Col. Salas' Carranzistas, gave them a sound thrashing. He continued southward, finally calling a halt only scant miles north of the sizeable town of Guerrero. He broke his piddling little army down into three strike forces. The first contingent, under Gen. Beltran was sent to attack Miñaca; the second force under Col. Cervantes was to his Guerrero, while the third group was to remain with him as a sort of mobile reserve.

The detachment under Gen. Beltran caught the settlement of Miñaca sound asleep and the garrison surrendered without firing a shot. In Guerrero the Villistas found the same situation. The Carranzistas surrendered. The attempt was then made to overrun

San Ysidro but by this time the garrison was alerted and they drove off the raiders.

The post was commanded by Gen. Jose Cavazos and once he had the Villistas on the run he hotly pursued them. Villa, from an OP near the scene of the battle, saw his people were getting the worst of it so he sent 50 of his Dorados down to turn the Cavazos' flank. This they did but Villa, while riding too close to observe the fray, took a bullet through the calf. It broke the bone and un-horsed him.

Villa was transported to a home in Guerrero and a local doctor was called. He dressed the wound. Col. Dodd, hard riding, heard the news that Villa has been wounded at San Ysidro and, spurring on his exhausted troops, galloped off toward Guerrero, in the hope that at long last he would capture the Mexican outlaw.

The 7th rode 55 miles in 17 hours to reach Guerrero before daylight. A Mexican who guided the troopers became very evasive about just which road should be taken in the darkness to invest the town. As a result Col. Dodd and his exhausted soldiery were compelled to wait until daylight to find for themselves the best approach. When the Villistas saw the U.S. Cavalry approach-ing as skirmishers, the horses at a high trot, they turned tail and ran. During the pursuit, which went on for 10 miles, the 7th Cavalry killed 37 Villistas and the wounded which were collected amounted to 67 casualties. These were turned over to the town as Dodd traveled without anything more than first aid men.

Never after that was Villa able to assemble a force of any con-sequence, neither to oppose the Americans nor to offer battle to the Carranzista. And as a matter of fact he was hard put to stay out of the grasp of the avenging U.S. Cavalry.

Realizing the seriousness of his wound, he early designated Col. Cervantes to assume command of his badly disorganized forces. And as for himself he was loaded in a buckboard by Nicolas Fernandez and with two soldados, an Indian named Cienfuegos and Joaquin Alvarez, they managed to escape the town and spent the first night at Hacienda Cienguita. Next morn-ing they went on to the Sierra del Oro. Villa was moved into a cave and there he remained for three weeks while his leg healed.

Pershing, who most of the time was out of touch with his forward elements, had moved his headquarters in a series of leaps to the tiny pueblo of Bachiniva about 150 miles north of the sizeable town of Parral. Here he sent for Maj. Frank "Tommy" Tompkins and directed the cavalryman to take Troops K and M of the 11th Cavalry and ride to Parral.

"We believe we have good intelligence which indicates Villa will hole up there for further treatment of his wound," Pershing told his subordinate.

Just to be sure that the 11th Cavalry troopers did not bite off more than they could chew, the commanding general also directed Col. Bill Brown of the 10th and Maj. Bob Howze, with other units of the 11th Cavalry, to follow in trail behind Tommy Tompkins.

While Tompkins had a flying start over his support units, Brown's 10th caught up at San Antonio. Word was passed along that indeed Villa had been at San Borja.

At San Borja, which was on a sort of roundabout track to Parral, Maj. Tompkins was stopped by Gen. Jose Cavazos who will be remembered as the commander who first routed the Villista attackers at San Ysidro and during the following battle was badly beaten off by Villa's Dorados, the elite palace guard.

Cavazos told the American officer that he should turn back, that the townspeople and the Carranzistas in the town would most surely attack him if he dared to enter. Tompkins turned aside and went into camp at Santa Rosalia. About that time Col. Brown and his contingent arrived and told Maj. Tompkins they intended to enter Parral via the Valle de Zaragoza.

Tompkins delayed his further advance. On the 10th of April a Mexican who stated he was Capt. Antonio Mesa came into the 11th bivouac and informed Tompkins he was from the Carranzista garrison in Parral and that it would be agreeable for the American troops to enter the town, reprovision, and move on out again.

On the 12th the cavalry squadron rode into Parral and pulled up in front of garrison headquarters. There Major Tompkins was greeted by the commander, Gen. Ismael Lozano. The Mexican professed complete surprise when he was informed that his captain, Antonio Mesa, had assured the Americans they would be welcome in Parral.

"But Senor, I have no officer in this command named Antonio Mesa," he exclaimed.

The American officer explained that all he wanted was to buy some rations for his troops and corn for his badly ridden horses. This the general agreed to. By this time a crowd had gathered about the soldiery and it was glaringly apparent it was a savage, ugly and threatening group.

Interestingly, the mob (for it soon turned into just that) was led by a German woman named Elisa Griensen, married to a Mexican national. This woman was armed with a Mauser rifle and she fired the first shot at the Americans. By this time the cavalry was moving out smartly, escorted by a company of Carranzistas provided by Gen. Lozano.

While shots were fired none of the U.S. troops had been hit but when Maj. Tompkins reached a railroad embankment, which he could see would provide a breastworks for his people, he deployed them and by this time his escort had all evaporated.

Despite the fact that Tompkins now had a thousand Carranzista and sympathetic Parralenses allied against him he did not give the order to return the fire which had killed all his pack mules and had accounted for two wounded troopers. 1st Sgt. Jay Richley stuck his head up above the railroad embankment to see what the enemy was up to and took a bullet through the right eye. His was the first death.

Maj. Tompkins, badly outnumbered, called his bugler and sounded recall. His people mounted up and commenced an orderly withdrawal. The Mexicans, by this time screaming "Matan los gringos cabrones" (kill those American SOB's) pressed closely behind the retreating squadron. The squadron commander fell back to Santa Cruz de Villegas, a village miles north of Parral. Here he set up a strongpoint on the high ground before the pueblo. He had by this time one Pfc. Albert Erickson killed and six wounded as well as one trooper missing.

He sent three troopers on the best horses out of the squadron to find Col. Bill Brown and ask him to send forward reinforcements. Capt. George Rodney, commanding "B" troop of Col. Brown's force, intercepted the hard riding cavalrymen and asked them where they were going in such a tremendous hurry.

"We're lookin' fer the 10th. Maj. Tompkins is surrounded by 'bout ten thousan' Mexicans an' we're goin' fer help."

According to George Rodney, who afterward wrote a book about the punitive expedition, he said, "You bastards are just plain runnin' away. I can tell by looking at you how scared you are."

Col. Brown, when he got word from Capt. Rodney, sent a light squadron under the command of Maj. Charley Young, a Negro officer, and when he got there the Mexicans pulled off about a half-mile. But they continued to fire at the Americans. They kept on shooting until Capt. Aubrey Lippincott (unquestionably the best rifle marksman in the Army of that date) climbed atop an adobe jacal, and in the prone position and with his sling tightened on his rifle, the leaf sight raised and set for 800 yards, proceeded to shoot a Mexican out of the saddle at what had to have been a full half-mile. This had a remarkably salubrious effect on the attackers. They drew off about a mile and went into bivouac.

Six hours later, Col. Brown arrived with the remainder of the regiment and the force remained in position for the next week, stayed until Pershing, under orders from Funston, ordered the cavalry back to San Antonio, Chihuahua.

General Pershing divided his command and by this time, pretty well satisfied he would never bring Villa to bay, assigned the 7th Cavalry to the area near Guerrero, the 5th to the pueblo of Satevo, the 10th to Namiquipa, the 13th to Bustillo, and the 11th to San Borja. While he had the 6th and 16th Infantry Regiments in his command it was simply no country for foot soldiers and these poor doughboys marched southward but played an insignificant part in the actions of the expedition.

At any rate on the 11th of April, the commanding general sent Maj. Bob Howze at the head of six troops and cavalry plus a machine gun platoon toward Cusihuriachic where two loudmouth Villistas, Cruz Dominguez and Julio Acosta, claiming to be in command of a thousand well-armed Villistas, had publicly stated they were making ready to march northward and overrun San Antonio, taking Gen. Pershing captive during the proceedings.

Howze commanded "forward" to his over-strength squadron at 8 a.m. and at midnight he was a bare mile short of the pueblo of Cusihuriahic. The Americans overan a small garrison of Mexican soldados who claimed rather fervently they were Carranzistas. They alleged the Villistas were at a ranch some 20 miles distant.

But they refused to provide guides to lead the troopers to the rancho. Pushing on through the town, and picking up guides enroute, Maj. Howze and his hard-galloping troopers reached the ranch called Ojos Azules (Blue Springs) just after daylight.

With a thousand yards still to go, the Villista pickets saw the approaching horsemen. They fired wildly and raced for their horses which were behind the main house. Howze split his troops, the main force moving around the headquarters to the left and the lesser group to the right. Villistas spewed out of the main building and from around the corrals. They were mercilessly gunned down. Those who managed to reach their mounts attempted to ride away without saddles or bridles. The Mexicans lost 60 dead and 72 wounded. There were seven Carranzista prisoners, all scheduled for execution at daylight. These were released by Maj. Howze.

It was the best bag of the Pershing expedition. Bob Howze, first of a long and distinguished line of Army people, went on to command a division during World War I. His sons saw outstanding service during World War II. Fort Bliss, Texas, long the home of the cavalry, has a stadium named for the family.

An account of the Pershing Penetration of Chihuahua would be incomplete without the mention of the aide to Black Jack. This aide, afterward probably the most outstanding general officer in American Forces during World War II, George S. Patton, Jr., was at the time of the Mexican adventure only a lieutenant. He was assigned to the 8th Cavalry, Fort Bliss, Texas, and when orders came for Pershing to move out he was ordered to take the 7th and not the 8th Regiment. Patton was beside himself with anxiety. Although only a mere 1st Lt. and in the military which at the time was simply stiff with protocol, he bearded the Old Lion in his den and went directly to Gen. Pershing's quarters after duty hours and asked the commander if he could accompany him.

Pershing, who was a stickler for discipline, simply glared down his nose at the upstart Patton.

"Get out of here!" he blazed. "Who gave you permission to come to my quarters at this time of night?" It was 8 of the evening. Patton, ever the brash one, replied, "General, I beg your pardon. But I sure want to make this one with you."

The next morning, young Patton found that overnight he had

been transferred from the 8th Cavalry to the 7th and besides that had been designated as Pershing's aide!

Now situated in San Antonio, Chihuahua, the horses in the headquarters of Gen. Pershing were, like virtually all the mounts in the expedition, short of grain. A detail of 16 troopers, in the charge of a sergeant and commanded by the General's aide, Lt. Patton, pushed off to purchase shelled corn. The party utilized three Dodge touring cars, one the personal auto of Pershing. With the group were a number of civilians, the best known a sort of soldier-of-fortune type named Emil Holmdahl. This adventurer had fought all over the world. He had been in the Boxer uprising, had been with the Boers in South Africa, and now, with an uncanny nose for action and war, had attached himself to the Pershing expedition as a guide.

The convoy reached and passed the pueblo of Rubio and turned on the well traveled road to a Rancho, San Miguelito. After seven miles of dusty travel, the 3-car cavalcade drew up in front of the high wall which surrounded the main ranchhouse and the patio. There was a great arching entrada and just in front of this entrance were four vaqueros busy butchering a beef. Patton and Holmdahl, who were in the first Dodge, had alighted and at the precise moment a half-dozen horsemen burst through the arched gateway, all of them firing busily at the nonplussed American cavalrymen. The yardage was something like 10 long steps and as the riders swept by shots rattled off the old Dodge, breaking the windshield and penetrating the door where the driver, Pvt. Lunt, sustained a flesh wound to his calf.

Patton, afterward to shoot the high score in the Olympic Pentathlon pistol event of 1924, hauled forth his .45 Model 1911 auto pistol and shot the first rider through his right arm, the second rider through both lungs (he died) and the third rider was spilled when Patton luckily hit the horse in the neck. The fourth rider, the redoubtable lieutenant was struck fairly in the spine just above the saddle cantle. It was some of the best shooting of the campaign.

Interestingly the first rider Patton had nicked through the arm was Col. Julian Cardenas who had led the raid on Columbus. As he rode toward the hills, Emil Holmdahl took a snap shot at the rider with the '03 Springfield from a distance of not less than 350 yards and put the .30 caliber bullet through his heart.

It has always been a moot point whether the Villistas who had executed the cowardly attack on the little town of Columbus were led by Julian Cardenas or in fact were under the command of Col. Candelario Cervantes. Be that as it may, on the 25th of May, Cpl. Davis Marksbury led a detail out of the Namiquipa headquarters to sketch roads. There were 12 troopers in the party, this to include Cpl. Marksbury. About 10 miles southwest of Namiquipa the party entered a broad open-mouthed canyon called Los Alamos. Suddenly from a trifling stand of cottonwoods (the canyon name means cottonwood) came a charge from at least 20 Villistas.

The Americans barely had time to dismount and drag forth their Springfields when the Mexicans were upon them. With no time to take aim the U.S. troopers stood behind their mounts and exchanged shots with the guerrillas. Cpl. Marksbury was hit on the first exchange. The 7mm bullet penetrated his throat and he died almost instantly. Three other American soldiers were wounded. For all that Pfc. George Hewlett shot two Villistas out of the saddle. It was an excellent demonstration of coolness under fire. One of the pair was Col. Cervantes. The other was an ordinary foot soldier named Bencomo.

So whether it was Cardenas or Cervantes who pulled off the hit-and-run raid on Columbus, both were now dead.

By the middle of June the situation between the punitive expedition and the Mexican provisional government had grown quite critical. Carranza sent word to Gen. Pershing through Jose Trevino, one of his innumerable generals (there were 1400 generals in the Mexican federal forces) that he must not move his forces either south, or west or yet east. The only direction he could move freely was north. Of course that was toward the U.S.-Mexican frontier. Pershing replied that he took orders only from the U.S. Government and would move in whatever direction he minded in his search for the brigand, Villa.

It was reported by American intelligence that Carranza had massed 10,000 troops at Villa Ahumada and was prepared to harass the various U.S. Army headquarters not only in the towns where the forces were stationed but as well along the lines of communication.

In a demonstration of force, Pershing ordered Troop C of the 10th Cavalry, an all-Negro outfit, into the saddle and directed its commander, Capt. Charley Boyd, to proceed eastward toward Villa Ahumada. Troop C of the 10th departed Casas Grandes on the 17th of June and the day following Black Jack also directed Capt. Lewis Morey with his Troop K of the 10th to follow in trail behind Boyd. Not satisfied with these forces, the General then ordered the 1st battalion of the 11th Infantry, under the command of Maj. Martin Crimmins to proceed by forced march toward Carrizal. This small hamlet was on the route of march to Villa Ahumada.

Charley Boyd, in command of C Troop and by seniority superior to Lewis Morey who had K Troop, was a firebrand, a real going-hell-for-leather hothead. He was not a young man; he had seen action in Cuba during the Spanish-American imbroglio, was with Pershing in the Philippines chasing Moros, had been 18 years as an enlisted man, had been fortunate in coming to the attention of Gen. Pershing while in the Philippines and had been given an outright commission as a 2nd Lieutenant. Now with 26 years continuous service he had a brand new promotion to the lofty stature of company commander.

He rode off toward Villa Ahumada not without first telling other company grade officers in the 10th, "We'll whip hell out of thim dirty greasers. Never was a Mex that'd fight nohow!"

With Boyd was Lem Spilsbury, a Mormon scout from Colonia Dublan, the largest Mormon settlement in Mexico. Spilsbury, who had lived all his life on the border, had chased Apaches, renegade stock thieves, served as a deputy sheriff, Arizona Ranger, and a member of Roosevelt's Rough Riders, simply shook his head at all this tough talk.

Boyd had 51 troopers, about a third the normal strength of a cavalry troop. Capt. Morey, with the K Troop, had even fewer, only 36 men. To reach Villa Ahumada the little force pushed through Colonia Dublan, thence took the road toward Carrizal, a pueblo on the road toward the larger town. That evening they went into bivouac at the Rancho Domingo. This sizeable cattle ranch belonged to an American syndicate and had as foreman a gringo, Bill McCabe. After the frugal chow of the evening, Boyd called together his 2nd in command, Lt. Adair, Lewis Morey, the ranch foreman, McCabe, and Lem Spilsbury.

Capt. Morey had been specifically enjoined from passage though any towns enroute to the objective. Boyd, ever the pugnacious one, insisted that he had not been so specifically ordered and he told the assemblage that on the morrow the stripped down squadron would not only move directly through Carrizal, which was now only eight miles over the next low line of hills, "But we'll go through any of the other of these pueblos," he challenged. "An' iff'n the greasers wanna make a fight of it the blood will be on thar heads."

Spilsbury and McCabe, both old hands along the border, tried to dissuade the troop commander.

"Stay in tha' rear iff'n yer afraid," he barked at the scout, Spilsbury.

The U.S. Cavalry trotted briskly up to the outskirts of Carrizal, and despite his boast that he would ride through the pueblo and any others along his route of march he sent a note by Capt. Morey's Mexican guide to the commandante of the garrison. He stated that he was passing through on a peaceful mission. The ranking Carranzista, a general named Feliz Gomez, came riding out with a retinue of ragtag soldiery at his heels.

A pow-wow ensued but meanwhile the Americans observed that large numbers of federale soldiers were taking up positions about them. Impatient with the delay and impervious to the arguments of the Mexican general, Boyd turned on his heel and retraced his steps.

"Mount up," he commanded, "we're going through." He brought his little force up against an irrigation ditch, ordered a dismount, sent the horses back in the direction of Rancho Santo Domingo, and at the same time directed Morey with his 36 troopers to move off to the right flank to cover him.

Dispersed as skirmishers, the cavalrymen forded the irrigation ditch and commenced an advance on the village. The Carranzistas, who numbered more than 300, opened fire with at least two old Hotchkiss machine guns. Despite the fire, which was mostly high and not effective, the 10th moved out behind Captain

Boyd. The second or third burst from the nearer machine gun hit three troopers and wounded Boyd in the right hand. He swapped his pistol to the left hand and charged down on the machine gun which was in plain view on a slight rise before the town. He was shot in the head at point blank range.

Lt. Adair then took command and, rallying his people, overran the position. His troopers had been firing so wildly they were running out of ammunition. Adair directed that bandoleers from the dead and wounded were to be retrieved. About that time he took a 7mm Mauser bullet through the chest. This left C Troop under the command of 1st Sgt. Alwyn Bloodgood, a veteran of the 10th.

Capt. Morey, who had been directed by Boyd to cover the right flank, moved out but soon found he was almost surrounded by Carranzistas to his front and on his left flank. Troopers of K Troop commenced to fall back. Morey was wounded. Once the commander fell panic ensued and the soldiers ran. Some raced toward the defilade where the horses were being held but others simply raced across the irrigation ditch, the fields, and into the brush, making generally in the direction of Rancho Santa Domingo.

Bill McCabe reported afterward that troopers singly and in twos and threes straggled back in a state of shock and fear. Some were mounted but others had fled on foot. It was a complete debacle, a rout, and the worst defeat of the punitive expedition.

There were 40 casualties, with seven dead. There were 23 prisoners, all of whom were lodged in the Chihuahua State Prison, stoned on the way by villagers, and reviled by all the population. They were released after an interchange between Carranza and President Wilson. In addition the President called out 75,000 National Guardsmen and closed all the International bridges over the Rio Grande.

The campaign wound down after the Carrizal episode. Although the punitive expedition did not quit Mexico until 1917, in time to prepare for World War I, the fighting virtually ceased with the debacle just described. American forces lost in all actions 15 killed and 61 wounded. The best estimates for the Villistas and Carranzistas were 251 killed and 166 wounded.

24

THE BORDER PATROL

Directly after World War I, the economic situation in Mexico grew more acute due to the interminable revolutions which had plagued the country since 1900. Essentially part of a farming–ranching economy, the peon had no land of his own and was dependent on the land-holding haciendado for employment. When markets faltered or droughts struck the farm laborer suffered. He was immediately thrown out of work, and there were no state or national programs to offer food or money to support him and his family. They simply went without, and many were on the grim brink of starvation.

In the United States there was an ever growing demand for farm help. New land to the tune of millions of acres was turned to the plow throughout the 1920s, cattle herds were vastly expanded, the national forests were opened to sheep grazing, roads and highways were abuilding, and the cities were expanding. These many enterprises beckoned to the impoverished Mexicano below the Rio Grande. He heard about it as far away as Yucatán, and he and his fellows flocked to the border and crossed into the promised land. Crossed without the formality of passport or formal immigration. Sometimes he came with his entire family, but more often he left the señora and the muchachos back in his native village, to be sent for after he got located. Or, as many did, he simply sent them funds and did not fetch them forward.

An entirely different breed of Mexican also flocked to the United States–Mexican frontier during these years. The second influx was not made up of the simple country Mexican intent on finding a job on farm or ranch. He was a *contrabandista*—a smuggler—and the evasion of the Volstead Act, the prohibition of liquor in the United States, beckoned to him. The dry law had scarcely been written into the books when the flow of whisky, tequila, rum, and kindred spirits commenced to move across the Rio Grande. It was transported by a class of latino who was a direct descendent of the border renegades of the seventies and eighties. A gun-swinging, hard-drinking, fast-riding outlaw who would carry a sack load of bottles across the Rio Grande, the cargo swung over his shoulder, and with a nickelplated six-shooter in his free hand, cheerfully shoot it out with those officers who aimed at intercepting him. And all for $3 which was standard pay for a full night's work.

From this situation—on the one hand the rising tide of illegal aliens entering to swell the ranks of the labor force in this country without regard to existing immigration law, together with the increasing traffic in illicit liquor fetched in by Mexican smugglers—a new law enforcement organization came into being. The Border Patrol.

The year was 1924, and the new outfit, created by an act of Congress and placed under the Department of Labor, was hastily recruited and scattered along both borders, the Mexican and the Canadian, and in the State of Florida. While the organization was created to stem the flow of alien labor into this country, the fact that virtually all the liquor and other contraband, such as drugs, gold, and foodstuffs, were also imported by aliens made it mandatory that the new force operate against these lawbreakers too.

The Border Patrol had six hundred officers to cover approximately four thousand miles of land boundaries, and the shoreline of Florida. To say that this was a skimpy shield against the army of aliens rolling across our frontiers would be gross understatement. It was a force so ridiculously inadequate that it was at once decided to concentrate the few officers available around the larger cities along the borders and let those vast reaches of sand, mountain, and brush go virtually unguarded. This decision probably accounted for the apprehension of ten percent of the incoming aliens and possibly slightly better percentages of the bootleg rum.

There was another Border Patrol operating along the Canada and Mexico borders, but this second service was a branch of the U.S. Customs, and its interests were solely in smuggled goods. It did not concern itself with aliens and usually ignored them. The two patrols ofttimes overlapped in their activities and occasionally got into gunfights through mistaken identity. Fortunately no one was hit during these unintentional exchanges of hot lead, a circumstance which did not speak very well for the marksmanship of either side. Our story here is not concerned with the Customs Border Patrol but with the other outfit, for years known as the Immigration Border Patrol, a title now dropped in part since the organization was transferred thirty years ago to the Department of Justice. It is now known simply as the U.S. Border Patrol.

The newly formed agency had scarcely commenced to function before it learned that the Mexican *contrabandista* was a fighter. He had a good thing going in smuggling booze, and he did not intend to let any high blown bunch of *"federales"* put a crimp in his activities. He shot when he was halted and was quick to do it. He laid ambushes and put rifles and shotguns in the hands of his liquor runners. It was war from the very beginning.

The patrol along the Mexican border was a magnet for many a cowboy. He gyrated to it as naturally as he had gone into sheriff's office or Texas Rangers. When he took the oath he fetched along his shooting irons. And it was well he did, for the service offered the old World War I Enfield rifle and the Model 1917 .45 revolver. The latter was okay, but the bolt-action rifle when in a close-up gun battle with six or eight determined *contrabandista* was far too slow and awkward. There were Thompson submachine guns available from the War Department but the Labor Department was without influence in military circles and made no effort to secure them.

The need became so acute, however, that finally a supply of Winchester Model 1897 shotguns, 12-gauge, fetched home from the trenches, was issued. These old cornshellers were just the medicine for eyeball-to-eyeball confrontations—the usual gunfighting yardages were never more than twenty steps. Ammunition was likewise war-time issue, and the big 00 buckshot had been loaded so long the outside of the cartridge was lumpy and out of round. But it invariably fed through the 97 shotgun, and many a smuggler felt the lethality of the whistling load of nine big pellets.

In no time at all the boys who were doing the fighting—it was confined to the Mexican border almost altogether—purchased their own fighting hardware. Just as the Rangers had done in the mid-seventies when the Winchester Model 1873 came along. They had paid a month's wages for the .44 and thought it a good bargain. Border patrolmen did the same and thought the bargain was a sound one. And again the choice was a Winchester, but this time a Winchester selfloader. The Model 1907 .351 autoloading rifle. It came regularly equipped with a five-shot clip-loading magazine. Patrolmen tossed this clip aside and bought three ten-shot clips. One for the rifle and two to carry in the belt. This rifle became virtually the unofficial long arm of the service. It was never purchased by the Department of Labor but was obtained on the part of the individual. The .351 figured in almost all the gun battles between the federal officers and the smugglers. The fighting grew so frequent and the gangs got so large that in most of the border districts the officers were compelled to work in parties of three. Two of the officers were armed with the .351 auto, and the third packed the old Model 97 shotgun. It made a lethal combination and one that accounted for the demise of many a gun-swinging *contrabandista*.

Tired of the life of a forest ranger, an existence a good deal like that of a sheepherder, and filled to the eyeballs with the glamor of the Border Patrol as relayed to me by my lifelong pardner, George Parker, who was a fighting member, I quit the Apache country of northern New Mexico where I'd held down the Vaqueros Ranger District for a year, and rode down to El Paso, Texas. Sworn into the Patrol at noon one day, that eve by nine o'clock, I was up in the mountains west of the smelter helping to load a very dead smuggler on a recalcitrant pack burro. I had not been a party to the shooting; it had been done earlier in the evening by another border patrol team, but the very idea that on my first day of duty I could see the evidence of high adventure in the shape of one slain border rat—he had essayed to fight it out—simply had me enthralled.

The days and mostly the nights after that were lively ones. In eastern El Paso is a peculiar geographical phenomenon which was a boon to the smugglers. This is Cordova Island, a misnomer since the Rio Grande a great many years ago while on a high-water rampage had switched its channel and left Cordova high and dry. There was a riverbed but no water. The so-called island stuck out into the Mexican settlement in El Paso like a sore thumb. It was a sore point with us, for the *contrabandista* could move their liquor onto the island and await a likely time after darkness had fallen to rush it across the dry sandy bed of the old stream. There were houses on either side of the international boundary, and it was a matter of only a few minutes to shift the contraband from a shack on the Mexican side to one on the Texas side. The riverbed was grown up in a dense stand of willows, and this made detection all the more difficult. It also made ambushes almost a cinch and to move into the cover after the sun had dropped beyond the Juarez hills could sometimes be quite sporting.

Around Cordova Island we exchanged shots with the smugglers through a long hot summer. Frequently we gathered up the incoming aliens, the impoverished Mexican laborer whose only crime was that he wanted to cross out of Chihuahua and better his livelihood, and that of his family left behind, with a job in the United States. These fellows gave no trouble. They had scarcely any desire to make a fight of it, and our detention at Border Patrol headquarters was crowded with them constantly. It was the liquor smuggler who was mean and ornery, and it was he who put spice into the job. He was big game in my book, and I hunted him industriously.

During some skirmishes of the summer, I had tried a lever action rifle and it appealed to me as lacking in firepower and accuracy in the darkness. I switched to the 97 Winchester shotgun. Around the muzzle I tied my white handkerchief so that it made a considerable lump at the snout end. This bandage was visible even on dark nights. I aimed over the top of it and pointed the shotgun at the opponent's thighs. It was brought home to me that when gunfighting at night the natural reaction is to be scared. Because of this the gunner raises his cheek off the comb of the stock so he can watch for the other fellow's muzzle flashes. When he lifts his head he overshoots. The wrapped handkerchief plus pointing at the enemy's upper legs kept me from pouring my 00 buckshot over the target.

I'd entered the patrol in March, 1930, and by December of that year was still patrolling Cordova Island in company with a couple of other officers who were good sturdy comrades. We moved in an old worn-out sedan, and it was our habit to leave the old car a few blocks from the international line, and move stealthily forward on foot until we reached the willows in the riverbed. The smugglers had confederates on this side, and it was their habit to cross at more or less regular trails so that they could make early contact with their cohorts. We had moved forward this night and crouched in the bushes alongside one of the much used trails. After a couple of hours this had produced no action. We got up and returned to our tired old sedan and commenced to move down a back alley hard against the frontier.

This was really not good judgment, as the car was a likely target and an ambush was probable. We rounded a corner within thirty yards of the international boundary and saw several shadowy figures dash back across the riverbed. These were likely smugglers, or bushwhackers, so we fell out of the old machine, guns at the ready. We dropped to the ground and moved forward to the corner of an adobe building which looked down on Cordova Island. In seconds, five men appeared from the direction of the international line. It was brightest moonlight, a commonplace on the desert, and in their hands we could see the glint of their guns. My two partners were armed with the .351 Winchester auto, and I had by this time swapped off the old Model 97 repeater for the Winchester 12-gauge autoloader. This old baby now long disappeared was known as the Model 1911. It was a real jewel. I had a gunsmith make an extension for the magazine tube so that it held nine cartridges. With the round in the barrel

I had at my command ten rounds. Each of the 10 buckshot loads contained nine pellets, so I had, in effect, ninety slugs at my disposal.

We were in position at the corner of the adobe shack which looked down onto the border. The smugglers came up this alley toward us in Indian file. They were closely bunched, one treading on the heels of the fellow ahead. When they got to within nine steps of us we challenged. All hell broke loose! The cholo in the lead had a ten-gauge Westley Richards double-barrel hammer shotgun. I had seen the moon reflected off the barrels of this old fowling piece, and when the first cap was busted I laced a pair of shots into him. He fell atop the ten-gauge, both hammers back but the gun unfired. After the scrap I gathered up this gun and after carefully lowering the dog-eared hammers, broke the gun open and found it was loaded with Winchester Hi-Speed No. 5 shot. If he could have set off those two charges before he took the double load of my buckshot he'd have evened the odds considerably!

The bucko immediately behind him had an old Smith & Wesson .44 Russian six-shooter. He was busily engaged in thumbing back the hammer on this gun and got off two shots before a bullet from one of the .351 rifles hit him on the breastbone. This slug knocked a hole in the outlaw as big as a four-bit piece, but it did not take any of the fight out of him. He dropped to his knees and crawled behind a small cottonwood growing in the alley. There he spun out three more shots from the single action revolver before my buckshot found him out and settled his hash. The third man in the string had a rifle, and this he fired from the hip as fast as he could flip the lever. He was shot in the groin but managed to get back to the Mexican side of the border. The two remaining bravos also wheeled around and ran for the protection of the willows. There they took up position behind adobe buildings on Cordova Island and made the alley an exceedingly hot spot with their fire.

At the morgue where we delivered the two gunmen, the leader proved to be the hombre with the old .44 Russian. In his watch-pocket we found a well-folded ten-dollar bill. His pay for the attempted ambush. This was a real curly wolf; the autopsy showed his heart was pierced by the .351 slug which penetrated his breastbone. Despite the wound he had fired three shots from the single-action .44. And would have fired more if the buckshot had not knocked him over.

Another night along the same part of the international line things did not go so well for us. This time the smugglers drove their pickup car into the willows in the river bed and in a twinkling had it loaded with booze. There were three *contrabandista*, all armed. As they pulled out of the river bottom the patrol car swung alongside and the liquor runners were commanded to halt. The two cars, the liquor laden sedan and the officers' vehicle, were stopped side by side. The border patrolmen alighted from their car on the side next to the *contrabandista*.

As they stepped out, a smuggler riding shotgun in the front seat swung a short carbine over the door and fired a shot at the officer alighting in front. The bullet struck the patrolman in the head and as it was a sporting softpoint slug it broke up; a portion of the bullet completely penetrated the skull, and flying off at a tangent hit the officer in the head who was alighting from the back seat. He fell unconscious. Thus with one shot the smugglers had changed the odds from three on either side to a seeming sure thing of three-to-one. But they had not counted on the last remaining bucko.

He had stepped out of the patrol car on the far side from the gunmen. He ran around behind their vehicle and opened up with a .351 automatic. He shot the rifle-wielder in the right eye, the bullet striking the outlaw at an angle so that it exited through the temple. It did not kill the man, did not indeed even so much as knock him out. However, it took all the fight out of him and he dropped the rifle. The patrolman kept on firing, and one of his bullets struck the driver of the liquor car in the kidneys and he died. The third smuggler, in the back seat with the load of contraband, raised up in the back seat with a six-shooter, his intention to fire out through the back glass. Seeing the movement, the federal officer concentrated on him and shot the gun out of his hand.

Thus in the space of a few heartbeats the border patrolman had managed to take care of the trio in such style as to avenge the death of his partner and to haul the killers into custody. The second border patrolman struck in the head by the bullet jacket which had broken up in the skull of his teammate was not badly hurt and quickly recovered.

After a space on Cordova Island, I was transferred to a horse station twenty miles west of El Paso, at Strauss, New Mexico. There with a single partner, we rode from Monument No. 3 West to Rodeo, New Mexico, if we wanted. This was 150 miles— across the entire southern border of New Mexico—and the only town was Columbus, where Villa had made his well-publicized raid in 1916. The country is all desert wasteland, scanty of grass and cover, and unwatered except for an occasional windmill. Juarez, a hotbed of smuggling activity, directly across the Rio Grande from El Paso, and only twenty miles from our camp at Strauss, spawned an endless succession of tough hombres who, guns in hand, sought to fight their way through the light screen we interposed.

Smuggling gangs, after they operated for a while, all tended to develop patterns of movement. They would cross the border in the same area, move across the desert, passing landmarks which they could find in the darkness, and finally wind up in the Rio Grande Valley above El Paso to make rendezvous with the awaiting auto which would whisk the contraband off to interior points. We rode the international line—it is an old rusting five-wire fence—each morning at daylight and soon picked up the tracks of a passing gang. We followed these out, tracking for a dozen miles until finally we arrived at that spot near La Union, New Mexico, where the loads of booze had been piled into an awaiting car.

In a few mornings we again struck this sign and again traced the route of the smugglers to the auto. After a third and a fourth passage we were ready to move against the *contrabandista*. We had noted that this gang varied by a half mile or so the place where they straggled through the old barbed wire fence. Far back into the country we saw that they inevitably passed around the brow of a low hill. Here, if we laid in wait for them, the runners would be nicely silhouetted against the sky. For good shooting at night this is essential. When we decided the outfit would run again we moved in after darkness and took up vantage points around the low hill. It was winter and a cold night, and by the time we heard the unmistakable noise of the group as they shuffled along, single file, striking now and then a rock on the desert floor or brushing a mesquite, the 4½-gallon cans of alcohol gurgling, a common item of the smuggling trade. It was 2:30 A.M.

As we had anticipated, the gang came directly toward our ambush. They would pass around the point of the low hill exactly as they had done before. Very soon we saw them silhouetted against the sky. In the lead was a burly cholo, no liquor visible on his back. Instead the dim light glinted on a six-shooter in his right hand. Behind him, strung out like a bunch of raiding Apaches, were the *cargadores,* the carriers. When the jefe was directly opposite our position we challenged.

He wheeled at the sound of our voices and commenced to unload the six-shooter. He was hit with a load of buckshot in front, but this did not knock him down. He wheeled to run, and a second charge of the big 00 pellets struck him in the back. He still did not fall. He ran back down the trail and passed my partner who let drive at him with a Model 54 .30-06. The bullet struck him in the left hip and ranged upward and went out under his right arm. He ran another fifty yards before he tumbled. He was dead when we picked him up. Another of the gang had a revolver, and he was busy with it. He got hit in the leg above the knee, and the limb was so badly mangled from the buckshot it had to be amputated. He developed syphilis of the bone in the wound and eventually died. The others of the gangsters dropped their rum and legged it off in the darkness to eventually work their way back to Juarez. Their pay for trudging all night, with forty pounds on their backs, risking capture and even death if caught in a crossfire, was $3.

Occasionally we would journey into Border Patrol headquarters in El Paso for a powwow with the chief of the outfit, to pick up mail, checks, and gossip. One fine bright afternoon we were trundling down the river levee in an old truck we used to haul horsefeed, en route to Patrol headquarters. We were only some half dozen blocks from the Patrol home base when we looked up, and here in broad daylight and right before our eyes, some five or six *contrabandista* were wading the Rio Grande with loads on their backs. This was not an uncommon stratagem, and ofttimes it caught the patrol unawares and was successful. On the El Paso side of the river were Mexican *jacales* (shacks), and into these the runners would dash with their liquor and thus be lost to the federals.

Old Bill, my partner, had a bad habit of leaving our camp unarmed unless we were going out to ride the line. This time was no exception. He had left his gun back in camp. I was armed but had only a six-shooter. We threw on the brakes on the old truck, and I bailed out, ran down the levee side, waded the irrigation ditch, and entered an alley in the settlement which showed a dripping trail. The smugglers had disappeared, but gun in hand I was loping along on the wet track. Suddenly at the far end of the alley, a passageway that was so narrow I could have extended my arms and touched either wall, an armed man appeared.

I noted he had a Winchester Model 95 rifle in his hands, and as I checked up from my headlong run, he threw down on me. The distance was about forty feet, and down that constricted alleyway it was like shooting fish in a barrel. I concluded he was riding shotgun for the smugglers and had been waiting for them to appear. At any rate it looked like a good time to start shooting. I dropped to my knees and triggered off a shot just an instant after this rifleman threw a shot at me. Both of us missed. He shot over my head as I went to my knees, and I reckon I also overshot him. I was packing an old Colt New Service .45 with only a two-inch barrel. I had hacked the barrel off, dehorned the hammer, cut out the trigger guard, and made it a fast draw gun. It was for close-up work and certainly not quite adequate against an hombre who was armed with a Winchester Model 95.

The gunman triggered off only the one shot, then he legged it out of my view. I ran to the entrance of the alley, carefully stuck my head around the corner of the adobe house which constituted one wall of the passage, and looked for my antagonist. He had driven up in a car which was parked about twenty yards directly to the front. I could see a portion of his legs behind the front wheel where he had taken cover. As I watched, a partner of his ran from the buildings on his left and attempted to make it to the car. I let one go at him as he ran and hit his rifle, another Model 95, in the small of the stock and broke it completely in two. He let out a yelp like he had been hit, undoubtedly splinters from the wood had struck him in the side. He was too fast for me, and I got only one shot at him. He dropped down behind the smugglers' car at the rear wheel.

This was a pretty kettle of fish. I was outnumbered two to one, the opposition both armed with rifles and me with a bunty-barreled .45, plus a partner who was standing on the levee behind me completely unarmed. I dived into a Mexican shack and motioned the people inside to get in a back room, and I went to the window and watched for a chance shot at the pair behind the car.

About that time reinforcements arrived. As I've said it was only a few blocks from Border Patrol headquarters. The shooting had been heard, and officers commenced to arrive in numbers, everybody with his rifle at the ready. The pair behind the auto came forth sheepishly. The gent who had shot at me was a Customs border patrolman, his partner was a Mexican stool pigeon whom he had armed to help him. He was completely out of his territory; we had divided the Rio Grande through El Paso to prevent this very thing. This smart aleck believed he could dash into our area, knock off the load of contraband, and get out again before our people knew about it. It was lucky we had both missed each other although it did not, certainly, reflect much credit on our marksmanship!

Midway on the international line between El Paso and Columbus is a waterstop on the South Pacific Railroad called Mount Riley. Near the cluster of right-of-way laborers' shacks is a ranch which was owned by Ed Cox. An old Texan who migrated to New Mexico, Ed was rawhide tough. He had lived there on the border for thirty years and had seen revolutions come and go below the border, each of them giving him problems with the inevitable rustling of his cow-flesh. He always rode with a Winchester .38-55 under his saddle fender, and when the occasion arose he was not hesitant to use it. One time he had trailed a band of rustlers with a gaggle of his cows into Chihuahua. The thieves had seen him coming and had abandoned the cows and ridden after Cox. The rancher turned tail, the odds being five to one, and rode for the border. The rustlers were overhauling him after a few miles, and so Cox simply dropped off into an arroyo, fell off his horse, and dragged the old .38-55 from its leather. As the outlaws topped the rise above him, he let them get well strung out and working on them from rear to front proceeded with some terribly lethal rapid fire to kill all five of them.

This was another day and another situation. Two border patrolmen riding the border struck Cox and his cowboy, Roger Pickett, far off the Cox range. As a matter of fact the country on the United States side of the rusty fence belonged to Glen Durrell. Said Cox, who knew both the officers, "Glad to see you fellers. Me an' Roger was jus' gettin' ready to make a Mexican invasion. Glen Durrell is gone an' he asked me to look after his stock. Las' night three dam' coyotes run off seventeen head of Glen's cows. I aim to go git 'em back."

The patrolmen looked at each other. This was just the kind of a show they were looking for. It was strictly against regulations to ride into Mexico but here they were thirty miles from head-quarters, a major cow rustling had been staged, and before them was an old friend. "We'll go 'long and give you a hand, Ed," the older of the two officers said with a grin.

The foursome trailed the rustlers all day, until they had swung around the Juarez mountains which lie on the west and south-west sides of the Mexican town. They were finally thirty miles below the border and were now southwest of Juarez. In the late afternoon, riding slowly and cautiously because the sign was smoking fresh, they looked ahead and in a dense stand of mesquite at a distance of about three hundred yards they saw a little wisp of smoke arising. Without a word everyone stepped off his horse, tied the animals, and went forward on foot, rifles cocked. They soon broke into a little clearing and there about a tiny fire lay three riders. The cows, dead tired, were scattered in the brush, and the jaded mounts of the thieves were picketed nearby.

One of the bandits, a big Indian-looking hombre, must have heard the gringos pushing through the brush, for just as the foursome cleared the last of the mesquite, at a distance of about forty feet, the big leader awakened, and on the instant he rolled over on his elbow, snatched up a .30-30 carbine lying alongside his body, and commenced to trigger off shots. The first two bullets in reply from the Americans caught the copper-colored cholo through the body and in the small of the stock on the rifle. It broke the stock into two pieces. But this did not slow the leader. Despite a body wound, he continued to fire the rifle with the stub of the stock in his hands. Three more shots hit him in quick order and he went down dying in minutes. The other pair had been slower to awaken, but they also showed fight. Both were armed with six-shooters and had been sleeping on their guns. They were killed in the exchange.

The border patrolmen, Cox, and his cowboy had escaped unscathed. They cut loose the played-out horses of the rustlers, gathered up the tired cows, and riding cautiously now back-tracked to the border. It was a slow ride, and darkness found the drive still many miles from the line. However by first light of morning the outfit let the barbed wire down and drove the animals back into Glen Durrell's pasture. So far as Ed Cox was concerned it was all in a day's work. A neighborly gesture which was no more than Durrell would expect of him. Ed Cox is dead now, a salty old hardcase who typified the Texan of yesterday.

The end of the Prohibition Act resolved a great many Border Patrol problems. The repeal of the unpopular liquor law reduced the gun fighting along the frontier until the patrol lost a lot of its glamor and attraction. By the same token as the rough old days past, the service commenced to get the money, guns, and equipment that it should have had when during a ten-year interlude in the El Paso subdistrict alone there was an average of a gun battle every seventeen days for the entire decade 1924 to 1934.

Now the Border Patrol has thousands of officers along either border, is equipped with light aircraft, helicopters, the best in firearms, two-way radio, and funds to pay informers on either side of the line. There is a recruit school where fledgling officers are taught law, procedures, language, and marksmanship. Each year the service sends a select team of Border Patrol shooters to the national police matches, and this team in 1968 and 1969 won the national championship. Border patrolmen have also won the national police individual championship. But it is not like it was in the old days when the recruit pinned on a badge and buckled on a six-shooter and went out to pack in a dead *contra-bandista* that same evening!

25

BONNIE & CLYDE

Texas felt the Big Depression of the early thirties touched off by the Wall Street crash of 1929. The state was hard hit when the price fell out of cattle and farm products. By 1934, when prohibition went by the board, even the bootleggers and the gangsters were crying hard times. The banks had little money in them, but they were more solvent than many other establishments, and they became the target of many an ex-liquor runner. Among these was a half-pint named Barrow. Clyde Barrow.

Raised in the slums of Dallas, he had quit school in the fifth grade and commenced to steal hubcaps, bust pay telephones, and do house robberies before he was into his teens. By the time he was fifteen he had a record with the local police that covered more than sixty arrests and was three pages in length. He had been to the reformatory three times and was out on parole after each sentence. When he was sixteen he graduated to the big time. He commenced to steal cars and was a part of a well-organized theft ring which ran the cars to Piedras Negras where the hot autos were turned over to confederates south of the border.

Between knocking off occasional Cadillacs, Barrow heisted gasoline stations, isolated grocery stores, and post offices. The latter were burglaries and put him in a higher bracket, for the federals then got on his trail. He was picked up by the Dallas sheriff's office, tried, and sentenced to two years for car theft. He was out in eleven months. And busy again.

He fell in with Ray Hamilton who was on the way up too,

very much by the same route that Clyde Barrow had followed, from small pilferage to increasingly serious crimes to finally becoming an accomplished car thief. When he and Barrow met, Hamilton was two years older and was bigger and more husky than the diminutive Barrow. Hamilton weighed 175 pounds and was five feet, ten inches tall, with a boxer's square jaw and heavy shoulders. Clyde stood five feet, five inches and dripping wet would not go more than 125. He was thin and stoop-shouldered and had a weasel's sharp face with shifty eyes that hid the killer's instinct which lurked just behind.

It was 1934 and Hamilton and Barrow had been teamed for nearly a year. During that time they had knocked off almost a dozen banks throughout Texas, Oklahoma, and Missouri. They had killed a bank cashier or two, gunned down several possemen, and accounted for at least three highway patrolmen. The year before, when they commenced the mutual operation, Texas had had 4000 indictments for murder, there had been 982 homicides, 685 of them involving gunfights. The Barrow-Hamilton duo had contributed their share. Some gangsters were being knocked off by the lawmen of the Lone Star state but the odds were about six-to-one in favor of the outlaws. None, unquestionably, more lethal than the two toughies from Dallas.

By a process of cut-and-try, Barrow and Hamilton had discovered how to evade capture. They would dash into a small town, a moderate size city where the cops were not equipped with patrol cars, had no radios, and were not concerned with big-time crime. The gangsters would pull up in front of the only bank, go inside, shoot anyone who gave them the slightest trouble, sweep up all the cash in sight, scurry out to the waiting auto, and be gone. Before a pursuit could be organized they were thirty miles outside the little burg and making tracks at a speed of one hundred miles an hour. The car was invariably the Ford V-8, which in those days was one of the fastest autos on the road. As darkness approached, the pair would pull into a town, steal another V-8, shift the loot and their guns to the new bus, and keep on going. They would flee for twenty-four hours and might drive a thousand miles. Quite often they drove into Illinois, Iowa, Nebraska, and Kansas after a bank heist.

If anyone among the pursuers managed to overhaul the getaway car, Barrow would get over in the back seat of the careening Ford and knock the back glass out. After that he would lay a Browning Auto Rifle, familiarly referred to as the BAR, over the back cushion and give the following auto a series of bursts from the .30-06. When he was killed he had three BARs in the car with him. He knew full well the potency of these rifles. Unlike a lot of his contemporaries, Clyde knew where to get his ordnance. He would simply drive around behind a National Guard armory in Texas, Oklahoma, or Arkansas, break in, and help himself to the automatic rifles, the .45 auto pistols, and a plentiful supply of cartridges.

About this time in his career, having given over all the small-time crime—sticking up filling stations and lifting new Buicks off the streets of Dallas—to bank robbery, he fell in with Bonnie Parker. Bonnie had a husband and worked in a greasy-spoon beanery in south Dallas. She was a hasher, the wife of a con doing life for a murder, and only twenty-two years of age. She was red-headed and hard-faced and stood four feet, ten inches in her bare feet. Barrow, who frequently slipped into Dallas to see his mother and brother, got acquainted with Bonnie, and the two instantly went for each other. On the first date Bonnie showed Clyde an obscene tattoo on the inside of her right thigh, put there by her hubby before they shut him up in Huntsville. Right after that she threw up her job and went with Barrow and Ray Hamilton. She and Clyde were made for each other. He was a two-bit unimpressive little runt who was made to feel strong and possessive by the diminutive Bonnie. They were good for each other, and there sprang up between them a strong bond of affection. A love which persisted to the death. Bonnie became the driver of the get-away car. She would sit in front of the small town bank while Clyde and Ray Hamilton were busy inside scooping up the cash and gunning down any banker who offered to resist. Once they roared away, she drove with skill and verve, and when it came to fighting their way through road blocks she could handle the hurtling V-8 with all the finesse and skill of a racing driver, giving the gangsters full time to climb over in the back seat and hold off the pursuit with the deadly BARs.

After a bank holdup in Drumright, Oklahoma, the trio took it on the lam for Dallas. They made it okay and went into hiding in the old home town. Only this time the cops had heard about their arrival and swooped down. Clyde and Bonnie, with an intuition which never seemed to fail them, took it on the lam, not stopping until they pulled up over in Bossier Parish, Louisiana. Hamilton, who had separated from the others once in town, was shacked up with a girl friend and was picked up at 3:00 A.M. completely nude and in bed with his inamorata. He was hustled off to jail, promptly tried and convicted for bank robbery and murder, and sentenced to life imprisonment. He was first sent to Huntsville and later transferred to Eastham Prison Farm, which is near the main prison.

It was then up to Clyde and Bonnie to operate alone. They managed. Always driving a new car, usually the favorite Ford V-8, with the back seat filled with an arsenal which consisted of submachine guns, sawed-off shotguns, the inevitable BARs, plus six-shooters, the robbers left a trail of busted banks and dead and crippled lawmen behind them. Take a seventy-year-old butcher in Sherman, Texas, who resented Barrow ramming his pistol in his navel. He reached down to push the barrel aside, and Clyde let him have it through the guts. He died the next day. Another day the pair were cruising through Lawton, Oklahoma, and were stopped by a speed cop for running a stop sign. When the officer approached the stolen car, Clyde panicked and shot him. Bonnie hopped out, turned the man over on his back, and shot him between the eyes.

On April 3, 1934, near Grapevine, Texas, which is between Dallas and Fort Worth, a car from the highway patrol pulled up behind a Ford parked on a lonely stretch of road. The officers had the report from a passing farmer that a wild party was going on. The pair were drinking out of a half-gallon jug and had made profane and obscene gestures at him when he slowly tooled by. The lawmen came up on either side of the sedan, and as they reached the front doors, both were struck in the faces with buckshot. Bonnie used a twenty-gauge sawed-off, and Clyde had a sixteen-gauge pump repeater with the barrel shortened to fourteen inches. An examination of the scene afterward produced the whisky jug with Barrow's fingerprints on it.

Three days afterward, Constable Cal Campbell of Miami, Oklahoma, drove up to a Ford V-8 bogged to the axles in the mud just outside the little hamlet. Old Cal was sixty-three years old, not accustomed to anything out of the ordinary in his quiet town, and all he wanted to do was help. He pulled alongside to offer help, and as he stepped out of his venerable pickup his coat fell open and revealed both his badge and his old single action six-shooter. It was all that the pair in the mired auto needed. They both opened up. Again with the deadly little 20 and the lethal 16. Struck in the face and head, Campbell was dead before his feet touched the muddy roadbed.

Clyde missed Hamilton, although Bonnie did a capable job of driving the get-away car. He determined to spring his erstwhile partner in crime, and to this end wrote to Ray in Eastham Prison. He gave him specific directions as to what to do and how he and Bonnie would support his break for freedom. The letter was passed by an accomplice to Hamilton. On the day set for the attempt, Hamilton, who was at the job of clearing brush along the borders of the farm, walked over to a pile of leaves and under it found two .45 automatics and a .38 revolver. There were three others in the plot with him. All rammed the pistols under their shirts and kept on with the brush clearance until the appointed hour. The foursome had meanwhile worked their way toward a line of trees and heavy brush.

Suddenly a car horn began to beep from behind the screen of brush. Hamilton commenced to run and so did the others. The guards, Major Crawson, Olan Bozeman, and another pair of guards, shouted at the racing cons and threw up their shotguns. About that time the staccato bark of the familiar BAR was heard from off one flank. Crawson was killed instantly, and Bozeman was seriously wounded. The other guards dropped to the ground and crawled for cover.

The car beeping was Bonnie; Clyde was at the trigger of the Browning. Bonnie turned the auto over to Hamilton who sped away with his three companions. She leisurely strolled over and joined Barrow, and they loaded up in their indomitable Ford and motored away, driving for Bossier Parish where they had friends and a secure hideout.

Whether Hamilton and Barrow ever got together afterward is not known. If they did, the meeting was a brief one. Within thirty days not only was Hamilton recaptured but so were the other cons who had made the break with him. But Bonnie and Clyde, by almost constant movement, sleeping in the same spot never more than two nights in a row, by driving sometimes a thousand miles in a twenty-four-hour period, and through the frequent change of autos, managed to elude all pursuit.

About this time Chief L. G. Phares, who headed up the Texas Highway Patrol, decided the time had come to take a decidedly different tack in running this pair of killers to earth. He called in Captain Frank Hamer, formerly of the Texas Rangers but at the moment at loose ends for a law enforcement job.

Hamer had been in and out of the Rangers for twenty-six years. At the time Chief Phares approached him he was no longer a young man. He was fifty years of age, six feet, three inches in height, and weighed 220 pounds, with a history of innumerable gunfights behind him and not a few bullet scars to attest to the fact that he had not come through all of them unscathed. He had gone in the Ranger force when twenty-two years old and had been in and out of the outfit, depending on who was governor and whether the politics of Hamer and the incumbent measured alike, through his entire lifetime.

The head of the highway patrol, an old friend of Hamer's, told him what he wanted. The ex-Ranger was to get on the trail of Bonnie and Clyde and to stick with that trail until the two "mad dogs" were brought to justice. It did not matter where the pair might go, whether in Texas or beyond, nor what might be needed to apprehend them, Hamer was to follow.

From here on the story is best told in the words of Hamer himself:

I took the trail and followed it for 102 days. Like Barrow I used a Ford V-8, and like Clyde I lived in the car most of the time.

I soon had valuable sources of information but these cannot be revealed without violating confidences. The fact that I never betray a confidence even from a criminal has resulted in bringing me inside information which every officer to be successful must have.

I soon learned that Barrow played a circle which ran from Dallas to Joplin, Missouri, to Louisiana, and back to Dallas. Occasionally he would leave this beat but he would always come back to it as most criminals do. One time he and Bonnie went as far east as North Carolina for no other purpose it seems than to visit a cigarette factory. Again they would go to Indiana, Oklahoma, Iowa, New Mexico, but like wild horses would circle back to their old range. The thing to be decided was whether to set the trap in Texas, Missouri or Louisiana. I decided that Barrow could be most easily caught in Louisiana because he was "hot" in Texas and in Missouri, having killed men in both states, but he had killed no one in Louisiana, and would probably make this his hiding place.

It was necessary for me to make a close study of Barrow's habits. I had never seen him and never saw him until May 23, but I interviewed many people who knew him and studied numerous photographs of him and Bonnie. I knew the size, height, and all the marks of identification of both of them. But this was not enough. An officer must know the mental habits of the outlaw, how he thinks, and how he will react in different situations. When I began to understand Clyde Barrow's mind, I felt I was making progress. I learned that Barrow never holed up at any one place; he was always on the go; and he traveled farther in one day than any fugitive I have ever followed. He thought nothing of driving a thousand miles in one stretch. Barrow was also a master of side roads which made his movements irregular. Around Dallas, Joplin, Missouri, and into Louisiana, he seemed to know them all.

Before the chase ended, I not only knew the general appearance and mental habits of the pair but I learned the kind of whisky they drank, what they ate, and the color, size, and texture of their clothes. I first struck their trail at Texarkana, at Logansport they bought a half-gallon of whisky; near Keechi they bought gasoline, and then they went in the night to a Negro house and had the Negroes cook them some cornbread and fry a chicken. In Shreveport they bought pants, underwear, gloves and an automatic shotgun. In their camp on the Wichita River, near Wichita Falls, they lost or threw away some bills for goods bought in Dallas. From the clerk I learned the size, color and pattern of Bonnie's dresses, and the kind of Ascot tie and belt buckle she wore. A description of these was sent to Ed Portley of Joplin, with information that Clyde and Bonnie were probably hiding in some abandoned mines near by.

The trail always led back to Louisiana, where I located their hide-out. I cannot give the name of the parish because of what followed. Because I was outside Texas it was advisable for me to take the local officers into my confidence. I discovered the sheriff of this parish could not be trusted and so it was arranged to have Barrow's hide-out moved into a parish where the officers were more reliable. In a comparatively short while the hideout was established in Bienville Parish at a place well known to me.

The next task was to catch Clyde when he was "at home." On several occasions I went alone to this secret place. It was my hope to take him and Bonnie alive; this I could only do by finding them asleep. It would have been simple to tap each one on the head, kick their weapons out of reach, and handcuff them before they knew what it was all about. Once the plan came near succeeding but for one of those accidents which will happen over which the officer has no control. There was always plenty of signs of the pair in the camp— Bonnie's Camels—Clyde smoked Bull Durham—lettuce leaves for the white rabbit; pieces of sandwiches and a button off Clyde's coat. I found where they had made their bed.

The end would have come two or three weeks earlier had not some local and federal officers made a drag on Ruston, Louisiana, and when Clyde heard of it he quit the country and I had to wait for him to return.

I traveled alone until shortly before the middle of April. On April 10, I called Chief Phares of the Highway Patrol to tell him that Barrow had used a Pontiac sedan to make his getaway after killing Constable Cummings and kidnapping the chief of police of Commerce, Oklahoma. I gave Chief Phares the license and engine number of this car and also numbers of extra license plates from Oklahoma and Louisiana which Barrow carried in that car. Phares told me that the Highway Patrol had decided to hire an extra man to travel with me. I asked for Manny Gault who had served with me in the headquarters company of the Rangers. Gault met me in Dallas on the 14th and traveled with me until the chase ended on the 23rd of May.

Bob Alcorn and Ted Hinton, from the sheriff's office in Dallas, gave me information. They also joined me a bit later on. I made contact with Sheriff Henderson Jordan of Bienville Parish and after I had told him of my plans he agreed to assist me and pay no attention to other officers, state or federal. He had as his deputy, Jay Oakley.

We did not find Barrow in his hideout but at his "post office."

All criminals who work in groups must have some way of communicating with one another when they are separated. I learned that Clyde had his post office on a side road about 8 miles from Plain Dealing, Louisiana. It was under a board which lay on the ground near the stump of a pine. The point selected was on a knoll from which Bonnie in the car could command a view of the road while Clyde went into the woods for his mail.

By the night of May 22, we had good reason to believe that Clyde would visit his mail box within a short time. About midnight we drove out of Gibsland, hid our cars in the pines, and made arrangements to furnish him with more news than he had ever received at one time. No detail was neglected. The road here runs north and south, and the knoll over which it rises is made by a spur or point which slopes from east to west. The stump that marked the location of the post office is on the west side of the road. We, therefore, took our positions on the opposite and higher side so that we could look down on the car and its occupants. Within an hour after we reached the place, which was about 2:30 in the morning, we had constructed a blind from pine branches within about twenty-five or thirty feet of the point where the car would stop.

We expected Barrow to come from the north or from our right as we faced the road. The six men were spaced at intervals of about ten feet, parallel to the road. I held the position on the extreme left, and next was Gault, Jordan, Alcorn, Oakley, and Hinton in that order. Gault, Jordan and myself were to take care of the front seat, Oakley and Alcorn of the back seat if it was occupied, while Ted Hinton at the end of the line was to step out and bust the engine with a BAR he had. Jordan and I had automatic shotguns while the others all had Winchesters. Everybody had either a six-shooter or an automatic.

We agreed to take Barrow and the woman alive if we could. We believed that when they stopped the car, both would be looking toward the post office and away from us; such action on their part would enable us to escape observation until we demanded their surrender.

With everything ready we had nothing to do but wait about seven hours without breakfast or coffee. Waiting is about the hardest thing an officer has to do. Many men will stand up in a fight but lose their nerve completely if required to wait long for the excitement. On this occasion I did not detect the slightest nervousness on the part of a single man.

As daylight came a few cars passed, and occasionally a logger's truck. The sun came up at our back which was in our favor. It was probably about 9:10 A.M. when we heard a humming through the pines that was different from that made by other motors. A car was approaching from the north at terrific speed, singing like a sewing machine. We first heard it when it must have been three miles away.

Finally it came into view at a distance of about a thousand yards and though it was still coming rapidly, it began to slow down as it climbed the hill toward us. We first recognized the color of the car, a gray Ford V-8 sedan, then the license number; then we saw two persons, a small black-headed man and a small red-headed woman. We recognized Clyde and Bonnie and knew there was no mistake. The speed continued to slacken under the brakes and the car came to a full stop at the exact spot that we had previously decided it would.

When Barrow brought the car to a standstill, he pressed the clutch down and slipped the vehicle into low gear with the engine idling. Just as we had figured, both he and his woman companion peered with all their attention toward the stump.

At the command "stick 'em up" both turned, but instead of obeying the order as we had hoped, they swung up their guns which were either in their laps or resting on the seat between them. When our firing began, Barrow's foot released the clutch and the car, in low gear, moved forward on the decline and turned into the ditch on the left. I looked at my watch and it was 9:20.

There can be no question raised as to who fired the first or the fatal shots. All fired as we had agreed to do and every man in the squad did everything he was supposed to do. It was not a pleasant duty, but it was a duty which no one shirked. Should I ever go on such another case, I hope I shall have the help of such men as the five who were with me that day.

An examination of the car revealed that the shots had been accurately placed, most of them ranging from the position of the driver's feet upward at an angle that would take into account the entire body. The examination also revealed that the car was nothing but an arsenal on wheels. The inventory included:

3 Browning Auto Rifles	Cal .30-06
1 sawed-off Winchester Mod 12, 16-gauge	
1 sawed-off Winchester Mod 12, 20-gauge	
1 Colt New Service revolver	Cal .45
7 Colt automatic pistols Model 1911	Cal .45

1 Colt automatic pistol   Cal .380
1 Colt automatic pistol   Cal .32
100 loaded magazines for BAR
3,000 rounds of assorted rifle, shotgun and pistol ammunition

As soon as possible I called Chief Phares at Austin and told him the job was done.

Frank Hamer had been on the trail of the bloodthirsty little gangsters for 102 days. He was paid by the State of Texas the munificent sum of $180 monthly for his efforts. He had made a practice of calling the chief of the highway patrol to keep him abreast of developments. When he submitted a voucher for these phone calls, they were disallowed because he had not gotten receipts for them.

BIBLIOGRAPHY

A Texas Ranger, N. A. Jennings, Steck Co., Austin, Texas.

Rangers and Sovereignty, Dan W. Roberts, Wood Printing & Engraving Co., San Antonio, Texas.

Texas Rangers, James B. Gillett, World Book Co., Yonkers, N. Y.

The Texas Rangers, Walter Prescott Webb, University of Texas Press, Austin.

The Plains of the Great West, Col. Richard Irving Dodge, Archer House, Inc., New York.

Fort Griffin on the Texas Frontier, Carl Coke Rister, University of Oklahoma Press, Norman.

The Quirt and the Spur, Edgar Rye (published by author).

Texans with Guns, James Farber, The Naylor Co., San Antonio, Texas.

The King Ranch, Tom Lea, Little, Brown & Co., Boston.

Gun Digest, John T. Amber, Editor, Gun Digest Publishing Co., Chicago.

Trails & Trials of a Texas Ranger, William Warren Sterling, University of Oklahoma Press, Norman.

Western History Collections, University of Oklahoma. Permission to reproduce photos from the Rose and Campbell collections in this book is gratefully acknowledged.

George W. Littlefield, Texan, Everts Haley.